COUNTY COURTHOUSES
OF PENNSYLVANIA

COUNTY COURTHOUSES OF PENNSYLVANIA

A GUIDE

Oliver P. Williams

STACKPOLE
BOOKS

Published by
STACKPOLE BOOKS
5067 Ritter Road
Mechanicsburg, PA 17055
www.stackpolebooks.com

Printed in the United States of America

10 9 8 7 6 5 4 3 2 1

FIRST EDITION

Cover design by Wendy Reynolds

Photographs by the author unless otherwise noted.

Cover: Philadelphia City Hall, photo by Greg James, courtesy of the Foundation for Architecture.

Back Cover: *Top left,* Somerset; *top right,* Franklin; *bottom left,* Dauphin; *bottom right,* Luzerne.

Library of Congress Cataloging-in-Publication Data

Williams, Oliver P.
    County courthouses of Pennsylvania : a guide / Oliver P. Williams.—1st ed.
        p.   cm.
    Includes bibliographical references and index.
    ISBN 0-8117-2738-6 (PB)
        1. Courthouses—Pennsylvania—Guidebooks.   2. Public architecture—
Pennsylvania—Guidebooks.   3. Pennsylvania—Guidebooks.   I. Title.

NA4472.P4 W55   2001
725'.15'09748—dc21
                                                                00-069821

To
Mary Ann

CONTENTS

ACKNOWLEDGMENTS

I have many people to thank for their help in making this book possible, particularly those who staff the county historical societies, many of whom are volunteers. Many courthouse employees showed me countless courtesies and gave me building tours that sometimes included attics, towers, and basements. I am indebted to all of them. In the early days of my research, I thoughtlessly did not record the names of those who helped me, and so they are missing from this list. From the counties, I wish to acknowledge Jim Scahill, Daniel R. Vodzak, Andrew Vesloski, Jeff Marshall, Rebekah A. Sheeler, Hugh Manchester, Barbara L. Weir, Warren W. Wirebach, Iva A. Fay, Annita Andrick, Kerlin Merill, Murray Kauffman, Jerry Pollock, Brenda Giles, Tom Clouser, Nancy List, Kip Van Blarcom, Beverly Zona, William Philson, Jean Suloff, Rene Drago, Robert Currin, Herry Knowles, Betty Smith, Scott Gitchell, Carolee K. Michner, Robert C. Scott, Chase Putnam, June L. Lloyd, William Murray, Jean Groner, and Greta Greenberger. Greg Ramsey of the Pennsylvania Bureau for Historic Preservation was very helpful in canvassing the files of courthouses on the National Register. Anna Coxe Toogood pointed me to sources on Congress Hall. Bruce Goetzman gave me useful bibliographic leads. Hyman Myers was always cordially responsive to my amateur queries about architecture, as was Richard Webster, who was especially helpful on Philadelphia City Hall. Finally, I thank my good friend Larrick Stapleton, who read most of the manuscript and gave me his lawyer's perspective and many stylistic suggestions.

INTRODUCTION

This is a guidebook to county courthouses, courthouse squares, and their immediate surroundings in the state of Pennsylvania. Its genesis was a personal fascination with the monumental Victorian courthouses in the small towns of the Midwest, which began in the 1950s. Just as the spires of smaller cathedral towns of Europe signal their presence from afar, on the flat midwestern plains the courthouse bell tower often loomed on the horizon and beckoned in a similar fashion. Later, when I moved east, I found that those monumental county structures were present here as well; indeed, it was here in Pennsylvania that some of the flamboyant styles were first introduced. Being interested in politics by profession, I often wondered who built these older monumental structures that stood in sharp contrast to many uninspired newer county buildings. Most county courthouses that were built in the fifties and sixties looked like warehouses and lacked the monumental spaces or decorative features of the earlier one. For buildings to have monumental elements, someone has to take pride in them, and in the case of county courthouses, this means *public* pride. Public pride was fashionable at the county level for much of our nation's history, but at times in this century, public penury has been more in vogue. While this guide focuses on the historic county buildings, it is gratifying to note that pride in public buildings is alive in some places, and there are some new county buildings worthy of note.

In those early visits to courthouse squares, I often found myself in a quiet and restful space with shaded benches and picnic tables. Plaques, fountains, and mementos had dedications that piqued my curiosity about local history. The more courthouses I visited, the more variety I discovered. I became a full-fledged courthouse junkie. As I began to share my observations with others, I found I was not alone in my interest, hence this guidebook to all the county courthouses of Pennsylvania, my adopted state for the past forty years. The book's emphasis is on the more historic buildings, interpreting them architecturally, politically, and sometimes socially, with the intent of helping viewers understand what they are seeing. It sometimes guides the viewer in a walk around the immediate environs, including the courthouse grounds, nearby buildings, and any other objects of interest. Additionally, further possibilities for exploration of the county seats are at times suggested, though this is not a guide to the county seats as such.

This guide describes many buildings using an adaptation of the procedures outlined for documenting buildings being nominated for the National Register of Historic Places. It may seem redundant to read a guide that describes the building you are observing. Actually, such detailing is an aid to seeing. It is commonplace to take in a complicated building at a glance and think you have really seen it. But once you start going over it piece by piece, you will discover much more about the building.

The premise of this guide is that the joy of viewing is enhanced by knowledge. The first thing to know about courthouses is that they are built with public funds, and their designs are chosen and approved by people who stand for election; thus, in a sense, this is a guide to a particular category of political art and architecture. It is about what communities, primarily counties, have thought their public buildings, as well as memorials, murals, and statues, should look like at particular places and times. Public art and architecture tend to follow fashion rather than to be innovative. Local elected officials are rarely great risk takers, particularly in the area of public esthetics, which means they often copy what other politicians are doing in similar places. The result is that courthouses built during a particular period tend to look alike. This is not necessarily bad, because it establishes a kind of architectural grammar that helps us read and recognize our built environment.

Courthouses and county buildings are influenced by their functions, and some knowledge of county government and its change over time will aid in better understanding the architecture. Because the design styles tend to reflect prevailing tastes, a historical review of styles may help place specific structures in context. The public space provided for the county functions is affected by the layout of county seat towns and cities, so a brief discussion of town planning—or lack of planning—is also in order. Finally, there is the issue of the politics of pride and penury. What explains why one or the other prevails at various times and places? The remainder of this introduction will address these topics generally, and then place Pennsylvania in that context. It is hoped that this background will enhance your visits to each county.

COUNTY GOVERNMENT

The county as a unit of government existed in Colonial times; thus, some Pennsylvania counties are older than the United States. As Americans moved into the frontier, the county was generally the first form of organized local government. When Penn founded Pennsylvania, he established three counties—Philadelphia (of which the city of Philadelphia was but a small part), Bucks, and Chester—even before he created an overall government for Pennsylvania. This is an indication of how basic a unit of government the county is. It is more basic and universal than other types of local government, such as towns and cities. Every part of a colony—or later a state—lies within one county or another. By contrast, towns and cities are limited and bounded areas, and not all citizens live within one. When new counties are formed, it is always by dividing the existing ones; this is rarely the case in creating new municipalities. This creation through division leads to a unique form of politics, described later.

The first need for local government on the frontier was for justice, thus the call for local courts. The need for courts was not just related to crime, but more importantly, to property law. Disputes over land titles were common, as property surveys were often crudely executed, deeds inexact, and squatting a common practice. The next governmental need was for record keeping, particularly descriptions of real property, because once a dispute was settled, it could not be made permanent without an official record. Other early record needs pertained to births, marriages, wills, and bequests. Because someone had to pay for courts, record keeping, and places to house these functions, county taxation arose simultaneously, hence tax collectors and property assessors. As the initial need for government was for courts, the name *courthouse* was given to these first county buildings, and the name remained even when the building housed other functions—at least, until modern times.

Early criminal punishments included use of stocks, whipping, branding, and hanging. These measures were gradually replaced with incarceration, but that created the necessity of a jail, and a jail in turn required a jailkeeper on duty around the clock. Many early jails were a kind of log cage, but soon courthouses, even very modest ones, began to include jail sections and a residence for a jailkeeper, usually the sheriff. Some of the surviving courthouse buildings once included jails and residential quarters for the sheriff/jailer, and the architecture still reflects these past uses (see Sullivan County). By the second half of the nineteenth century, as prison populations increased, counties began building jails separately from the courthouses. In the nineteenth century, they were generally one of two

The jail as residence. Former sheriff's house, Indiana, Indiana County.

types. One looked much like a residence from the front, because it was, in fact, the residential quarters of the jailer and his family. The other was a grim, crenellated medieval fortress. Many of both types of structures still stand, though many have been converted to alternative uses.

The justice function remains a very important part of Pennsylvania county government. Counties have criminal courts, called courts of oyer and terminer or courts of quarter sessions, juvenile courts, orphan's courts (probate and other family law jurisdictions), and courts of common pleas, which have civil jurisdiction. The same judges may preside over all of these courts. There are separate clerks for various categories, the prothonotary being the clerk for the court of common pleas. Many of these terms are part of our inheritance from English institutions in legal matters. In Pennsylvania, the sheriff is less a peace officer than in other states. Here, the local peace is

The jail as medieval fortress. Pottsville, Schuylkill County.

largely kept by municipal police and state troopers, and the sheriff is more an officer of the courts, executing court orders, delivering prisoners to and from the jail, and in smaller counties, administering the jail itself.

County services other than law enforcement were rudimentary until modern times. In most states, the county was in charge of rural roads and bridges, but not in Pennsylvania. Along with other Middle Atlantic states, Pennsylvania divided each county into townships, and one duty of these county subdivisions was to provide roads. Education was an early county function until it was spun off into independent school districts. The county provided rudimentary health and welfare services, and the latter led to the creation of county poor farms or almshouses. They were invariably built in the country outside the county seat. Few of these structures survive in Pennsylvania, and those that do are outside the purview of this guide.

Nineteenth-century courthouses were often treated more like community facilities than strictly government buildings. The courtroom was often the largest auditorium in town, and it was treated as a resource. Sunday church services were commonplace, as they were a way new congregations could get organized while they were constructing their own church buildings. Courthouse bells called people to services throughout the town on Sunday. Often nongovernment groups, such as veterans' organizations, were provided courthouse space, particularly after the Civil War. In some cases, offices and even the courtroom were available for private rental to provide county income for easing the tax burden.

A big change in county government began with the New Deal and accelerated after World War II. In most states, including Pennsylvania, the county role in welfare expanded exponentially. County health and inspection duties increased. Economic development and land use planning became politically important. Many of these expansions were stimulated with the availability of federal funds. With many new functions, county governments began to occupy many buildings. Today, many county governments occupy a large complex, or there are county buildings in many different locations. It is common to find huge, complicated directory signs to help citizens find where to go for a particular service. Criminal justice has become a major growth industry, and the term "criminal justice center" has become part of our building vocabulary.

Besides the county government's judicial and executive functions, there is also the legislative branch. Counties have a governing body, which in most states, including Pennsylvania, is called the county commissioners. County government typically differs from state and particularly the federal government in its legislative-executive relationships. Part of the difference dates from the time of Jacksonian democracy, when just about all public servants were elected. As counties added offices such as the sheriff, treasurer, surveyor, clerk, or auditor, they were directly elected and answerable only to the electorate. This Jacksonian practice is still retained today in most counties. County commissioners rarely have had any direct administrative oversight over these elected officials, other than budgetary leverage. The result was that the county government, until about fifty years ago, comprised a series of autonomous fiefdoms that often occupied the same building but otherwise had little to do with one another. The courts were one of the fiefs. The commissioners were in charge of what was left outside of these fiefs, and in those areas they were both legislators and executives.

In the nineteenth century, most county commissions did very little. Today, the newer twentieth-century functions—welfare, planning, economic development, health, parks, recreation—fall under their jurisdiction, and these are the parts of government that most citizens care about. The Pennsylvania county commission as created in the nineteenth century was composed of three members elected at large. Technically, it was a bipartisan board, as only two commissioners could be from the same political party. This reform feature, which was supposed to reduce party politics in county government, usually had the opposite effect. The minority party member could greatly enhance his or her power by driving a wedge between the two majority party members. Another strategy was for the majority party to give covert support to a selected minority commissioner in order to neutralize potential opposition. A modern constitutional amendment has provided for county home rule. The number of commissioners can now be changed, they can be elected by district, and they can appoint an executive, who works for them somewhat like a city manager. Most of the burgeoning county bureaucracy works under the commissioners or the courts, while the old row offices that were once so important are now a smaller part of the action.

In Colonial times, the royal governor had the power to create counties, and in the case of Pennsylvania, this meant William Penn initially and subsequently the proprietors. After the revolution, this power passed to the state legislatures. Counties in the settled areas were relatively small in size, but counties in the less populated areas could be huge. This meant that citizens in outlying areas were often far from the county seat, and going to court was a great hardship. In the early part of the nineteenth century, the state legislature was besieged with requests to divide up the counties into new ones.

Most citizens in the new areas had to deal with county courts. Part of the cause for this was the way land was sold to speculators and settlers. Surveys did not precede sales. Instead, purchasers would mark a piece of land and bring a description to the land office, which would enter the description. Claims were recorded sequentially and without regard to location in the state, making title searches tedious affairs. Boundary markers could be trees, streams, or tomahawk marks. While the claimant was supposed to pay for the land, many settlers did not. Title disputes usually favored primacy of registration and proof of occupancy. The opportunities for conflicting claims were legion, however, and the courts were kept busy sorting all this out.

During the Revolutionary War, the radicals took over the state government, with substantial western support. One issue for the western settlers was the need for more counties so travel to the county courts would be less arduous. The radical victory was a major upset, and men of common station for the first time ran the government. Their first move was to secure their victory by legislating that only citizens who took an oath to support them could vote. They also passed a tax law and exempted themselves from paying it. While part of the agenda that brought them into office was a promise to create more western counties in order to bring courts closer to the people, they created only one, Washington County in 1781. They were surprisingly fearful about the uncertainties of an open democratic process. New counties meant new state senators, a possible source of change. These politically inexperienced radicals were also inept in running the government, and this led to their downfall.

When the "aristocrats" returned to power, they proved to be more skillful than the egalitarian radicals at democratic politics. They quickly created seven new counties. A lesson soon learned by the politically astute was that one way for a party to increase support was to extend the franchise to the previously disenfranchised and thereby earn their gratitude and allegiance. The new constitution that Pennsylvania adopted in 1790 gave the governor power to appoint county officials, a measure that merged county politics inextricably with state elections. This practice continued until the constitution of 1838, in which county offices were made elective.

The key body in the county creation process was usually the legislative committee in charge of preparing the bills. County creation was a very political matter, as it contained elements of a zero sum game. There were always winners and losers. A new county meant a new county seat and a new set of county officers, but it also meant the old county seat lost business. Furthermore, the property tax base had to be divided. Some campaigns for new county creation went on for decades. Issues at stake included party politics, land ownership (speculative interests), and political ambitions. It is clear in some cases that the legislators were mainly interested in making as few enemies as possible and tried to wring grudging compromises from the parties affected. An interesting by-product of this process was that the county name was chosen by a political body in which the new county area was not represented. As a result, county names reflect the politics and values of the committee, not the people in the new county.

County functions shaped courthouse architecture. The early county courthouse function was record keeping. Because the records were so important to the inhabitants, their safekeeping was a major concern. The greatest threat to records was fire. Many early courthouses burned down, and the legal consequences were painful. There were cases of arson in which culprits tried to destroy evidence by burning the courthouse. Safety concerns led taxpayers to invest in well-built courthouses, which meant using brick and stone rather than wood. Early courthouses often were the only nonwood structures in town. Because they were so well built, many have endured. As the county clerk kept the important court records, special care was devoted to the clerk's quarters. In some states, though not Pennsylvania, the clerk was placed in a separate fireproof building. By the mid-nineteenth century, each county office was provided with special fireproof iron vaults. Their ornately decorated doors still exist in many buildings. Second to fire, the next major destroyer of courthouses was population growth. Growth meant more records, more employees, and more courts, and so even sound courthouses were razed so larger ones could be built. The oldest surviving courthouses in continual use are in counties that have had the least population growth.

While record keeping dictated the choice of fireproof building materials, the central influence in the building layout was the courtroom. In this country, trials have always been public events, and in early days, they were well attended. Before movies and television, they were often the best show in town. Many trial lawyers and judges became local celebrities as the result of trial performances. This meant that courtrooms had to be built large enough both to accommodate the public and to stage the show. In contrast, trials in nineteenth-century British colonies were not public, and the courthouses in places such as Australia provided no seating area for the public and only a small standing area for witnesses. Early American county courthouses were largely composed of a single large courtroom. As courthouses were enlarged to house other functions, the courtroom remained the largest room, and its design bore some resemblance to a theater. Many had a presidiumlike structure on either side of the judge's bench, suggestive of a stage. Balconies were common, as they enabled more spectators to be closer to the action.

Prior to this century, only larger cities had courthouses with multiple courtrooms, but today, only the smallest counties have but a single courtroom. Most modern trials are attended by only a few interested parties, and so recently built courtrooms are small. Perhaps because they no longer stage a public show, they are also exceedingly plain. Paradoxically, the greatest county court show trial of our time, that of O. J. Simpson, took place in one of these small, unadorned, nondescript courtrooms designed for current, commonly unattended, trials. As civil cases increasingly are handled by arbitration and criminal cases end in plea bargaining, judicial architecture is moving away from courtrooms and toward conference rooms, and from public spaces to office space for large bureaucracies. This new type of judicial structure is unlikely to inspire the writing of a future guide such as this one.

Some of the most delightful spaces covered in this guide are the older courtrooms. While the subjects of style and decor are treated below, a few observations about the organization of the courtroom is in order. Just as there is a clear separation between audience and stage in a theater, such is also the case in courtrooms. The dividing line is the *bar*, which usually takes the physical form of a railing. Lawyers practice before (beyond) the bar, where they have a domain that is barred to the public. The actual barrier is often handsomely crafted in wood, marble, or in rare cases, metal. The bench and beyond is the judge's compartment and space. Benches can also be elaborate pieces of furniture, but whether simple or elaborate, they are always raised, ostensibly so the judge has a clear view of the courtroom, but also to symbolize his or her importance as the embodiment of the majesty of the Law. Nearly all benches cover the lower part of the judge's body. Perhaps this is also a psychological ploy. A judge, manifested as a talking head (although no longer wigged), adds an air of authority. Dangling feet beneath the elevated bench would detract from the symbolism. Today, most solid benches have bulletproof shields as added security for the judge. Frequently, the space behind the bench is designed to further exalt the place occupied by the judge. There may be a niche or alcove laden with classical forms or other symbolism. Sometimes there are quotations for the edification of the audience.

Other furnishings behind the rail include desks for the clerk and court reporter, tables for counsels, a witness box, and a jury box with chairs. The prosecutor or plaintiff usually occupies the table closest to the jury, and the accused is placed at a distance from them. Just as the audience is physically separated from the trial area, the jury usually has a physical barrier that sets it apart. The accused may be further separated from the audience and jury by use of a separate entrance, particularly in the recently built facilities. Underground tunnels or "bridges of sighs" provide secure passages from jail to courts. Courtroom ancillary spaces now include judges' chambers, law libraries, jury deliberation rooms, witness rooms, and consultation rooms for lawyers and clients. Other than courtrooms, law libraries are often the next most interesting spaces. At least, that was true in the precomputer days, before case law was digitized.

A number of the early courtrooms did not provide for clear separations between audience and jury space or between audience and court personnel. The courtroom in the old Philadelphia city hall was particularly deficient in this regard. There are stories of spectators taking seats next to the lawyers and chatting openly with jurors during the trial. However, most of the courtrooms covered in this guide have the features just described. The very newest courthouses and courtrooms have completely separate spaces for the public, court personnel, and prisoners, including distinct entrances for each.

The court was the largest room in the courthouse in nineteenth-century buildings and was nearly always on the second story. Because of the audience effect on air quality, adequate heating and ventilation systems were important parts of the courthouse architects' craft. Large, high windows on either side of the room, opening from the top, allowed hot air to escape and encouraged a cross draft. Ceiling vents, sometimes elaborately engineered, were common. Stained glass in a skylight was a powerful decorative effect and diffused the rays of the noonday sun. The larger late-nineteenth-century courthouses often had huge central rotundas that also had an air circulation function. Sadly, the very devices used to make buildings comfortable in the days before air conditioning—high ceilings, huge windows, transoms, skylights—and that also defined the esthetic of their interior architecture, are the first to be sacrificed by expedient modern air-conditioning engineers.

Because of the second-floor location of the courtroom, most courthouses had wide, often double stairways to accommodate the spectators. The stairs afforded the architects an opportunity to add decorative flourishes. In the earlier courthouses, a pair of stairs, often gracefully curved, was located immediately inside the front door to take the courtroom audience upstairs without traipsing through the building. With the later rotundas, huge central stairs were often a principal monumental decorative feature in the building.

In addition to the courts, courthouses housed what are often referred to as the row offices—clerk, treasurer, assessor, recorder of deeds, and so on. These offices had little to do with one another—the employees in each had separate (elected) bosses—but the public needed direct access to each of them. Architecturally, the typical arrangement was to array the offices along a center hall on the first floor, which facilitated direct access to each office. The walls of the hallway were usually load bearing to support the second-floor courtroom. There rarely were interior doors connecting the row offices, but in some buildings, each had its own exterior entrances.

Surprisingly, most early courthouses did not provide a space for the commissioners, who held part-time positions and had no employees. There was not even a public room in which the commissioners could address or meet with the public. As new county functions were added in this century, they were rarely assigned to row offices, but instead came under the jurisdiction of the commissioners. Thus, modern courthouses have commissioner offices and public meeting rooms akin to those in city halls. After all the twentieth-century changes, the old-fashioned courthouse is obsolete. The primary need now is for office space for bureaucrats. The new county buildings being built today are rarely called courthouses.

ARCHITECTURAL STYLES OF COURTHOUSES

What should a county courthouse look like? With the earliest courthouses, function rather than fashion was probably uppermost in the builders' minds. It was a matter of constructing a usable space large enough to house the court function with limited resources and available materials. The first court sessions in most counties were held in houses or taverns, and in a few cases, in churches. There were court cases to be decided as soon as there was a government, and some trials took place in the open air. The first specially built courthouses were simple structures built of wood, often logs. An unrestored example of this survives in Waynesburg, Greene County. Another early style has been dubbed "coffee mill," describing a boxy building with a central tower that resembled that household implement. There are no extant examples.

The question of style usually came up when a courthouse was being replaced and there was time for planning. It was common to copy what other nearby counties were doing. County officials frequently visited other counties, the building committee junket being a perk of the office. There are a number of examples of commissioners hiring someone to copy an existing courthouse. One of the first successful lawsuits by an architect to stop such practices was by Philadelphian Samuel Sloan against Northumberland County.

Because most courthouses were built according to prevailing styles, one can usually date a courthouse by looking at it. One problem in doing so is that many courthouses have been modernized or added on to. This guide covers many of these hybrid buildings, and they will be pulled apart, figuratively, so the pieces can be dated, when possible. As when examining an antique, one asks what is original and what is a replacement part.

While many courthouses were copied from others, this was not always the case. There are very definite style differences, but styles tend to cluster at various points in time. Transitions in style were usually derived from influences in the larger society. These style shifts are national or even international in scope, and Pennsylvania courthouses tend to reflect these larger trends. There follows a classification of these national styles that have surviving examples in Pennsylvania. All buildings cannot be fitted neatly into these classifications, and from a national perspective, the Pennsylvania examples are a skewed sample. The goal here is to use a more general architectural vocabulary to discuss courthouses in this state, rather than create a set of terms that apply only to Pennsylvania.

Federal. The Federal style is very much derived from the residential tradition, and early courthouses, particularly during the first years of the republic, had a residential look. The same style was used in many public and commercial buildings. There are no pure Federal-style courthouses in use today in Pennsylvania. The only surviving example is Congress Hall in Philadelphia, which was constructed as a county courthouse. Some of the characteristic elements of the exterior facade are symmetry in the window pattern and a front gable, usually low. Windows are usually double hung, multiple paned with thin muntins, often shuttered. The main entrance often has architectural elaborations, such as pilasters, a fan light, and side lights around a paneled door. Congress Hall has most, but not all, of these characteristics. The older part of Tioga County's courthouse has Federal elements. Adams County has a modified Federal-type entrance, and several indigenous local builders who built Classical-style buildings incorporated Federal touches.

Congress Hall. PHOTO BY W. A. McCULLOUGH, COURTESY INDEPENDENCE NATIONAL HISTORICAL PARK.

Classical. The association of justice with the Roman law tradition and Greek philosophy may explain why the Classical model was adopted as the first self-consciously selected style as appropriate for courthouses. Thomas Jefferson advocated this style for public buildings, and he is often credited with starting the vogue. From about 1820 until the Civil War, the Classical temple was *the* courthouse form, not only in Pennsylvania, but also in most other states. The Classical temple of antiquity employed post-and-lintel construction and did not enclose a large interior space. It was a place people could flow through, not an enclosure for people to assemble to meet or work. Consequently, it was an awkward model for nineteenth-century government buildings. Jefferson adapted the form for the Virginia capital, retaining the Classical symbolism but creating a building that was practical for the time. He used the freestanding columns only on the front, where they supported a portico. By using pilasters rather than columns on the other three sides, they became part of the walls needed for an enclosure while retaining the Classical architectural language. This use of columns on the front and pilasters on the sides is a feature that appears time and again on courthouses described in this guide, including the later Eclectic styles.

The early temples of justice courthouses used the simple Doric or Tucson orders (Bedford County); later they were more likely to sport the fancier Ionic (Centre County) or Corinthian (Lancaster County) orders. There is some evidence that the Roman model was identified with the politics of Jefferson and Jackson, and the Greek with Federalists and their successors. While that degree of sophistication may have been followed in big cities, it probably does not explain the choice of architectural orders in most county courthouses. Many of these early courthouses were not architect designed, but built by local artisans who had only pattern books as their guides (Cumberland County). The more common fronts were tetrastyle (four columns) or hexastyle (six columns), but occasionally there are only five (Mifflin County). An alternate type is the distyle *in antis,* which, instead of having columns all across the front, has two columns standing within a recessed entrance (Bedford County). Because the major decorative features of the temple were on the facade, this building style could be given an addition to the rear without destroying its appearance. This may explain why so many of these early facades have survived.

Some Classical courthouses confined the orders to a porch or portico over the entrance rather than across the entire building facade. An early Pennsylvania example is Mifflin County. This device was sometimes used to Classicize early simple buildings (Tioga County), a widespread practice in eastern states. Modernization, that is, updating the style of an old building, is a practice that existed before our modern times.

Italianate. Americans experimented with many styles in the first half of the nineteenth century for nonpublic buildings, while Classical Revival dominated public architecture. Just prior to the Civil War, this experimentation began to extend to county courthouses. The most popular alternative to the Classical was called Tuscan Villa, a term also used in describing its application to residential building. Characteristic features included a boxy look with prominent brackets supporting the cornices. The invention of the power scroll saw enabled highly ornamental bracket designs. Hood moldings are extensively used over windows, which frequently had round-topped upper sashes or transoms. All the Pennsylvania examples have prominent bell towers, a feature not always present in Italianate courthouses in other states. There are a number of strongly Italianate courthouses in this state, such as that in Sunbury, Northumberland County.

Eclectic. From the beginning of the economic boom after the Civil War, and continuing for half a century, county courthouses became much larger. The increase in scale was not only a response to the need for more room, but also an expression of local community pride. Pride in this context took on competitive overtones and a desire not to be outdone by neighboring counties. Symbolism became primary, and utility was sometimes a secondary concern. A courthouse often was the largest, most elaborate structure in the county, containing monumental interior spaces. These spaces at a later, more pragmatic time were viewed as wasteful and hence were targets for elimination. Some architectural historians label the late-nineteenth-century architectural styles as simply Eclectic, as they borrowed forms from many times and places. However, there are discernible subtypes.

Second Empire. Second Empire was named for the form that found favor in the French urban building boom at this time, the Louvre (1852–57) being the quintessential example. Its central features as adapted to courthouses are the mansard roof with elaborate dormers, corner pavilions, and a prominent clock/bell tower. The quintessential expression is the Philadelphia city hall–county courthouse. The peak period is the 1870s.

Renaissance Revival. The great Renaissance palaces of northern Italy supplied the prototypes for a number of buildings. Elements were taken from all of the orders of Classical architecture, which were often used in combination. However, the forms in which they were expressed reflected the inventive combinations of the northern Italian architects. In the Eclectic tradition, only parts of buildings might reflect this style. There is only one Pennsylvania example, in Towanda, Bradford County.

Gothic. Throughout the earlier part of the nineteenth century, the Gothic style was reserved for churches, and to a certain extent, residential cottages. However, Gothic decorative flourishes, such as trefoil windows and pointed arches, became part of the architectural vocabulary for the Eclectic architects of this period and can be seen in courthouses in Blair and Butler Counties.

Romanesque. The Romanesque style is often associated with architect Henry Hobson Richardson, who began his professional career around 1865, following a European education. Hallmarks of his style included the Roman arch in windows and entryways, short, sturdy columns, elaborate carved stone or terra cotta foliage decorations, and masterful management of stone surfaces. His Allegheny County courthouse (1883–87) was the defining building. He died before it was finished, and it has been said that as a consequence of his early death, other architects were freer to copy his ideas. In any case, designers of county courthouses all over America began introducing the Richardsonian look. While Romanesque elements had been introduced by other architects before Richardson, he integrated and shaped the elements in a fashion that left his personal mark on the style.

Classical Revival. While Classical elements were incorporated into many of the Eclectic styles, some buildings were more pointedly derived from the earlier temple of justice tradition. As the courthouses need to be much larger late in the century, the Classical order was often confined to the entrance portico, rather than the full front facade. The Classical form seems to be the permanently politically correct look and the refuge of timid building committees who want to avoid public criticism. A late example is Indiana County.

Beaux-Arts. By the turn of the century, American architects increasingly went to the École des Beaux-Arts in Paris to finish their education. This near educational monopoly was bound to have its effect on the looks of American buildings. Its influence was coalesced by the World's Fair of 1893 in Chicago, where the orthodox École style was embraced and viewed by American visitors from all parts of the nation. It took a few years for the new generation of French-trained architects to start getting the counties as clients, but by the turn of the century, they had. There were several contextual factors that led the counties to adopt this new influence. As America industrialized and urbanized, the function of the courthouse was changing. The communications role of the bell and clock tower was a thing of the past, even in small towns. The buildings had to be bigger to provide for more employees and more courtrooms for larger populations. Big buildings require new solutions for internal lighting and air circulation in an era before air conditioning. A common response was the central rotunda, often covered by a monumental dome, and in many cases, the national capitol was the model. The dome was not for a bell or clock, but was sheer ostentation. Some architectural historians call them county capitols.

Pennsylvania is well represented by these, a good example being in Greensburg, Westmoreland County.

The Beaux-Arts style involved elaboration on Classical components, often done in innovative ways. The Neoclassical, often gray limestone, usually towerless buildings became the vernacular courthouse expression throughout the nation for several decades. For all their exterior drabness, they are often very exciting inside, with monumental spaces and impressive courtrooms.

Art Deco and Art Moderne. What we often call Modernism is the rejection of Classical models and the invention of a new building language. These ideas, from Wright to Bauhaus and beyond, occurred concurrently with the Beaux-Arts period. While Modernism banishes the language of arch, column, and cornice from the architectural vocabulary, there were styles, particularly in public architecture, that retained them in a modern way. The cleaner lines of Modernism were embraced, but the Classical forms were not completely rejected. Art Deco has its own peculiar style of zigzag lines, fake Mayan bas-reliefs, and curved edges, some of which can be found in the unusual courthouse in Reading, Berks County. Art Moderne was more likely to retain Classical elements, particularly the pilaster and surface ornaments, but they are so muted that they barely interrupted the building plane. This style is also identified with distinctive building materials: Decorative metal, bronze, and for the first time, aluminum, came into use, and travertine was the stone of preference. Doorways, lighting fixtures, and elevator surrounds were favorite locations for these materials. There are Art Moderne features in a number of Pennsylvania courthouses and annexes, but the purest example is in Harrisburg, Dauphin County.

In the 1930s, most new courthouses were built with the aid of federal public-works funds. Simplicity and economy became political priorities in design choice, because cries of federal waste were in the air. The WPA courthouses incorporated the prevailing Art Moderne style, but often in a very bare-bones fashion. There are no pure WPA courthouses in this state, although there are some annexes and interior renovations.

Modern. Most courthouses built in the 1950s, 1960s, and 1970s are the kinds that give Modernism a bad name. All monumental elements, both inside and out, were minimized. During this period, some states were assuming responsibility for the courts, and local pride was disassociated from courthouse construction. Parsimony and even penury became a standard principle at the county level. Lebanon County is a Pennsylvania example of this style. Pride could still be expressed in the Modern style, however, as in the one example in the state in Bucks County.

Postmodern. The reaction against the dismal Modern warehouse styles and air-conditioned, boxy office buildings has led to the reincorporation of some purely decorative forms and monumental spaces into building structures. This is the current design fashion in both modernizing and building new structures. A good example can be found in Philadelphia's Judicial Administration Center.

Modernization and Preservation. Modernization is a very old economic trick. To update a building inexpensively, a new trendy facade can be the answer. Classical porticos were used to adorn Federal-style courthouses along the East Coast before the Civil War, and after the war, ornate Victorian towers were often added to old temple-style buildings. Pennsylvania's modernization between 1930 and 1950 often meant stripping off all adornments and encapsulating the building in a box. Though there have always been people who objected to such practices, it was not until the preservation movement of the 1960s that the reaction against modernization affected public policy. There were still some terrible modernizations of courthouses in the 1970s, but slowly the message seems to have gotten around. Though modern systems must be installed, there has been an increasing effort to preserve and restore the original architectural style. These achievements are highlighted in this guide.

THE PLACE OF THE COURTHOUSE IN THE TOWNSCAPE

One of the enduring American townscape images is that of a courthouse in the center of a full square, surrounded by grass, trees, benches, a veterans memorial, a bandstand, and perhaps plaques dedicated to local heroes. There are examples of this scene in Pennsylvania, but that model is more widespread in the nation's heartland. It occurred more frequently when a new town was platted specifically to be the county seat and was a concept that evolved with the westward expansion of America.

In Pennsylvania, there is an interesting mix of courthouse locations in the townscape, of which this courthouse square type is but one example. When county seat status was awarded to an already developed town, the courthouse had to be crowded into the commercial area. This made land acquisition expensive; consequently, open space around the courthouse was often limited. Most of the courthouses covered in this guide are located downtown, as is the case in most eastern-state counties. It is not till one gets to the railroad towns of the northern plains that courthouses are relegated to the residential areas and the railroad station is given the central place.

Geographers have developed a vocabulary for classifying county seat towns by types. When the courthouse takes up a full block in the rectilinear street grid and commercial establishments are located across the street on all four sides opposite the courthouse, it is called a Shelbyville Square, named after the town in Tennessee that first employed this plan. A variant on this is the Lancaster Square, named for Lancaster, Pennsylvania, which sets aside a complete central square, but one offset from the regular grid so that the courthouse is at the center of the two major intersecting streets. The result is to visually highlight the courthouse as it is seen straight ahead by approaching traffic from four directions. Philadelphia now has this plan, but the square on which the courthouse now stands was for a long time vacant. Lancaster no longer uses the plan to which it gave its name. A variant combining elements of both these types, called Harrisonburg after a town in Virginia, has a square offset from the street pattern in only one direction. Pennsylvania has one example in Mercer County.

A New England tradition provides for a central open space, often called the green, but has the important public and religious buildings facing it, rather than in it. Symbolically, this placed the community sectors of government, religion, and social on an equal status. Interestingly, commercial establishments did not face the green, implying a lesser status for them. As northern Pennsylvania was settled initially by New Englanders, we find courthouses facing a park that is sometimes called the green. Churches and other community institutions may also be arrayed around the park, but not always. Some Pennsylvania counties have a central space, often adjacent to the courthouse, that is called the diamond. This term is unique to Pennsylvania and shows another early immigrant influence, in this case the Scotch-Irish. It was the English practice in what is now called Northern Ireland to arrange the public buildings around an open space that was called there the diamond, evidently because of its shape. The Scotch-Irish brought this concept to many towns in the state, not just to county seats. An example of where the term is retained among our county seat towns is Butler.

Finally, many courthouses were simply assigned a place at the end of the business strip, and they faced the main street, just as did other buildings. The only difference is that the courthouse usually has a setback and often side yards, while commercial businesses do not.

The placing of the courthouse or city hall in the middle of an open square has no precedent in England or continental Europe. Evidently, like the diamond, this is a planning concept brought from Northern Ireland by the Scotch-Irish. There, it was the constabulary that was so situated. One cannot but wonder why it caught on in America and became popular even where there were no Scotch-Irish immigrants. A building placed in the center of a square tends to have entrances on all four sides. This makes it very accessible to the public and therefore symbolic of democratic access by the people to their place of government. This accessible building type was particularly appropriate for the county government as it evolved, in that the public needed direct access to many separately administered functions. These nineteenth-century courthouses are poorly designed for our present security-consciousnesss, however. Many of the fine old entryways are now closed, and the public must enter through metal detectors often set up at narrow basement doors.

The town plan can influence how well nineteenth-century courthouse buildings have been preserved. Those placed in the center of a square have three or four facades and cannot be expanded without ruining the design, whereas those built facing a street or square usually have only one facade and can be given rear additions. Because those located in the center of squares are difficult to add on to, they are often gutted to cram more office space into them and consequently lose their monumental interiors.

How do you find the courthouse in a strange town? This guide will supply street names and routes in most cases, but a few other tips are helpful. Always try the very center of town first. If there is no center square, the courthouse will usually be within a few blocks of the main intersection. The sheriff's radio tower can sometimes be a clue.

For Americans living outside the large cities, the county has been, through much of our history, the principal place of identity. Many professional and nonprofit organizations are organized by county, such as lawyers, doctors, and veterans and charitable groups. Thus, it follows that the courthouse and the courthouse square collect a large share of memorials, statues, and plaques honoring local persons and events. Most county courthouses have a veterans memorial, including Civil War statues. Some of the earliest Civil War memorials are in Pennsylvania, and interestingly, there was no initial consensus as to their desirability. (See the entries for Wayne and Erie Counties to learn about the controversy.) The square across from the Tioga County courthouse provides a good distribution of county memorials, which are illustrated here.

Memorial to coal mine owner John Magee, Wellsboro, Tioga County.

Typical veteran's memorial, Wellsboro, Tioga County.

When plaques are not self-explanatory, this guide tries to provide information, but there is little point in repeating information that is clearly provided on the site. Particular attention is given to statues of or memorials to local heroes, identifying why they are heroes and how they came to be memorialized.

The guide covers the decorative arts in the vicinity of the courthouse, particularly those of a public nature. In the nineteenth century, wealthy citizens often donated fountains or bandstands to decorate the squares, often as memorials. The 1930s brought on a wave of public art through federally sponsored art programs. Murals, often placed in post offices, portrayed local themes and gave local citizens a say in their contents. Thus, what is portrayed usually says as much about local views and tastes as those of the artists. There are some purely esthetic examples of sculpture as well.

THE ARCHITECTURE OF PRIDE AND PENURY

When I first began this project, I assumed that the prevailing public attitude toward public buildings was different in the nineteenth century than today. The monumental buildings suggested as much, for it is difficult to imagine today's county taxpayers approving such ostentatious displays. As I delved into the contemporary accounts, I found evidence to support this view, but the story is more complicated than I first thought. There are reasons for changing attitudes, and these must be part of the story.

There was an opposition that fought the construction of nearly every great courthouse. There is always a faction that does not want to spend any money, and there is always a faction that wants a new facility that will serve the needs of the county well. The penurious group always says that the existing buildings are adequate, or that with a modest set of changes the county government can get by. The advocates for a new building are guided by various motives, only one of which might be properly labeled civic or local pride. Sometimes the argument is simply that a new building is a sound investment. Old buildings may have high maintenance costs, they may be firetraps, or they may be so small that auxiliary rental space is inevitable. What is predictable is that there will always be a pro and con faction for every building proposal.

The squabbles over building proposals in the nineteenth century were probably exacerbated by newspapers and, at times, by electoral politics. Most counties had two or more newspapers all fighting for circulation. Taking sides on local issues was one way to get readers. And candidates challenging incumbents always need issues. But were these factions rooted in real interests? A reading of newspaper accounts is suggestive. The propride, monumental courthouse advocates in the post–Civil War period were the same interests who were identified with growth and development generally. The courthouse was a leading physical symbol of civic status aspirations. The dedication ceremony for a Victorian courthouse is indicative of how emphatically the symbol was exploited. These ceremonies were huge affairs. Parades and activities lasted all day. Most people in the county attended, and the backup of horse-drawn vehicles trying to enter town would stretch for a mile or more. Special trains often brought out-of-town visitors. The main speaker was an important figure, the governor or the chief justice of the Supreme Court. Predictably, the bar association always had a prominent presence in these ceremonies. One surmises that a monumental building reflected favorably on their profession. References to the new buildings at the ceremony and in the newspaper accounts emphasized the grand and sumptuous features. There were never any apologetic or defensive notes expressed.

It is fascinating to observe the stratagems that the promonumental group used to prevail over opponents. One of the most common was to specify a cost that was unrealistically low, then start the building anyway. Sometimes the advertised estimate would cover only the exterior, sometimes not even the roof. It appears as if the building committees had confidence that the public would get behind the project once it got started.

The debate between the two factions did not always end in a clear victory of one party or the other. Some of the buildings covered in this guide are clearly compromises. They were built less grandly than some advocates wanted. Building costs can be reduced by choosing inexpensive materials. Limestone can be substituted for marble, brass plating for solid brass, tin for copper, scagliola for stone, decorative paint for coffered ceilings. Many examples of downgrading are described herein. What is surprising, however, is the number of times that in the course of construction there was an upgrade in materials. Building committees got carried away, and material change orders moved up the quality scale.

The grandness of the courthouse is not just a result of a tussle between the pride and penury factions. Some counties were simply wealthier, and others very poor. There were also some very definite secular political trends in new construction over time. The period of monumentalism lasted from the post–Civil War years until the Great Depression. This was a period of great growth and recurring optimism. The towering Berks County courthouse was built after the stock market crash of 1929. There is no hint in the words of the building commission that any cutbacks should be considered. Indeed, they were determined to give the county a building that "the people deserved." Even the Dauphin County courthouse, built during the early part of World War II, continues the monumental tradition unabated.

To determine what effects the Great Depression may have had, it may help to look beyond Pennsylvania at what was being built elsewhere. Many county courthouses were built over the country with the help of WPA funds. For the most part, they were simple structures that used less expensive materials. Most were built in the Art Moderne style, though some Classical Revival examples can be found. The WPA was very sensitive, not only to local opinions in matters of style, but also to criticisms about waste. WPA releases and handouts stressed the practicality and serviceability of the structures. What was built may have had local input in the choice of style, but the national political agenda dictated much of what was done. This suggests that when two or more levels of government share financial responsibility for building a structure—when a courthouse is partly financed by national or state funds—parsimony, if not penury, is likely to prevail. Interlevel transfers come as gifts in which the interests of nonlocal taxpayers are involved.

This supposition is given added support if one looks at the many county courthouses built with federal aid in the 1960s and 1970s. In many rural counties of Appalachia and the western plains, economic development grants could be used to build courthouses. These are mostly very dreary buildings. Urban county buildings built with federal economic stimulus funding have a similar institutional drabness. Yet more recent court buildings, which have been built nearly entirely with county funds, indicate that pride was present. In states where the former county courts have been integrated into the state court system and the state is building the courthouses, the results can be uninspiring.

It is not just intergovernmental financial transfers that portend the end of monumental architecture, however. With the great expansion of county functions and the explosion of county employees over the past decades, county governments are now housed in complexes. Consider the justice function and the courts. The largest share of judicial employees do not work directly for the judges. Criminal justice is a major county growth industry. Mandates from above result in increases in criminal justice personnel, separate facilities for juveniles, and standards for prisons. There are public defenders, parole officers, probation departments, family counseling, witness protection, and large prosecutorial staffs. All this leads to a new set of county buildings, usually called a judicial center. There are more trials and more courts, but large audiences are a rarity. Many new courtrooms have only a few benches for ten or twenty people. This book visits few of these courts. Any monumental spaces in the newest county buildings are not likely to be where the courts are located, but rather where the commissioners or county executive have their offices. Power and monumental spaces have a way of going together, but in a democratic society with elected officials, the story is never simple. Penury is sometimes good politics, and some commissioners will choose to occupy pitifully dreary spaces.

Most of the newer structures are of little interest because they are built without pride and are simply the kind of architectural space we pass through without notice in our modern lives. This guide visits the modern structures only when there is an interesting point to be made. The primary focus is historical.

ORGANIZATION OF THE GUIDE

This guide is written for those who wish to visit Pennsylvania's county courthouses. It covers every county. I can always find something of interest, but I would be the first to admit that some courthouses and squares are much more rewarding than others to visit. The descriptions in this book make those distinctions clear. Some of the courthouses have great historic interiors, and others have been completely modernized. This information may be especially helpful for weekend travelers.

Some of the most interesting spaces are the historic courtrooms, public places that can be visited even when in session, although juvenile and domestic cases can exclude spectators. Be prepared to pass through metal detectors. Do not carry a camera or a pocketknife unless you do not mind checking them as you enter.

The following section lists the courthouses by county name, in alphabetical order.

THE COURTHOUSES

ADAMS
County Seat: Gettysburg

Pennsylvania honored the first three sitting presidents of the United States by naming a county for them, including this one for John Adams. The county's creation in 1800 was the result of a twelve-year campaign in which western York County residents sought to end their fifty-mile treks to the county seat at York. Ethnic concerns and an orientation of west county residents to Baltimore rather than Philadelphia markets helped fuel the call for county division. To this day, many in this general area continue to be oriented to Baltimore in shopping and sports team loyalties. Samuel Gettys was a member of the original settler family.

Chances are that if you are in Gettysburg, it will be to view the battlefield and associated attractions. While the courthouse cannot compete with those spectacles, it is an interesting stop. It was built in 1859, so it was there when *the* battle took place. It was briefly captured by the Confederates, who used it as a hospital, where, according to neighboring residents, many amputations took place. Located at Baltimore and Middle Streets, a block south of the central square, it is

a brick building (1859, S. D. Dutton of Philadelphia, architect) constructed somewhat in the Italianate style, with rather restrained bracketing, but also with Classical elements. Dutton's building was three bays wide and six bays deep. A 1906 addition to the rear is in a compatible style. The central front bay is within a shallow pavilion framed by double square pilasters, which support a pediment projecting above the roofline. The pediment has modillions on the raking sides only and the county name and courthouse date are on the entablature. The entrance is modified Federal with a fanlight over the door. Above is a cornice, supported by consoles and small brackets, which fits between the pilasters. At the second

story, there is a Norman window with semicircular brick hood molding. A distinctive feature of the building is the tower, which projects 25 feet above the roof. Both its base and belfry tier have slightly slanting sides. The square base has engaged piers at each corner, and the belfry has a single arched louver on each side. The clock faces interrupt a bracketed cornice, and each has an ornamented, semicircular hood. There is an elaborate finial with a simple weathervane on top. The side bays of the facade are separated by pilasters, the first-story windows are rectangular with stone lintels top and bottom, and the upper-story windows are segmentally arched with hood moldings. There is a belt line high on the building at the base of the bracketing.

Adams County commissioners through most of this century were more parsimonious than prideful in their dealings with the courthouse. As a result, the building suffered a series of insults. Its bricks were painted, windows were glass bricked, the *trompe l'oeil* walls in the courtroom were covered with acoustical tile in the 1960s, and in the 1970s the county commissioners voted to abandon the building. There followed a protracted preservation battle. The commissioners wanted to build a new courthouse in the suburbs and relented only after being taken to court. Rallies were held to prevent the razing of the old building, and the preservationists mobilized no less a person than Mamie Eisenhower to their cause. Finally, the commissioners built the new courthouse next door, which the architects (Rogers and Frederick of Harrisburg) initially proposed with a modern design. The commissioners rejected that idea and chose the vapid, pseudo-Colonial design you now see. Curiously, the architects' names do not appear on the building, which is highly unusual.

The 1859 building was finally restored, and the job was done with care and sensitivity. Othmar Carli, a conservationist trained in his native Austria, was in charge of the work, and the results of his efforts are apparent by a visit to the upstairs courtroom. The glass brick is now gone, and the hundreds of acoustical tiles were removed from the courtroom walls in order to expose the *trompe l'oeil*. The plaster walls and ceilings had to be stabilized with hundreds of shots of resin. Tests revealed that the *trompe l'oeil* had actually been painted many times with varying levels of skills. Carli chose to preserve as much existing paint as possible, and the result is most attractive, though it is not exactly the same *trompe l'oeil* that was first painted in the late nineteenth century. The restored images include a coffered ceiling, pilasters, and a niche behind the bench. The bench and nonmatching witness box are old, the former probably original. The audience benches were made in 1934. Carli designed the chandeliers based on detailed studies of fixtures used in churches and public buildings at the time the courthouse was built. John Gibson, whose portrait is paired with John Marshall, was chief justice of the Pennsylvania Supreme Court from 1827 to 1851. For years after renovation, the courtroom was used only for weddings and ceremonial affairs, which seemed a waste of good courtroom space. Recently, the gavel again has been heard here, as it is used for jury trials when the modern courtrooms are unable to handle the caseload. The downstairs hall and stairways were also restored and now have a nineteenth-century look. The center hall has wood-framed honor rolls of county veterans.

Originally, the town was built on the Lancaster plan, with the courthouse in the middle of what is now Lincoln Square. The square was formed by nibbling four corners off the adjoining blocks, providing room for the roadway around the courthouse. Just as in Lancaster, the square could not accommodate a larger building, hence the choice of the present location. Ironically, in this town that lives off the Civil War, there was no monument to local Union soldiers until 1991. Perhaps all those in the battlefield park were enough. The modern monument is located on the south side of Lincoln Square.

ALLEGHENY
County Seat: Pittsburgh

Allegheny is of Indian derivation. The county seat is indirectly named for William Pitt, the British prime minister. When General Forbes conquered the French Fort Duquesne on this site in 1758, he renamed it Fort Pitt, and the city, which came later, assumed the name of the fort. Allegheny County was established in 1788.

The courthouse on Grant Street is one of the most significant county courthouses in the United States from an architectural perspective. Designed by H. H. Richardson, along with the adjoining jail in 1883, it was com-

pleted in 1888, two years after the famous architect's death. His first important building was Trinity Church in Boston, built in the 1870s, and his last major work, conceived in 1885, was the Marshall Field wholesale store in Chicago. The Pittsburgh courthouse and jail rank right up there among them. He is one of the few American architects for whom a whole style is named, and this Allegheny County building had a major impact on the look of new county courthouses for several decades, particularly in the Midwest and Texas. The main elements of the Richardsonian Romanesque style are described in the Introduction. To the admirers of this building, it is poetry in stone and has all the trademarks of the Richardson genius. Its beauty does not overwhelm on first sight, but requires observation and attention. In examining the exterior, it is helpful to have a pair of binoculars.

The courthouse is primarily built of Milford pinkish gray granite, quarry faced on most surfaces and smooth for accents, such as the water table, belt courses, cornices, and archivolts. Follow the red grout lines and note the varied but highly controlled masonry patterns. The surface texture changes under differing angles of light. The window arrangements were designed to give as many rooms as possible natural light from two directions, using the huge interior court. Since the visual dominant features viewed from the outside are the formidable stone walls, it is surprising how well the interior is flooded with natural light. The tall tower, in addition to providing a civic symbol, originally was intended to draw in a better quality air than was available at the very polluted ground level.

Looking over the facade, note that the window treatment changes with each story but is constant within stories except for the tower. However, that is not exactly true, as you can see by examining the mullion pilaster capitals through your glasses. If you want to try to count the variations, you had better give yourself some time. The front of the tower rises flush with the front facade. Above the building roof, it has turrets on the sides, centrally placed between two tall blind arches in the stone. The turrets at each corner rise to the roofline. Examine the tops of the turrets with your glasses, and then move over to what look like modillions under the open area of the belfry. Those faces are your next treat. The belfry has tall, narrow, arched openings. Again with your glasses, note the subtle curves on the cross braces, and then look at the stone leaf work of the cornice. Even the slate pattern on the various roof surfaces is a rewarding look. The sides of the building have varied planes, including two round sections on either side of the portals, each of which rises to a conical roof. Note the row of rosettes in the stones near the top of these round sections.

The front door opens into the basement, a very spare space with a low vaulted ceiling. If you are disoriented by this space, there is a reason. When Richardson designed the courthouse, there was a hill in front of the building on Grant Street, and his entrance led to the story above. When the hill was hauled away to level Grant Street, the entrance was shifted down a story. Find your way up a story, and you will discover a grand stairway that is the major decorative feature of the interior. Again, its beauty is austere and ordered like the exterior, featuring round arches, squat columns, and carved capitals. The corridors that connect the rooms of the lower floors follow the inside wall next to the courtyard and thus are well lighted and also provide a continuing view of the exterior walls opposite. The patterns are again worth observing. Each of the four arcades of arched windows is designed differently. The large arched windows originally acted as clerestories to illuminate the original banks of two-story courtrooms.

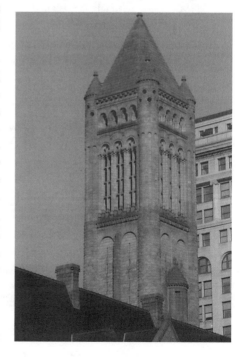

Richardson was chosen as architect in a competition. What impressed the commission that made the decision was not his bold design, but his practical organization of space. For example, next to each two-story courtroom, he placed two stories of auxiliary office space, which were connected by an interior spiral staircase. The courthouse interior has been greatly altered over time, and all of the original courtrooms have disappeared, although one has recently been restored to replicate Richardson's original look, including the furnishings.

The murals in front of the building were painted by Vincent Nesbert between 1934 and 1940 with WPA aid. The themes are mostly self-explanatory. The two military murals portray events that took place very near the site of the present building.

The jail to the rear of the courthouse was also designed by Richardson and built at the same time. To many admirers, it is an even more impressive work in stone. The stone "bridge of sighs," which connects the two buildings, was copied after its namesake in Venice. The bridge, in addition to being attractive, provided a very practical way to deliver prisoners to the courtrooms with minimal contact with the public. The jail was enlarged once, but in keeping with the original style. The county commissioners proposed to demolish it on several occasions but were stopped by public outcry. At this writing, the building is unused, but proposals for its reuse are under active consideration.

There are several other county buildings adjacent, one of which, the City-County Office Building (1929), is worth a look. As its title suggests, it houses Pittsburgh as well as Allegheny offices. While there are a number of architects' names on the dedication plaque, Henry Hornbostel, who worked for the E. B. Lee firm, is generally credited with the design. It features a grand arcade between the city and county sides. There are courtrooms on some of the upper floors, and one (number eleven on the seventh floor) has an interesting WPA mural entitled *Modern Justice,* painted by Harry W. Scheuch (1906–78). Scheuch, who called himself a regional artist, had some success as an easel painter and completed one other mural in the post office in Scottsdale, Pennsylvania. The trip to the seventh floor will also give you an opportunity to examine some of Hornbostel's design work on the inner atrium.

ARMSTRONG
County Seat: Kittanning

There were a number of Colonial generals named John Armstrong, many associated with deeds in the middle states, leading to much confusion about Armstrong place namesakes. The Gen. John Armstrong who is the namesake of this county, which was established in 1800, led an expedition in 1756 that destroyed the Indian town whose warriors had caused trouble for the residents of Kittanning. Kittanning took its name from the Indian town whose site it displaced, an action that may have caused the warriors to make trouble in the first place.

The Greek Revival courthouse is arrestingly sited at the end of the main street that runs from the Allegheny River Bridge. It was built on solid rock into the hillside (1858–60, Hulings and Dickey, architects), and its location and design both contribute to its striking appearance. It features a Corinthian portico, which rests upon a stone first-story triple arcade. The stone of the first floor, including the arcade, differs from that of the upper stories, and there is some evidence that the lower-story stone was salvaged from the previous courthouse, which had been destroyed by fire. The courthouse tower is centrally located, aligned over the apex of the pediment. It has an octagonal base, which supports a modified octagonal belfry; alternate faces have arched louvers with detached Corinthian columns at the angles and a denticulated pediment above. The main body of the tower is sandstone and the decorative parts are wood, thus it predates the period of sheet metal ornamentation. Its roof is a ribbed high dome, topped by a similar smaller dome and a finial. The white paint is a recent treatment. The now electrified bell, which rings out the daylight hours, may be from the first, 1818 courthouse. The absence of a clock is unusual for this date. The jail (1873) just to the north, which is made of somber red Clarion County sandstone, also has a tower. It is of the crenelated Pennsylvania jail genre. There are two additions to the rear dating from 1914 and 1950, both hidden from the front view.

Interior changes began in the early 1870s, including some acoustical adjustments in the courtroom. One source mentions local architect James McCulough, Jr., in connection with this work, but what he did remains sketchy. The interior has been altered several times in this century. The major, second-story front courtroom dates from 1954, and much of the remainder of the interior is a product of the 1990s.

The adjacent Postmodern administration building has a wall war memorial, which is unusual in several ways. It is one of the most complete in recognizing all local citizens who gave their lives in service. Second, it includes some Native Americans. The criteria for doing so is not clear, however, because Indians killed in the first battle of Kittanning are not listed. The panoramic plaque seeks to portray many of the scenes associated with the military actions in which the memorialized fell.

Given its location, there is little room for green space around the courthouse, but there is an attractive park being developed along the riverbank several blocks away.

Perhaps Armstrong County's most famous person was Nelly Bly, investigative reporter, steel barrel manufacturer, and most of all, circumnavigator of the globe in seventy-two days in 1889–90.

BEAVER
County Seat: Beaver

The seat and county are named after the eager little animal that was once abundant in this area. The county seat is a well-laid-out residential town in this largely industrial county. It predates the county, which was created in 1800, and was planned with a great deal of land reserved for public use, much of which remains in parks, including the area along the high bank of the Ohio River and the central part of the town.

The courthouse is located in Agnew Park, one of four contiguous public squares just north of the main business strip, which are part of that publicly dedicated land dating from 1792. It is an architectural puzzle of a building. It looks like Art Moderne, but the shape is wrong for that style. Art Moderne courthouses usually have wide frontal facades and no towers. The answer is that it is an 1875 building (Thomas Boyd, architect) that was badly damaged by fire in 1932. The architects, Edward J. Carlisle and Harry P. Sharrer, who were brought in to rebuild it, wrapped the salvaged remains in a stone skin, using the contemporary Art Moderne style. They followed the lines of the old building, including the stump of the old clock tower. The front lunette window, which is not part of the Art Moderne palette, is copied from the Boyd building, though it was formerly higher up on the facade. The bas-reliefs are strictly Art Moderne.

Along the north side of the building, you will find a series of annexes. The first one, added by Carlisle and Sharrer in 1922 before the fire, was originally red brick like the Boyd building. Note that its three stories are lower than the 1875 two-story building, indicating the passing of those Victorian fifteen- and twenty-foot ceilings. This annex was also encased in the new stone veneer. Next comes a 1974 annex (Carl G. Baker, architect), and then a 1989 addition (Wallover and Mitchell, architects). The latter has a composite mural of county scenes by Ray Zielinski, a county resident.

In the 1933 rebuilding, there was a big debate about the exterior stone veneer. In this Depression time, bricklayers, including some in Ohio, protested the use of imported stone and urged support for the local brick-making industry. As it turned out, the architects probably should have heeded the protesters, as the stone veneer has turned out to be a problem and is now being replaced in stages.

The attractive adjoining well-planted squares contain cannons, bandstands, veterans memorials, benches, and all the traditional elements of courthouse grounds. There is a plaque commemorating local boy, Matt Quay, who became one of the leaders of the powerful state Republican political machine that held sway over Pennsylvania for decades. At the other side of the square, across the street from the courthouse, is an 1858 sheriff's house and jail, built of cut limestone. Throughout its long history, many prisoners have found ways to escape from it and those that did not, at times, lived in rather uncomfortable conditions. As of 1997, it was still in use.

All of the above sites are within a nationally registered historic district, which includes all the area of the original village.

BEDFORD
County Seat: Bedford

The county, created in 1771, was named for the town of Bedford, which took its name from a fort named for the fourth duke of Bedford, John Russell. Russell, who was prominent in British politics largely because of his enormous wealth, was reputedly most interested in cricket. He was associated with the party opposite Pitt and was no friend of the colonists. When the county was formed, the fort had been in existence for decades, and there probably were few thoughts about Russell when Gov. John Penn gave the county its name. The town of Bedford was laid out with a generous set of reserved public squares in the tradition of William Penn. Unlike Philadelphia, here the squares are adjacent, and the courthouse occupies one of them. Various veterans plaques and memorials are located on the other three and are mostly well marked. This courthouse placement in the town plan is unique and falls outside the geographer's classification of county seats.

Bedford County claims that its 1828 courthouse, at Juliana and Penn Streets, is the oldest in the state in continuous use. There are other counties that have older building portions, sometimes only remnants embedded in their courthouses, but this one remains substantially intact as built. It was built by a young local carpenter and builder, Jason Filler (1797–1855), and is an example of the "temple of justice" style, although it incorporates some Federal elements, such as the lunettes. A red brick building, it has two Doric columns *in antis* and four square pilasters at the angle of the forward sections. There are two handsome lunettes, the more interesting one being in the pediment. It is entirely designed by compass, as all muntins are circle arcs. Chimneys that once serviced the fireplaces are still arrayed along the roofline. A wooden tower with clock faces is attached to a rather

bulky square base. A smaller cylindrical belfry tier has louvered openings and a plain cornice. The shallow, round cap supports a flagpole. All and all, it's a very attractive structure. A small rear section was added to the building in 1875. The bricks were painted through much of its history, being variously tan and red. The present natural appearance dates from 1968. The building was restricted to public use by an 1832 resolution, an unusual nineteenth-century measure. Many counties rented their courtrooms to entertainers and used them for other nonpublic purposes, including lectures and religious services.

The interior, though somewhat modernized, retains a nineteenth-century style, particularly the courtroom. Note the unsupported front curved stairs. The steps list to the right from the weight of a century and a half of court-bound persons, but Filler built well for them to have remained in place.

The attractively maintained squares contribute to the general amenity of this small town, and the main street, one block away, also remains reasonably intact and exudes a quiet vitality. In the summer, flowers are very much in evidence, even atop the parking meters. Most of the historic buildings in or near the squares have their dates and pedigrees attached. Two undated ones are the Lutheran Parish House (1872) and Lawyers Row (1870). The 1914 post office opposite the courthouse is worth a look. Oscar Wenderroth was the supervising architect, and not many of his Classical-style buildings remain. When built, this post office had a set of secret surveillance passageways for Secret Service personnel, who could enter unannounced to check on post office workers.

The county is using nearby historic buildings for its office expansion, and one of them (annex #3) is also a Filler building. Filler's own residence is a white house a little farther down this street (marked and privately owned). Its appearance has been altered by the loss of the large Filler porch that ran across the entire front. One block north, at Penn and Thomas Streets, is an 1895 sheriff's residence and jail built by Van Dorn Iron Works of Cleveland. It lacks the forbidding fortress appearance of many Pennsylvania county prisons of the earlier period.

During the Whiskey Rebellion, the ill-disciplined American army passed through here, often stealing provisions from farmers as they traveled. Bedford was the westernmost point of George Washington's travels in overseeing this assertion of the new federal authority. Washington established federal authority but did little to address the injustices that lead to the troubles. His Bedford headquarters have been preserved by the community.

BERKS
County Seat: Reading

As with most early place names dating from Penn's era, both Berks and Reading are named after a county and city in England.

Berks County was created in 1751 and has had a remarkable architectural record in its county buildings. The second courthouse (1840) was designed by no less an architect than Thomas U. Walter, designer of the U.S. capitol dome (see Chester County). By the 1920s, the county had outgrown this building, and despite newspaper citations of Oliver W. Holmes's *Old Ironsides,* it was not preserved, though there were some feeble efforts to save the facade by moving it to a park. Two large statues of the Goddess of Liberty, which once stood on the building's 146-foot-high spire, one of wood (carved by John Rush, son of Benjamin) and one of copper, may be seen in the Berks County Historical Society Museum at 940 Centre Street.

In the unlikely year of 1931, the county constructed the $2 million, nineteen-story structure that still absolutely dominates the downtown of

Reading. Its architect was Miles Boyer Dechant of the local family firm, William Dechant Sons. He was an artist (his plan to personally paint a mural in the courthouse never materialized) as well as an architect. In the latter capacity, his commissions were mostly residences for the local elite, so this building was his most important commission.

The courthouse is essentially in Art Deco style, and the only example of this esthetic among the state's courthouses. While many of its materials and patterns are straight out of the Art Deco traditions, they also reflect Dechant's Eclectic propensities. The nineteen-story (plus a water tower on top) central shaft of the building rests on a broader nine-story base. The exterior, clad in Ohio limestone, rests on a granite foundation below the water table. It has typical close-to-the-surface Art Deco bas-relief decorations on the base and stylized eagles on the central tower. The taller windows on the fifth and seventh floors light four two-story courtrooms that we will visit inside.

When it was constructed, the architectural firm bragged of its up-to-date systems. These included staged elevators copied after the Empire State Building; something called "tele aura," a precursor of the fax, which allowed clerks in the courts to post messages in the lawyers fifth-floor lounge about the progress of cases; a mail chute system; and levers instead of door-knobs so clerks carrying heavy paper-filled baskets could open doors with their elbows. Alas, time has not been kind to most of these, but a few surviving fragments can be found. A sensitive restoration-renovation in the 1990s (John M. Kostecky Jr. and Associates, architects) has done much to bring the building back to life. The interior deserves attention. There are three circulation systems for people in this building, one each for the public, county employees, and prisoners. This was a very advanced idea then, but it has become common practice in the last few decades. This guide sticks for the most part to the public passageways.

The vaulted foyer on the first floor features walls of sienna travertine and floors of plain travertine, a favorite Art Deco stone. At the Sixth Street entrance, there are massive solid bronze fixtures and typically Art Deco pseudo Mayan bas-reliefs on the walls. A dolphin theme is used in the foyer's five-foot bronze light fixtures. Half of these are original but formerly located elsewhere. The blue earth globe is a replica of the original made by a local artisan in 1931. The foyer ceiling opposite the main entrance is of pecky cypress and appears to be painted with Pennsylvania Dutch designs, showing Dechant's eclecticism. The room on the northwest corner of this floor was originally for tax collection; if it is open, do take a look. It originally featured hand-hammered wrought-iron cages, parts of which have been moved to the east room of this floor. There remain two stunningly impressive marble and wrought-iron wall desks, great capitals atop the pilasters, and other decorative flashes. There are also decorative iron cages and wall cornices in the southwest room (originally for the county treasurer), but at this writing its use was not determined, so it may not be publicly accessible. Most of the first-floor plaques are self-explanatory, but the significance of the one for James Wilson is that he first practiced law in Reading (1768) before moving on to Carlisle. Note the black and gold decorations over the doorways featuring a pair of horses. The elevator signs are reproductions of the originals. The fine elevator doors have been restored, but the elevator interiors that were originally paneled in walnut have been greatly simplified. The remnant of the mail chute system can be found in the large disused metal mailbox.

There are five courtrooms of interest in this building, pairs on the fifth and seventh floors and one on the ninth, but the courtrooms are locked when not in use. The pairs on the fifth and seventh floors have similar decorative themes but differences in their execution. On leaving the elevator on the fifth floor, note the flamboyant marble wainscot in the hallways and the colorful modillions accenting the ceiling. Preliminary plans prescribed that the two fifth-floor courtrooms were to be early American, and from appearances, this seems to be the decorative theme, with traditional elements, such as broken pediment and pilasters. The unusual chandeliers, restored after the originals, feature eagles and Federal-period forms. Both courtrooms have similar ceilings, marble baseboards, attractive long seating benches, and an interesting bar rail with a shelf on the audience side. This Dechant feature is used in all his courtrooms and may have been to accommodate newspaper reporters attending trials. The rooms differ from the bar and beyond, as the east one uses wood and the west marble. The painting scheme differs between courtrooms 5A and 5B, and therein lies a tale. There was a big local row over the paint colors chosen by the renovating architects, who used hues favored by the Art Deco tradition. The sitting judge of courtroom 5A would not allow the architects to touch his room, and the color scheme there is of his choosing, presumably resulting from his own historical research. The controversy over the colors seems still alive, based on my visits. The architects' color preferences are well expressed throughout the building, perhaps most cheerfully so in the lawyers' lounge and the law library. However, some local folks do not think these are appropriate colors for the somber and grim events played out in the courts.

On the seventh floor, the wainscot is yellow marble. The two courtrooms were specified as Early Italian Renaissance on the preliminary plans. It is difficult to put a label on what one sees there, so let us stick with that designation. Whatever the style, it is certainly colorful. The two courtrooms are similarly decorated, having the same ceilings, unusual vaulting with colorful corbels on the side walls, and fancy air vents at the rear. The corbels and air vents are paint on plaster. Both rooms have highly colorful alcoves behind the judge's bench, each with a pithy aphorism. The audience seats are handsome and a bit more sturdy than those on the fifth floor. As on the fifth floor, one side uses marble around the bench and the other wood, in this case finished in walnut. In the back of both rooms, there is a surviving example of Dechant's door levers, which here are of elaborate wrought iron. One suspects these were deluxe levers for the courtrooms and not the pattern used throughout the building.

The ninth floor has a brown marble hallway. The single courtroom on the south side of the building, unlike the others, is decorated in contemporary rather than historical style and is a one-story space. The style is Art Deco, and a telltale pseudo Mayan band of silver and gold runs around the upper part of the wall and envelops the clock at the rear. The segmental arched ceiling has modern square recessed lighting. The custom-made wood furnishing has fine detailing throughout. This more intimate courtroom has a greater affinity with the remainder of the building than do the others.

There is no observation deck on the tower, but there is a publicly accessible north window on all floors, which gives a fine view over part of the city.

The attached Berks County service center (1991, John M. Kostecky Jr. & Associates, architects) is a striking postmodern structure and continues the Berks County tradition of quality courthouses. The architects wanted to repeat the form of Dechant's building, but the space needs of the county were great, and the site so constrained by the railroad and bridges, that the only alternative was a massive rectilinear floor plan. Nevertheless, the form does manage to pay homage to the old building. The central curved portion exactly conforms to the width of the Dechant tower. The baseline is the same, so the two buildings rise together (viewed from the south). A perch in front was intended for the Justice statue from the nineteenth-century Walter courthouse, but squabbles over ownership defeated that idea. There is an urban courtyard in front of the annex, including a day-care play space. Note how the "bridge of sighs" is Postmodern on the court side but traditional on the outside. Go inside and check out the ceiling over the elevator lobby.

There are interesting things to see in the environs, including the shaded seating area down the path opposite the Court Street entrance of the 1931 courthouse. If you proceed to 5th and Penn, you will be at the site of the Walter courthouse. The downtown area is amply supplied with historical markers that need no augmentation from this guide.

BLAIR
County Seat: Hollidaysburg

This is the only Pennsylvania county named for one of its own native sons. Those proposing a new county are like supplicants before legislative committees, and those controlling the committees have their own agenda for passing out honors. In this rare exception, John Blair, who was a major booster of development in the area prior to the formation of the county in 1846, received appropriate recognition. The county seat, Hollidaysburg, was named for Adam Holliday, which explains the spelling. Today the seat is not the largest city in the county, but its prominence preceded that of the now larger Altoona. It owes its primacy to the Erie Canal in New York, which channeled wealth from the Midwest through New York City, giving that city a tremendous economic advantage over Philadelphia. The Allegheny Mountains thwarted the linking of Philadelphia with Pittsburgh and the burgeoning Midwest by water. In 1834, Pennsylvania, with great determination, linked the cities by an unusual system composed of a combination of canals and a remarkable inclined portage railroad. The railroad was used to cross the high point in the route, which was located in present

Blair County. It was at Hollidaysburg where people, freight, and later, whole boats were shifted from the canal to the portage railroad, a device that used gravity augmented by steam to haul everything over the mountain to Johnstown. (Remnants of this enterprise are being partially restored in a national park.) As the transfer juncture, Hollidaysburg received a developmental boost, and when Blair County was formed, it became the seat. By 1852, the railroad had made its way across the Allegheny mountains, rendering the Rube Goldberg gravity machine obsolete.

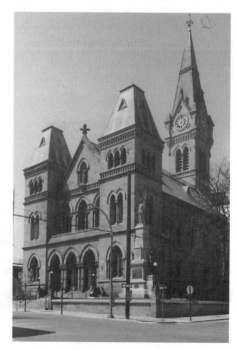

With Altoona's growth, the county needed a bigger courthouse, and as was often the case in this expansive era, they built a good one. The courthouse, located at Union and Allegheny Streets (1877, David S. Glendall, architect), is a monumental structure soaring upward to 177 feet at the top of the spire. Its Gothic style (note the pointed arches and trefoil windows with stained glass) is unusual for a courthouse, even in Victorian times. The "spire" placement and the facade make the building look a little churchlike. The building walls are of buff and peach stone, colors quickly dulled by air pollution, and contain an inch and a half space between the outer stones and the brick interior liner wall, thus providing an early example of using air space for insulation. The T-shaped building is five bays across the front. The outer bays rise to short towers, and the central bays are recessed above the first floor. The porch over the recessed entrance has an arcade of three Gothic arches supported by six columns with carved capitals, pilasters on the inside wall, and a solid parapet above, with a metal cresting. Above the porch, the three central bays repeat the porch facade, but with glazed windows and pilasters. At the gable level, there is a statue of blind justice. The corner bay's first-story windows are recessed within an arch with corner pilasters, the pair of second-story windows are separated by a column mullion, and the third-story windows form a small arcade. The truncated pyramidal roofs are pierced by small, triangular dormers with roundels. There are stone bands composed of miniature arches on the corner and main towers. The clock tower, which dominates the town, is at the rear of the main section of the building, an unusual location. It is essentially a square shaft pierced by double louvers with a column mullion and Gothic arch head moldings. The clock faces have steeply raking gable hoods with finial. The steep roof spire is banded at midpoint and topped by a finial and weathervane. In 1906, a section was added to the rear of the

courthouse, and portions of the interior were rebuilt. This addition (W. L. Plack, architect) tastefully matches the stone and the Gothic motif of the original building, albeit in a more restrained fashion. A major Postmodern annex to the left was added in 1998.

The interior has been altered but there are things to see. The front foyer is largely untouched, and the first-floor hall has traces of the original decoration and even some of the original brass hardware. On the second floor, the Lawyers' Lobby still has the original decor from the 1906 enlargement, as does courtroom 1. Its features include stained-glass windows and a large circular coffer in the ceiling, decorated with a zodiac motif. There is a large painting of the Declaration of Independence signing, which was executed by an art contract firm at the time of the renovations. The second and larger courtroom on this floor dates from the original 1877 building. It is worth studying a moment, even though it has been desecrated by 1970s alterations. It is one of the more insensitive butchering jobs in this part of Pennsylvania, which takes some doing. Go to the rear and sit down. The room was originally in the "modern" Gothic style, as it was described when built. The ceiling is wooden, of yellow pine and ash, and originally had a natural finish instead of paint. Ribs run upward from corbels anchored into the masonry walls. The ceiling is divided into three planes, and each plane is further divided into panels. There is a double row of bosses and decorative screens that once covered ventilation ducts across the top plane. The desecration is obvious in the front. Above the paneled box that juts into the room, one can see the top of a Gothic arch. Originally there was an elaborate Gothic niche, twenty-five feet high, behind the bench, elaborately decorated, including six columns. Given the size of the room, it was probably in scale. The judge's bench and other furniture are gone, but the audience benches are original.

The stone and iron electric light standards at the front of the building were installed about 1896. The ornate, upwardly thrusting Civil War monument is a fitting companion to the vertical architectural exuberance of the courthouse.

Need for space has led the county to take over an old Catholic girls school (Highland) a block away, on Walnut Street. On the porch of this building, there are graduation aphorisms on the rail, the older ones in Latin and the later in English. The foyer and fireplace have a few Mercer tiles (Bucks County). The old chapel has been converted to a courtroom, which makes for an unusual court setting, but given the Gothic-style courthouse, it is in keeping with the local tradition.

BRADFORD
County Seat: Towanda

Bradford County, established in 1810, is named for one of the many William Bradfords who were prominent in Colonial affairs. This William was the son of the William who was called "the patriot printer of 1776." The son was one of those bright, talented young men who seemed to be in abundant supply at our nation's founding, and many of whom were engaged by general and later president George Washington. This William Bradford was the nation's second attorney general, whose term was cut short by his untimely death before he reached age forty. He died of an illness he contracted during an arduous investigation of the political indiscretions of his predecessor, Edmund Randolph. Prior to becoming attorney general, he had served Pennsylvania well as lawyer and jurist. Among his services was the successful pleading of the case against Connecticut that gained the disputed Wyoming area for Pennsylvania, part of which is fittingly within this county. (The initial name proposed for the new county was Ontario, and as often happened, the name was changed by the legislative committee.) Towanda is located on the Susquehanna River, one of the great natural scenic assets of Pennsylvania.

The courthouse is located on Main Street, facing west on a lot that slopes down to the riverbank, and is fronted by a prominent Civil War

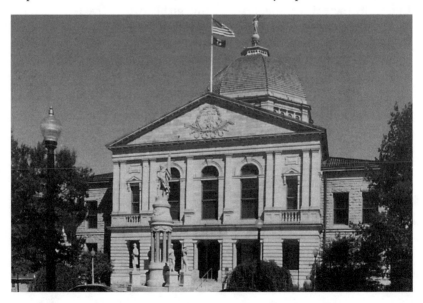

monument. It is among the few Pennsylvania courthouses built in a Renaissance Revival style and is well worth seeing. Built in 1896–97, the architects were Israel Lehman and Theodore Schmitt of Cleveland, who also did the Cuyahoga County, Ohio, courthouse and were chosen here in a competition with fifteen entries. The building has a cruciform layout and an exterior of gray sandstone from Barclay, New Hampshire. The west front has a prominent five-bay pavilion, the first story of which has rusticated piers and pairs of gray granite columns that frame rectangular openings. The pavilion second-story windows have arched transoms with keystones in the three central bays. Pilasters singly or in pairs separate the

bays. The pediment on the gable roof has block modillions on both its horizontal and raking lines. The tympanum contains a cartouche with the words "JUSTICE, LAW, MERCY" surrounded by olive branch garlands. The most prominent feature of the exterior is the ample octagonal dome covered with gray-green glazed terra-cotta shingles. Note the row of windows at its base and top, always a good sign that there is going to be a monumental interior space. A silver-plated statue of justice, with a few missing parts and without blindfold, stands on a ball at the top. The outer two bays of the front and the balance of the building are covered with rock-faced ashlar stone. There is a water table and belt course on all sides except the front pavilion. Over the attractive oak entry door are windows with lattice (clathri) bars. The ground floor may be entered on the west and east through arched doorways that have keystones. North and south entrances are to the basement level.

The rotunda is the major interior feature, nearly always the case for these domed courthouses. The floors are marble mosaics, and the walls have marble wainscoting. A second-story balcony is supported by a series of wide consoles decorated with the head of Pan at their base. A cast- and wrought-iron staircase occupies the center and connects the first floor to the balcony. The principle interior decorative form is the arch, whether in door transoms or on the walls around the rotunda. Decorative touches include extensive stenciling on the walls, and a massive, sixty-bulb central chandelier of antique copper provided by a Philadelphia firm ($3,000) and equipped for gas or electricity. Native white oak was used on all the interior woodwork, most of which is still in place. Courtroom 1 is in the front of the building and is illuminated by the three large front windows, as well as a small arcade of cut-glass windows on the rotunda wall. Corinthian columns support a cornice and segmental arched pediment behind the bench. A carved set of wooden panels featuring a large sunburst fills the space between the columns. A curved rail separates the bar from the audience. Note the heavy bailiff's chair. There is a beamed ceiling, and canvas was applied on the walls to improve courtroom acoustics. Courtroom 2 has been altered and made smaller.

Note the plaque just inside the building memorializing David Wilmott, the author of the Wilmott Proviso, who represented this area in Congress at the time of the Mexican War. He has been described as "stout, slovenly in dress, enormous in appetite both in eating and drinking, forceful in speech and lazy." He was also one of those otherwise obscure congressmen who do one thing that gives them everlasting fame. The Wilmott Proviso had great appeal to his constituents. It was tacked on to a $2 million appropriation bill to finance the aftermath of the Mexican War, essentially stating that the new territories won in the war would not allow slavery. It created what today's pundits call a "wedge issue," because it gave the national Democratic leadership fits. Their prowar coalition included the South, which hoped new states favoring their perspective would come from the conquered territories, thus offsetting the Senate votes of new free states destined to be added beyond the Mississippi to the north. The proviso never passed Congress, but it assured Wilmott hero status in parts of Pennsylvania. Wilmott's political career had many bumps, however, as he was a staunch free trader, reflecting a lumber industry perspective in a high-tariff state with coal and steel interests. He left the Democratic party and was instrumental in forming the new Republican party. He served briefly as a Republican U.S. senator during the first two years of the Civil War.

The Civil War monument was built in the early 1900s. An 1847 brick annex on the courthouse grounds was built to house county offices and has lasted through three main courthouses. A block to the south at Pine Street is the old unused stone jail, which once had a high tower. At the time of the last visit, it was under renovation for alternative use. It may be worth a visit. Main Street, going north from the courthouse, offers fine examples of nineteenth-century wood homes built from the bountiful supplies of local lumber.

BUCKS

County Seat: Doylestown

One of the three original counties, established in 1682 by William Penn, Bucks County was named after his ancestral English home of Buckinghamshire. Doylestown was named after a Doyle family that operated a tavern at present-day Main Street and State Street. Doyle's land had passed through at least four other hands prior to his purchase in the 1730s. His tavern at a crossroads became identified with the place, and the family name has remained indelibly attached to the site. Doyle sold his property, and it was in the hands of a Tory during the Revolutionary War, at which time it was confiscated. Consequently, one might say that the present courthouse square is war booty. The best time to visit the courthouse in this old borough is in April, when its cherry trees are in bloom, though it is an unusually interesting town to visit at any time, with its little museums, particularly Mercer and Michener, and crafts and antique shops.

Bucks County has had many courthouses before the present one, so many that the count is given variously as seven or eight. The present courthouse was dedicated in 1962 (Carroll, Grisdale & Van Alen and Fred F. Martin Associates, architects) and is a startlingly modern design for this ancient borough. Only a self-confident middle-class suburban and exurban

county with a cultural tradition like Bucks would have the public moxy to build such a departure from one of the politically correct styles. It is really two buildings, consisting of a round and a rectangular part. Airline pilots viewing it from the air have dubbed it "the toilet." The round section is the judicial portion and contains a number of attractive modern courtrooms. The furniture for them was handmade in Puerto Rico, an early example of the present offshore labor cost-saving practice. The judges' offices on the fifth floor, not open to the public, enjoy a nice panoramic view from the glass-enclosed round perch. The large, rectangular section houses administrative offices, or at least it did at the time of its construction. When the building was opened, a press release stated that the plaster walls were covered with "lovely, expensive, canvas-backed, hand painted and sprayed vinyl wall paper," but the "expensive" 1960s vinyl now needs to be renewed. The bell, which served in the previous two courthouses, is on display in the lobby, with its odyssey related on a plaque.

The 1878 courthouse, which the present one replaced, was designed by Addison Hutton (see Venango County) after the breakup of his partnership with Samuel Sloan. It contained a famous round courtroom, and the present circular judicial wing was inspired by it.

The courthouse triangular "square" is bounded by Main Street, Court Street, and Broad Street, with the sharp point of the triangle at the Civil War obelisk. One of the first Civil War monuments built in the north (1868), it celebrates the Pennsylvania 104th Infantry Regiment, which served throughout the war. Now marooned on a traffic island, it was less isolated when constructed. Numerous additional veterans memorials now occupy the courthouse grounds. At the opposite end of the "square" at Main and Broad is a fountain memorializing World War I veterans. It depicts a wounded soldier being given water from a canteen by a fellow doughboy and was designed by William R. Mercer, brother of Henry C., the anthropologist and tilemaker, using as models local veterans who had served in the war.

Most of the buildings facing the square have nineteenth-century cores, some older. The arrival of the county seat in Doylestown in the second decade of the nineteenth century stimulated new building construction, particularly by lawyers. Lawyers' Row on Court Street was built in the 1830s but most of the structures were later refitted with Victorian facades. Printers' Alley, which is perpendicular to Court Street, was an unpaved mud alley until Belgian blocks were laid in the 1920s and was so named because the prominent English language newspaper, *The Intelligencer,* was located there. It occupied 10 Court Street, which was designed by Addison Hutton and his new partner, Thomas L. Cernea. The office of the German language newspaper *Der Morgenstern* was in the small nondescript building next to the James-Lorah House, opposite the courthouse on Main Street. The early Germans kept their language for generations, and there was a time when German speakers constituted nearly half the population of Bucks County. Many of the larger houses facing the courthouse were built by lawyers or judges for their homes and offices, such as the James-Lorah Memorial House at 132 Main Street (1844), which was built by Judge Henry Chapman, whose grandson was Henry Chapman Mercer, founder of the tile works. Judge Chapman had married the stepdaughter of Pennsylvania governor Shrunk, which may have enhanced his legal career. Apparently, there was a bit of status competition in the designing of these houses. For example, the wife of Nathan James, who built the twin at 108–110 Main Street, was competing with the wife of the builder of 87 Broad Street for bragging rights, and the result is two unusual asymmetrical twins that still adorn the square today. The latter has gone through a recent attractive adaptive reconstruction for offices and is worth a peek through the front door glass.

Addison Hutton, the architect of the previous courthouse, was also retained to design a new jail, which was built on Pine Street. Eventually, it became locally referred to as the Pine Street Hotel. Part of it still exists, and it has been incorporated into the Michener Museum (just opposite the Mercer Museum). Viewing the museum complex from Pine Street, you will see before you the old sheriff's residence with its arched opening embedded in a section of the old high prison walls. Note that the walls were severed on the right by the museum architect and left unfinished, as if to provide a permanent reminder that a captive space had been breached. The brownstone residence housed the sheriff and family (later the warden), whose respective spouses were the matrons for women prisoners and in the early days took care of the juveniles as well. Note how the arched sally port has a gate at both ends. The outer one provided access to the residential quarters on the left and the sheriff's office on the left. The inner gate, built of heavy oak timbers and iron bands, was the entrance to the prison. Originally, new prisoners would arrive via wagons and pass through this sally port into a walled courtyard that connected the house with the guardhouse beyond. The sally port gate would be locked, and then the guardhouse gate would be opened to admit the prisoner, thus providing security at all times. The jail was copied after the Philadelphia Eastern Penitentiary, a Quaker-conceived facility that originally provided individual cells where prisoners were to reflect on their transgressions. Long corridors of cells radiated off the central guardhouse, from which surveillance was possible. In the Bucks case, the jail was T-shaped, and the central guardhouse was at the center of three corridors. The guardhouse, which is the structure with the closed arch just opposite the sally port, is the only part of the prison that was incorporated into the museum. It is now the first gallery upon entering the museum, and two of the arches that provided surveillance down the prison corridors have been retained. Note also how the Patricia D. Pfundt Sculpture Garden uses the old twenty-four-foot prison wall as a backdrop. The museum shop stocks a book entitled *The Pine Street Hotel*, which gives an interesting history of this old jail.

BUTLER
County Seat: Butler

Gen. Richard Butler (1743–91) served in the Henry Bouquet campaign of the French and Indian War in Ohio, became an Indian trader, served with Anthony Wayne during the Revolutionary War, became a Pennsylvania Congressman, and was chosen by Congress in 1786 as North District Indian Affairs superintendent. In that capacity, following the Treaty of Paris, he was charged with informing the Indians who had fought with the British during the war that as they were on the losing side, they must now do what the American government told them to do. Since the Indians had no knowledge of the treaty, this was news to them. The imperious manner in which Butler delivered this message caused great consternation and resentment among the tribes, who looked upon themselves as free nations, not a vanquished people. The consequence was repeated Indian depredations on the frontier, particularly in the Northwest Territories. Butler became second in command to Arthur St. Clair in the American military response, a horribly mismanaged campaign that ended in our worst military defeat at the hands of Indians. A contributing factor to the defeat may have been that Butler and St. Clair did not get along. Butler fought bravely in the battle and was wounded. Unable to escape, he was subsequently tomahawked to death. His body became the principle trophy for the victorious Indians, who distributed prized portions of it widely among the warriors. From the perspective of the time, Butler's behavior was deemed faultless, and he remained a hero to the people of the frontier area from which this county was formed in 1800.

The courthouse is that building you see on the high end of the main street, the one with the odd shiny, pointed tower. The building was first built in 1885, substantially rebuilt in 1907, suffered subsequent insensitive

interior alterations, and more recently, some comparatively sensitive
restoration. Parsimony, if not penury,
has often triumphed over pride in its
maintenance.

Viewed from across the street in
Diamond Park (see reference to Diamond in the Introduction), you see an
1885 facade designed by James P. Bailey of Pittsburgh, featuring a combination of Gothic and Romanesque
elements. Built with local stone,
quarry faced in thin ashlar blocks, it
has an attractive yellow cast in the
sunlight. The facade reads as five bays,
with the two corner bays and the central one brought forward. The central
bay rises to a tower that is the building's dominant design feature. Its first-
story entrance is behind an arch

supported by columns, above which is a balcony, and the second story has
triple windows and transoms set within segmental arches. The lower part
of the tower has two rows of three narrow windows, the lower ones rectangular and the upper arched. Next comes a half-bowl balcony with windows
(front side only), then the ornamented clock-face stage, an elaborate cornice
with a row of rosettes, and arcaded corbels flanked by corner turrets. Then
that strange top! In 1958, the offer from Aramco Steel of a free stainless-steel
replacement tower cap proved too tempting for the county commissioners.
This incongruous shiny cap simplified the contours and shortened the peak
of the original Bailey tower. Unfortunately, it is as durable as it is deforming.
On either side of the entrance, there is an open porch accessible from the entryway. The porches have a balustrade with portholes and columns that support blind arches with carved sun decorations. All windows on the first and
second stories are in sets of two within a Gothic arch supported by engaged
columns and have stained-glass transoms with Gothic hoods. There is a triple
window within a round arch at the third story. The side towers have pilasters
on each story, pyramidal roofs, and turrets on the two outer angles. When
the new steel cap was installed in 1959, it served to show how blackened the
rest of the building had become from air pollution. Unfortunately, the standard cleaning practice of the time was sandblasting, and that resulted in a
loss of details and a weakening of the surface.

In 1907, J. C. Fulton was retained to renovate and expand the building. The impact of his work is largely on the interior, which he essentially gutted. He did make one major external change. Bailey's original side walls receded just beyond the corner towers. Fulton widened the building by sixteen feet, moving the sides walls outward until they were flush, but rebuilding them in the Bailey style. Almost, but not quite, that is, for a close examination will show differences. For example, on the south side, Fulton used blind stone transoms in place of Bailey's Gothic glass ones. He replaced the roof, inserting skylights and installing dormers on either side. Toward the rear of the building, there are cross gables with angle turrets, which become engaged columns below. At the very rear angles of the building are turrets that rise from the ground. This rear part appears to date from the Bailey building.

Entering the front door, to the left is a Bailey iron staircase, which provides access to one of his Gothic stained-glass windows. Fulton removed the original stair to the right to gain space for an extra room, and he built the grand central stairway that is partly marble and has Beaux-Arts design features. Note the shell-and-dolphin fountains. The skylight Fulton had used to light the central stairway began to have maintenance needs about 1966, but rather than fix it, the dome was closed and the window plastered over, in another triumph of parsimony over pride. Recent redecoration is not exactly faithful to his design; however, the paintings surrounding the second floor of the rotunda, portraying various scenes of the county and its history, remain. Fulton retained the original eleven-foot office doorway frames on the first floor. The best surviving one is that to the prothonotary's office, which still has an etched-glass sign and a cranberry glass transom that has not been darkened by a dropped ceiling, as is the case for other offices.

Fulton built skylights in the two courtrooms, but in the intervening years, both were hidden behind dropped ceilings. They have both recently reemerged. One is in the old courtroom 2, which is now a passageway room to the skyway connecting the courthouse with the Government Center (1991, Foreman, Bashford, architects), built to the rear. This room is projected to contain historical displays and other exhibits. Courtroom 1 has been largely restored. It features a coffered ceiling with its now emancipated skylight, marble wainscoting, walnut benches, Corinthian pilasters, and a classical pedimented background for the judge's bench.

Behind the courthouse is an 1828 residence, originally built as a summer home for U.S. senator Walter Lowrie and now owned by the county historical society and open for tours.

CAMBRIA

County Seat: Ebensberg

Cambria is the Latin name for Wales. It was the name of an antecedent township, which was heavily populated by Welsh immigrants. Cambria was a favorite usage with nineteenth-century poets who wrote about things Welsh. Cambria County was created in 1804.

The central part of the courthouse was built in 1881 (M. E. Beebe, architect). It once had a huge tower that made it twice its present height, and given its hilltop location, when built the courthouse must have been an imposing sight viewed from the east. However, Beebe's tower failed and was removed when the building was comparatively young. The style is typical Beebe. The body of the building is Tuscan Villa, particularly the window treatment, while above the roofline, the style is more Second Empire with the mansard roof and corner pavilions. The Huntington County commissioners hired Beebe after seeing this building; the one he designed for them is similar, and the tower failed there as well. Beebe also designed the Warren County courthouse, built four years earlier in a similar style, and its handsome tower is still intact.

In 1913, the Cambria commissioners ordered a building enlargement, and a famous architect, James Reilly Gordon, was retained for the job.

Early in his career, Gordon had designed many courthouses in Texas and the territorial capital of Arizona. Later, after he moved to New York City, he designed several major county courthouses in New Jersey. To the Beebe building, he added three wings, one on each side and one to the rear, and nearly completely gutted it. Gordon made the exterior of the new wings compatible with Beebe's old central portion. The interior, however, is pure Gordon and is delightfully well preserved. The work was started in 1914 but was interrupted by World War I and not completed until 1923.

The visible portion of the Beebe facade is ten bays wide and in the form of an attenuated E, with the center and end sections brought forward. The central bays have rusticated stone around the two arched entrances. The whole building has stone quoins, not only at the outside angles, but at the inside ones as well, which is rather unusual. There are stone belt courses between the stories, and most windows have stone hood moldings. The first-story windows are segmentally arched, have keystones, and are connected, while the second-story ones are rectangular and unconnected. The central bays rise to a pediment, which was once at the base of the tower. The cornice, including the raking sides of the pediment, has dentils and modillions and is probably metal. Dormers pierce the mansard roofing of the end towers, while on the receding bays, the dormers are decorated roundels. The side towers have corner urns. There are prominent chimneys with corbel brickwork toward the rear. Gordon's wings copy the Beebe style and add only a parapet at the roof line, which was probably intended to hide his skylight arrangements.

Gordon tried for maximum natural interior lighting, which led him to use skylights in most of his courtrooms. Here he took advantage of the space previously occupied by the Beebe tower to introduce a rotunda with a stained-glass oculus in the central part of the building. On the second floor, the rotunda is surrounded by an octagonal, balustraded corridor that circulates the traffic toward his three courtrooms. The main courtroom to the east is circular and has Gordon's trademark balcony supported by scagliola (composite order) columns. The skylight is round, set at the center of a coffered ceiling, richly decorated with those Beaux-Arts Classical touches. The curvilinear theme is even reflected in the judge's bench and furniture beyond the rail. These were all designed by Gordon, as verified by extant original drawings. In this theaterlike layout, the jury is directly in front of the judge instead of to the side, as is conventional in rectilinear courtrooms.

The north and south courtrooms are smaller and horseshoe-shaped, with corresponding semicircular skylights. They have a single niche behind the bench instead of three, as in the larger east courtroom. The column orders are Doric, and the scagliola colors differ. Otherwise, the decor and furnishings are similar in the three courtrooms. Note the heavy oak plywood and leather audience seats with a wire hat rack under each. The iron and oak rails are the same throughout the building. The marble on floors and wainscoting throughout the building date from the Gordon expansion. The two murals on the second-floor rotunda walls are by Ralph Zimmerman Galbraith, a Johnston artist who was self-taught. They date from the early 1930s, and one notation indicates WPA support. In 1992, the whole building was given a general refurbishing using prison labor, including refinishing of the furniture in the courtrooms.

Incidently, the 1872 Haviland jail (see Carbon County) at North Center Street and Sample Street is still in use and worth a look. It was the scene of numerous hangings, which once were major social events. In 1906, over one thousand people witnessed a double hanging there. Hangings were so popular that sheriffs would limit the crowd to invitation-only viewers, a nice political resource for an elected official.

CAMERON
County Seat: Emporium

This county was named after Simon Cameron, who in 1860, when the county was established, was on his way to becoming a powerful force in state politics. Naming the county for him has all the earmarks of political promotion. Earlier, Cameron had a career that combined law, newspapers, insurance, industry, and banking and made him a wealthy man. He loved the wheeling and dealing of politics, and he was known for his shifting political alliances. However, he was a consistent supporter of high tariffs, a policy that became a central canon of the Republican party in this manufacturing state. He joined the Republican party at its outset, and it was during this period that the county was named for him. He was chosen for the U.S. Senate, was influential in the nomination of Lincoln, and as a result became secretary of war, but unfortunately, not a very able one. Lincoln got rid of him by sending him to Russia as ambassador. After the war, he continued as a power wielder in Pennsylvania politics and bequeathed a political head start to his son. The Latinized name of the county seat is an expression of economic aspiration. The founders probably hoped it would be a much more important commercial center than it has become. Emporium has always been a bit off the beaten path.

The courthouse, sited on a sloping lot one street up the hill from Main, is a simple Romanesque structure (1890, A. S. Wagner, architect) that features three round arches over the entry and a large but simple square clock-and-bell tower. The basic material is red brick, with accents of red sandstone. Viewing the building from the street, there is a prominent square tower on the right, four bays across the center, and an octagonal section on the left end. The octagonal form is repeated on the diagonally opposite northeast corner. The windows across the central bays and lower tower are arched. The three arches over the entryway have a Richardsonian look, as do the short columns and foliage carving accents on the sandstone. The central part of the building has a gable roof. The tower is divided into six sections, defined by horizontal sandstone belt courses. The uniformity of the sections is broken by varied window arrangements in terms of number, shape, and spacing. The tower roof is pyramidal and is topped by a platform that supports a statue of Lady Justice. (A fiberglass replica of the original was on order at the time of visit.) Wagner also designed the facade of Columbia County courthouse in a similar Romanesque Revival style.

The interior was decorated in wood, as marble was probably too expensive for a county so small in population. The courtroom has been largely modernized, but it still retains its original place. The old staircase is at the west end, and there is an iron fountain at its base that once served those

County sheriff's house in front of jail.

about to climb the stairs to attend court. Some original courtroom furniture remains, and the judge's bench has a classical niche behind it.

The Emporium newspapers were filled with bickering over the cost of the new courthouse in 1890. It was standard practice at a time when small towns had a number of competing newspapers for them to enter into spirited arguments about public matters. It is hard for a modern reader to distinguish between banter designed to sell papers and reports reflecting public sentiment. This courthouse came in overbudget, and as an economy move, perhaps influenced by the newspaper comments, the commissioners saved money by deleting the clock and ordered the clock face's holes to be bricked in. For the first ten years, these blind Cyclops eyes stared out over the town. The Ladies Chamber of Commerce took on the task of raising money for the clock. In 1900, after a two-year campaign that employed a variety of fund-raising ventures, including selling commemorative spoons, they raised the necessary $600.

The picturesque sheriff's house and jail on the courthouse grounds was built in 1867. The stone lower floor was the jail, and the wooden upper floors, including the balcony, were the sheriff's home. It is now used occasionally as a holding cell and for prisoners who are in leave programs. The residence is still occupied, and there is usually laundry drying on the balcony, which makes it look as it did over the many years when the sheriff and his family lived there.

CARBON

County Seat: Jim Thorpe

Carbon County, founded in 1843, is appropriately named for its famous hard anthracite coal, a mineral that was the reason for developing this area and for the founding of the seat town of Jim Thorpe, originally named Mauch Chunk. The name change occurred in the 1950s when a local newspaperman successfully promoted the idea of providing a gravesite for the famous athlete, thinking it might promote tourism. At the time, Mauch Chunk and an abutting borough were consolidated, thus the new name announced the creation of a new town.

Jim Thorpe is surely one of the most interesting town sites of any county seat in the state. Its central area lies in a narrow valley, and the main street, Broadway, winds along the Mauch Chunk Creek from its juncture with the Lehigh River. The courthouse is located on U.S. Route 209 at the confluence, where there is a small flat area, practically the only level space in the town. It is directly opposite a tiny park and old rail station. Because there is so little level ground, few houses have lawns, and most buildings, including the courthouse, are built to the sidewalk. The courthouse is a dark, reddish

brown stone Romanesque structure (1893, L. S. Jacoby of Allentown, architect) with a tile roof and a square clock tower containing a 2,122-pound bell cast in Baltimore. At one time, the bell was tolled thirteen times for murder convictions. The Panic of 1893 struck just as the building bonds were issued, and the financing was a struggle, but the builder and the community persevered and completed a simple but well-built courthouse that features an exemplary courtroom.

The building is L-shaped, occupying space behind the adjoining bank building. This section also has a 1937 New Deal–aided addition. The stone is from the county and is very high-quality, as indicated by the foliage carvings, which have lasted better

than those of most century-old buildings in this region (compare with the Lackawanna County courthouse in Scranton, for example). The main surface is quarry dressed and the accents are in smooth stone, a reversal of the more common usage. The rocklike surface seems appropriate for this location. The windows are both rectilinear and arched, alternating between floors on the side. A dormer projects from the roof in the front, and on the side, two dormerlike windows are actually continuations of the building wall. The tower rises from two projecting bays on the right side of the front, with the windows on the first three floors in rhythm with those on the east side of the building. Where the tower projects above the roofline, there are three nearly blind arches, pierced only by two narrow openings. A cornice separates this tier from the clock-face section, where the stone becomes smooth ashlar. The clock face is in a slightly recessed square section bounded by thin pilasters on either side and corbelling above. Above the clock face is an arcaded open belfry with two double columns, pilasters, and slightly recessed voussoirs, which give the arches defining shadows. The belfry section has a corbelled cornice. The pyramidal tile roof is topped by a finial.

Inside, the central portion is simple and plain except for the colorful tile floors and the two original decorative iron stairwells. Courtroom 1 occupies the second floor of the ell behind the bank. This nicely renovated room is a winner. An immediate impression is made by the triple, peacock-tail-shaped sections of fretwork above the large judge's bench. A second outstanding feature is the stained-glass skylight with its central panel showing the Goddess of

Former Carbon County jail.

Justice. It is a large room with an ample balcony, well lighted on both sides by a bank of windows, including three tall, beautifully shuttered ones on either side. Oak wainscoting with a carved foliage border surrounds the room, and in both front corners there are surviving fireplaces decorated with American tiles that feature a carving of a disembodied hand supporting scales. Frances B. Kramer of Philadelphia supplied the courtroom interior furnishings.

The tall, gray veterans memorial was erected in 1886 and not only memorializes the Civil War, but also includes the names Yorktown, New Orleans, Mexico, and Appomattox, sites all associated with moments of United States military success. However, while Yorktown and Mexico City were culminating American battle victories of those wars, the battle of New Orleans occurred after the peace treaty was signed, and Appomattox was not a battle, but a surrender site. Perhaps when there is room for only four words to be chiseled in stone, brevity is more important than historical accuracy. The modern 1972 annex is of little interest except for the outdoor plaque, which tells the town name-change story. In the small park across from the courthouse, note the large lump of coal, which needs no explanation.

Broadway, which curves upward from the courthouse, has such an inviting look that one can hardly resist exploring it. Besides the shops, there are a number of public buildings, including a Victorian library, which is worth a look inside. If you persevere to 128 West Broadway, you will find the old 1871 county jail, designed by John Haviland (architect of the Philadelphia Eastern Penitentiary and the famous New York House of Detention called "The Tombs") and the scene of hanging for six Molly Maguires in the first decade of is use. Its medieval fortress style was a standard jail design for much of Pennsylvania during the mid-nineteenth century. It is now open for tours during the summer.

CENTRE
County Seat: Bellefonte

Centre County, created in 1800, is at the geographic center of the state. While the largest city in the county is State College, home of Pennsylvania State University, the seat is the smaller but much older town of Bellefonte. Its French name, according to tradition, is attributed to Tallyrand, a 1794 visitor who suggested naming the town after a big spring, one that still flows in a local park.

The main street of Bellefonte is a striking museum piece, with its very large nineteenth-century commercial buildings. The surrounding steep hills make the setting all the more dramatic. Prominent at the head of High

Street is the very old courthouse. Its oldest portion dates from 1805 and 1811, but what you see is from an 1835 renovation attributed to Ezra Ale. While the original building had a cupola and weathervane, the ones seen today, along with the hexastyle Ionic portico, are from the later date. It is truly a classic Greek Revival "temple of justice." The rear was extended in 1911 and again in 1963. The porch has eight twenty-six-foot Ionic columns, six across the front and two next to the facade, under a pediment with modillions and dentils. The main building facade is five bays wide, with a door in the center. The cornice over the door may be original, but not the door itself. The cupola has a square base, upon which sits an octagonal clock-and-belfry tier.

Here there are Doric pilasters at the corner, and alternately single and double louvered openings under the clock faces. A copper roof is topped by a fish weathervane. Why a fish on this inland courthouse? A longtime local newspaper reporter gave this account. In the nineteenth century, Bellefonte twice built reservoirs for public water supply. The second reservoir, which was built higher up the hill than the first in order to increase water pressure, was at the level of the courthouse weathervane. At this time, around 1870, trout fishing was a big local attraction. These aquatic associations, in a town with an aquatic name, led to the choice of the fish, the original version having been made of wood. Though this explanation may be true, several other Pennsylvania courthouses also sport fish weathervanes.

The courthouse interior was redone in 1911 (Newman and Harris of Philadelphia, architect). Among the improvements was to introduce the first plumbing and hence flush toilets. Though the offices were rearranged and the hallways refurbished, the courtroom retained its place and the style dating from the Ale time. The interior is a well-maintained and attractive space. The floors and wainscoting of the halls are in white marble with black accents. The double staircases with marble newel posts fitted with brass lamps are in the Classical style as it was being done at the time of renovation. At the top of the stairs is a foyer decorated with Corinthian pilasters. The courtroom features a circular, decorated ceiling, painted pine furnishings, and a high-backed jury box. It is difficult to date all of the elements in the courtroom as to what is original, but presumably much beyond the rail is. The audience seating was replaced around the turn of the century, and there may have been other changes as well. The fourteen windows that bathe the room in natural light add greatly to its attractiveness.

Centre County can claim to have been the home of five governors, the most renowned of whom was the Civil War governor Andrew Curtin. He was an outstanding leader who mobilized the other Northern governors in support of Lincoln's war effort at a time when the Northern cause looked bleak. His bronze statue by W. Clark Noble in front of the courthouse is a local tribute to his national prominence. Curtin was a straight arrow who turned against the Republican party because of the corruption of the Grant administration. He was later elected as a Democrat to the House of Representatives, where he served from 1881 to 1887.

Few county seats have such a commercial architectural legacy in their downtown as Bellefonte, and let's hope it can find a new life. Noting just two buildings, at High and Allegheny, the Brockerhoff House Hotel is an 1860 Italianate structure (look at the windows) capped by a rather inelegant 1890 mansard roof. Brockerhoff was a wealthy global adventurer who found his way to this remote county from Napoleon's staff, arriving in 1825. He was an innkeeper and hotel operator for over fifty years when Bellefonte was host to legions of travelers. The Crider Exchange building, with its large iron-bound windows and Queen Anne topping, was designed by a talented local architect, J. Robert Cole.

CHESTER
County Seat: West Chester

It is the third oldest county in the state, formed by William Penn in 1682 and named after Chester, England. Chester and Delaware Counties share with New Castle County, Delaware, their unique circular county border. It came out of a boundary dispute compromise between Maryland and Pennsylvania in 1732 settled by the Privy Counsel. The negotiators used geometric calculations in coming up with the settlement, one of which was a circle centered on the city of New Castle. What looked simple on paper proved most difficult in transferring to the actual ground. A circular boundary was beyond the capacity of Colonial surveyors, leading to the re-

tention of two English mathematical astronomers, Mason and Dixon, to execute the settlement. They not only solved the problem of the circular boundary, but also ran their renowned line that became the symbolic demarcation between the North and the South.

The architect of the 1846 courthouse was none other than Philadelphia native Thomas U. Walter, successor to Thomas Mills as architect of the U.S. Capitol. Walter is renowned for his Classical designed buildings, including the Girard College in Philadelphia. In Chester, he created a Corinthian, hexastyle temple of justice with a prominent and curious tower. This was a replacement courthouse, and there was a huge public debate over whether it should face south or east. This indeed sounds like a petty issue, but politics is often petty. There may have been some economic considerations involved, because some commercial establishments wanted to be at the very door of the courthouse. One cannot help but think in reading contemporary discussions, including letters to the editor, that the newspapers were creating a tempest in a teapot in order to increase circulation. Walter dodged the issue by creating entrances on both the south and the east. The portico and main entrance are to the east, with fluted columns made of steel filled with stone. The southern door was at the center of a pavilion on that side. Its doorway has now been converted into a window, though some of the entrance surrounds remains. Of the nine side bays, the five middle ones rise to a pediment. There is no pavilion on the north side, which faced an obscure alley when the building was constructed. The blind window on the second story north resulted from an 1893 interior change in the courtroom described below. There are rectilinear panels in the stonework between the two rows of windows. There is a dentillated cornice around the building, but the raking angles of the pediments are unadorned. The bays on all sides are divided by square pilasters, except on the south, where they are more like attached columns under the pavilion. While all courthouse towers are unique (I have yet to find two identical), this one's shape is in a class by itself. Above its clock faces is an unusual elongated, copper-clad bell tier, which is capped and topped by a gilded ball, spike, and weathervane. The gilding materials have varied over time.

All of Walter's work on this structure was not successful. The exterior was originally stuccoed (called mastic), and it "peeled like a shedding snake." The building was re-covered after a few years with Pictou stone. The copper roof lasted only until 1856. In fact, the record of changes and correction goes on nearly annually for the next century and a half, but most changes were minor or interior. The building looks basically as Walter designed it. There is a great 1870 photo hanging inside the courthouse that shows the building without additions and surrounded by a splendid Walter-designed iron fence. It looked great all by itself.

The building is of vaulted construction, which can best be seen in the basement (not open to the public), the central hall, and the offices off the main central corridor. (Walter was using this construction technique concurrently in constructing the massive main Girard College building.) Originally, all the row offices were located on the first floor off the central hall. All the doors and surrounds are modern replacements, but probably follow the original design. Just inside the front door there is an oval foyer, now partially filled. The single curved stairs (a second north one was removed in 1892 to add an office) once led to courtroom 1. This staircase is partially original. The treads have been replaced, but the balusters and what must be the smallest newel post in this guide may be original. To reach the courtroom, you must now enter through the snitch box at the building's rear.

The impressive courtroom 1 occupies the original courtroom space, but what you see dates from 1968. The township engineer is quoted as saying they were seeking "an old fashioned look." The original courtroom had the judge's bench on the west, but it was shifted to its present location in a Victorian renovation in 1893. A window on the north wall was closed to make this possible. A newspaper reporter's sketch of the original Walter arrangement surfaced after the 1968 renovation, and it shows the bench on the west side. Behind it, there were four Corinthian columns, beyond which a corridor led to chambers or jury rooms and culminated in a window. That was a more sensible layout than the present one, from the standpoint of the judge, who no longer has a chamber behind his bench and must move through the courtroom each time he enters or leaves. The design sacrifice was probably made to facilitate access to attach the annex.

The 1895 addition (T. Roney Williamson of West Chester, architect) uses the hall that was behind the original bench as its second-floor entrance. The annex has two courtrooms worthy of a look. Courtroom 2 has a beamed ceiling and is lighted by large, round-topped, colored glass windows on three sides. The wainscoting, rail, and furniture are rather plain for the time. The fancier decoration was probably bestowed on courtroom 1, and to see the clue that supports that surmise, go to courtroom 3. This room is converted from the old law library, which explains the balcony arrangement. Note, however, the bench, which was built for the 1892 courtroom 1 but was thrown in the trash in the 1968 "restoration." A lawyer picked it up, and it eventually was used for a bar of a nonlegal sort in a local restaurant called "The Country Lawyer." When it closed in 1983, the old judge's bench was purchased by the Bar Association and stored in the barn of a local cabinetmaker. It was evidently an active barn, as chickens left their mark on it. When the county converted the library to this courtroom in 1986, the Bar Association donated the bench, and it was resuscitated and installed in its present place.

There is also a modern 1964 addition (Young and Schultz, architects), which has two courtrooms with medallions above the bench made by Bucks County artist Harry Roon, who also did the exterior bas-reliefs. These were part of the architect's effort to soften the impact of a five-story wall abutting the downtown sidewalk. The scheme of the bas-relief is based on four centuries of Chester County, with the seventeenth at the top and twentieth at the bottom. The personages portrayed, whose names are at the base, were selected by a local committee. Some selections may not be familiar to non-locals. In the nineteenth-century set, Darlington wrote on local botany, Taylor was a poet called the "bard of Kennett Square," and Lukens was one of the few women who ran a steel mill. Among the twentieth-century locals, Pennock is well known to old Phillies fans, and Philip was a teacher at West Chester University for forty years.

Continuing outside, note the stone water fountain (nonfunctioning) with a gargoyle on the curb. It was the object of much derisive comment when installed soon after the original courthouse was built. It was once suspected of spreading paludal fever. It featured a triple watering service: one for people, one for cows and horses, and one for dogs and hogs. It has had a peregrinating history in the town. It was originally placed in its present spot, got moved during one of the modernization frenzies, but found its way back in 1987. The 1915 Civil War memorial is surely one of the last to be built. Its design was debated for nearly ten years, and from newspaper accounts it is unclear whether the principle reason for the delay was commissioner parsimony or esthetic differences.

Across Market Street from the entrance to the Williamson addition is a brick structure with an iron second-floor balcony, a building that housed a press that printed the first biography of Lincoln. Across the street from the front of the courthouse is a Thomas U. Walter designed bank. It is the one with the prominent fluted Doric columns. The modest brick structure next to it also served as a bank and as residence of the bank president. If you want to see a Walter building with the third classical order, the Ionic, you only have to go several blocks to West Miner Street and South Darlington Street and observe the Presbyterian Church. It's worth the walk. Thomas U. Walter had a long and distinguished career and toward its end helped design the Philadelphia Centennial of 1876 and supervised the building of MacArthur's Philadelphia City Hall until his death in 1887.

CLARION
County Seat: Clarion

The name Clarion was first given to the river and then to the county, created in 1839, and county seat. Three early surveyors allegedly were resting in their tents near the river and were impressed at how the dense forest seemed to reflect the sound of the river with great clarity, like a clarion.

The courthouse (1882–84) dominates the townscape of Clarion. The architect, E. M. Butz, designed several other courthouses, including that of Salisbury, Maryland, and this one gives a good account of his style, which he

dubbed Queen Anne, probably because of the complex rooflines. While his designs are restrained, he liked to use materials with color accents. The red brick contrasts with the sandstone that is used for the water table, entryway, window outlines, belt courses, and decorations on the tower. Other design features include quarry-faced stone for the foundation, foliage carvings, and ornamental finials at every roof peak. The tower that rises over the entryway is of all-brick construction, with thicker walls at the bottom and stepped thinner from the inside toward the top. The three narrow windows on its second and third floors light interior stair landings. The bell is behind the balconies, which have hidden louvered openings to emit the

sound. The clock-face tier has many stone accents, with a denticulated equilateral pediment above each face. The sides of the steeply pyramidal roof each have one of Butz's small dormers. A galvanized Lady Justice statue rides high on the top. It was recently taken down for repair, and it contained twenty-five bullet holes, a common fate of these roof statues. It is now covered with fiberglass. Originally the tower was piped for gas in order to illuminate the clock faces at night.

Viewed from the sides, the building has six bays of double windows, with the central one extended forward and rising to a gable. Here, a large dormer pierces the roof. There are also two small, louvered dormers at the attic level. Because the courtroom occupies a space as wide as the building, the roof is supported from the exterior wall. The large attic (not open to the public) contains an impressive array of triangulated trusswork that supports the roof and carries the courtroom ceiling in a bridge construction manner.

Butz gave great attention to his interiors, and in this case there are fine wooden newel posts and banisters on the foyer stairs that leads to the courtroom. The colorful tile floors still sparkle and give life to the public space toward the front of the building on each floor. Many doors have the original hardware. The large courtroom has a wooden ceiling, a distinctive feature found in northern Pennsylvania counties. This may have something to do with the abundance of inexpensive local wood when the virgin forests of this area were being logged. Originally, there was a balcony and the walls had murals. The wooden window shutters are still there, as is most of the original furniture beyond the rail. There were modernizing renovations in 1947 and 1981.

The courthouse is on an ample square and fronts a park of equal size in which veterans of various wars are duly memorialized. The Civil War statue is one of the few funded by the state, which may explain why it has no dedicatory information. There may have been a desire to muffle this fact to ward off a line of supplicants for state–financed memorials. Beyond the park are two attractive old houses, one of which houses the county historical society (18 Grant Street).

CLEARFIELD
County Seat: Clearfield

The county, created in 1804, derives its name for the original feature of cleared land. The referenced clearings were not man-made, however, but rather, the intense grazing of a herd of buffalo eliminated the undergrowth. The county is the site of an ancient Indian village, the name of which meant "no one tarries here," perhaps prophetic, as the population growth of this area has remained limited.

The 1860 courthouse (Cleaveland and Bachus, architects) is located at the main intersection of the central business district, which is a block from the West Branch of the Susquehanna River. A nineteenth-century observer said of the building that it "was constituted with a view to utility and convenience rather than outward appearance and show." That fairly characterizes this two-and-a-half-story brick building with comparatively few decorative embellishments. The facade is a bit unusual and certainly unique among Pennsylvania courthouses. The bell tower stands in front of the gable front of the main building, with two one-story arcaded porches on either side. On first glance, one might conclude that these are later additions, as so many courthouses acquire new facades. Such is not the case here, however. It is unclear whether the present appearance is the original architects' plan. They ran into trouble building the tower, which began to lean, perhaps because of subsoil conditions. The tower had to be rebuilt and may have been shifted forward. The decorations on the porticos originally included roof balustrades, in addition to the cornice brackets and a decorative brick course. The tower rests on four arches at the ground floor, and these provide access to the main entrance. The tower itself is a straight, square shaft, which is articulated into levels by window placement and belt courses. The clock faces are mounted flush on each side without adornment, and the bell tier has double arched louvers. Moving to the south side, note that there are two cross-gabled sections. The rear one is an 1882–83 addition (Thorn and Burchfield, architects). While the addition is built in a style similar to the older part, small embellishments are introduced reflective of the later, more exuberant architectural style (compare Palladian windows). The addition is asymmetrical in order to provide for a new chimney and law library to the left.

Former Clearfield County jail.

There were originally three front doors and two interior staircases. When this building was constructed, court sessions would attract a full house of spectators, and there was a need to provide easy entrance and exit for substantial crowds. It is a testimony to the times that trials are no longer such a great community diversion, and this building has lost a door and a staircase to provide more office space. The remaining original staircase is a rather simple one, with a wood balustrade. The foyer has a tile wainscot, which originally probably went down the wide hallway now lined with display cases. The hallway has a fairly elaborate tin ceiling with a cornice. The old courtroom has been severely altered, essentially cut in two to provide a second courtroom at the rear. There are some original furnishings beyond the rail, and the pastel-colored window tops are attractive on a sunny day.

Several blocks north from the front of the courthouse on the left you will find the former jail (1870), which should be instantly recognizable. It has been shorn of its walled side yards, but it remains very much intact, and alternative uses are being considered.

CLINTON
County Seat: Lock Haven

Clinton is a late county creation for Pennsylvania, coming in 1839. It was the product of the dogged lobbying on the part of one Jeremiah Church, a transplanted New Yorker and founder of Lock Haven. Late county creations were always intensely political, because the new county had to be extracted from well-established ones that were being forced to give up territory and tax base. It took Church six years of persisted pleading, but in the end he succeeded, and the county was named after another New Yorker, DeWitt Clinton, the famed creator of the Erie Canal. The future county seat was located on a canal. It had a *lock* and it became a *haven* for the large number of rafters who came down the Susquehanna heading for markets farther south. The rafts hauled produce and were themselves made of marketable saw logs.

Accounts written seventy years ago are radiant with plans to improve and beautify the city. Some of them were carried out, such as to turn the canal locks, which had become dumps, into parkland. While the area in front of the courthouse is parkland, a river view is inhibited by the high

flood dike. The courthouse (1869, Samuel Sloan and Addison Hutton, architects), which faces the river on Water Street, has dual towers and is similar to other efforts of these architects (see Venango County). The building style is Romanesque before Richardson, but Sloan called it Norman. A distinguishing feature of the building is the tall Norman windows with double arches and circle at the top. The facade is five bays wide, with the three central ones brought forward as a shallow pavilion. The first story is rusticated around the three arched entryways, with a faux balcony above. Four square pilasters frame the three central Norman windows and rise to a pediment at the roofline. Sloan wrote with pride about the quality of the stone used as plinths, sills, caps, and balusters. While the towers still get your attention, particularly with their new multicolored paint job, they are but pale shadows of the ones designed by Sloan and Hutton. The top domes, now all shiny, were once taller, and each had four hooded dormers. The square bases have been simplified, the finials have been shortened, and detailing on the Norman windows is gone from the nonclock surfaces of the taller tower octagonal section. The building cornice has dentils and modillions, including on the raking sides of the pediment. Side windows on the first floor have a variation on a Gibbs surround. The rear addition, creating a T-shaped floor plan, was added in 1936 (Russel J. Howard, architect).

Inside, the central hall is stenciled and has a repeating arch ceiling treatment similar to the one in Venango County. This was a building device that Sloan used to strengthen support of the floor above. The courtroom retains much of its original look, but documentation on the specifics is lacking. It uses the ramped audience area also found in other north Pennsylvania courtrooms, such as at Honesdale and Tunkhannock. There is an Ionic broken pediment decoration behind the judge's bench and a nice abstract sunburst over the rear entrance door. The furniture is painted pine with grained highlights. The twelve tall Norman windows provide the lighting for this very satisfying courtroom space.

The small park across the street on either side of the Jay Street Bridge contains markers and memorials. Interesting old houses can be found in the first block both east and west on Water Street. Going west, note the Jacob Grofius House at 217. The nucleus was built in 1843 and housed a store, which faced the canal (where the dike now sits, there was a grass strip) and served canal-boat passengers. In 1853, it was enlarged and received its embellishments, including the floral band under the cornice, reputedly to outdo the neighbor's house at 201 (still there). To the east, at 362, is Heisey House, remodeled as Gothic Revival after the 1861 flood and now the county historical society museum. On its grounds are a gazebo and an interesting 1854 icehouse.

COLUMBIA
County Seat: Bloomsburg

This county, established in 1813, is one of the ten counties in the nation with a name that pays tribute to Christopher Columbus. Bloomsburg was an established town when the county seat was moved here in 1846. As is so often the case in this situation, the courthouse was crowded into the already developed commercial area, and the result was meager yard space around the building.

The courthouse on the main street (called Second) can best be understood if you walk to its left and view it from the west side. Note that it is composed of three sections, with the oldest part in the middle. This section dates to around 1850, and its plan is attributed to no less an architect than Napoleon LeBrun, the designer of the Academy of Music in Philadelphia. Its bricks were burned by Daniel Snyder, one of the local movers and shakers, who promoted the county seat and who was responsible for financing the jail and courthouse. The building was extended forward in 1868, after which it was described as being in the Ionic style with a bell tower. In 1890, A. S.

Wagner (see Cameron County) added a front section, and as a consequence, the building now reads Romanesque Revival with Richardsonian influence. Richardson's Pittsburgh courthouse had only been completed two years before, which shows how rapidly his ideas were adopted by other architects. It is a brick and brown Hummelstown stone building with galvanized iron cornices. The rounded arch, open balcony, window arcades with stone voussoirs, square tower, intricate foliage carvings, and short columns are all in the Richardsonian vocabulary. (Put your glass on the apex of the front gable.) The Wagner facade has three sections: the central tower, the gabled right side, and the octagonal left. The three are in a stepwise regression, but the arcaded porch adjusts the appearance of the front building line to make it more square with the street. The lower part of the tower is an integral part of the building, and its third story originally contained a small courtroom. Above, there is an open arcaded belfry tier. Octagonal corner turrets begin at this level and continue through the clock-face tier. The pyramidal roof culminates in a weathervane.

Going inside, the stairs to the second floor connect you with the courtroom, which is in the oldest, middle section of the building and still retains its classical look. The courtroom space is still intact and is lighted with ten windows. Its main features are the Classical cornice, door trims, and painted wood benches with natural finished trim. The newest rear section of the courthouse has nothing of interest.

There is a 1908 soldiers and sailors monument at a nearby intersection and an elaborate Victorian fountain that is partially functioning. Each has a complicated and colorful history. The monument was not completed until 1908, some forty years after the war. The delay started with the fact that this area was copperhead country, and the Civil War and the draft were unpopular here. Fund-raising caused many delays and required a third effort before achieving success. Then there was the issue of location, which finally had to be settled by a judge. Some feared an errant trolley might bowl it over if placed in Market Square, but there it stands long after the trolleys have gone. There was even a controversy over who would preside at the dedication. Reputedly, the usual speech by the governor for such occasions did not occur, as he wanted to steer clear of the local controversies. The fountain resulted from a gift by a thrifty local candymaker in the late nineteenth century, whose bequest included money for a water system. This was translated into the fountain, which was ordered from a catalog. By 1960, it had so deteriorated that it was removed during a downtown beautification effort, after which it was displayed in a local museum. The museum was closed due to Hurricane Agnes, but the fountain survived and was eventually reassembled by volunteers in its present location. Along the way, it lost some key adornments, but plans were under way for a complete restoration at this writing. The post office has a WPA-sponsored walnut relief by Roy King entitled *Pennsylvania Farming,* and flowers form the zip code on the lawn.

CRAWFORD
County Seat: Meadville

Col. William Crawford, surveyor, lifelong friend of Washington, and longtime Indian fighter, survived the French and Indian War, Pontiac's War, and Revolutionary War but was burned at the stake by Indians in Ohio in 1782 while leading an expedition. Crawford County was formed in 1800, and Meadville became county seat by promising to create a "seminary of learning," which it did by raising $4,470. Meadville is still the seat, but the seminary has long since gone. It is always noteworthy when a county bar produces a U.S. Supreme Court justice. Henry Baldwin, a Jacksonian appointee to the Supreme Court, started his law practice here. Industrially, Meadville is identified with the development of the slide fastener, which was dubbed the zipper when B. F. Goodrich installed them in his rubber galoshes, a product very widely used before America was paved over. It took decades of tinkering before the zipper was used in the many applications it is

today. Its growing popularity made Meadville prosper, even in the down times of the thirties. In observing Meadville, note the shade trees, something that the city promotes as a local signature. It has an active tree replacement program and a tradition of memorializing persons with a tree planting.

The courthouse faces Diamond Park, a full square that separates North and South Main Street, and is, characteristically, filled with attractive trees. At its core, the courthouse is an 1857 building, but what you see dates from 1954. The 1857 building (E. L. Roberts, architect), which replaced an 1825 courthouse designed by the renowned architect William Strickland, was early Second Empire. It differed from the later ones of this style, so it is unfortunate that we do not still have this example. In 1952, it could be derided as a monstrosity, at a time when modernity was in and historic preservation was yet to arise from the dust of rampant urban renewal clearance projects. When the Roberts structure was dedicated, the following was sung to the tune of "America":

Hail masonry Divine
Glory of Ages shine
Long mayst thou reign . . .

I am sure no such toast was uttered to the present "masonry profane." The 1952 red brick and limestone encasement (Hanna and Stewart, architects) is in a prosaic Colonial Revival style. At least, that is what it was called at the dedication, but Classical Revival fits as well. It has a quatrastyle Doric portico centered between two wings, which expand forward from the front plane of the embedded structure. There is little about it to inspire verse making. Perhaps by way of apology, the commissioners installed cases in the entrance of the present building showing memorabilia from the old one. On either side of the entrance, there is a set of bas-reliefs created by Carl Heeschen, then head of the Allegheny College art department. They depict county historical scenes, including the Titusville oil strike and a recognition of the zipper. There are also depictions of the 1825 Strictland courthouse and the later Roberts one, so you can get some idea of what a treat the last one was. It had a sumptuous courtroom that looked out over the park from a large second-story central section.

The park, called the Diamond since 1956, started as an open militia training space laid out as a parallelogram in 1795. There is a story of mule herds of over a thousand being driven through the town in 1833. The animals rolled in the bare dirt of the square, creating a huge dust cloud that settled over the whole town. It was fenced after the Civil War to keep wandering cows from eating the grass and drinking from the new Shippen dolphin fountain erected in 1863. E. W. Shippen was of a prominent family who owned the foundry in which it was made. The fountain has recently been given new anchors but still lists a little to one side; nevertheless, it is a handsome historical piece. The park also sports a bandstand donated by local musician Dexter Bulen, a centennial statue, and other memorials. Nearby residential streets are worth exploring, and one suggested stroll is out Chestnut Street to the attractive David Mead Inn, where you can obtain a brochure on the history and locations of some noteworthy tree specimens.

CUMBERLAND
County Seat: Carlisle

This Colonial county, created in 1750, is named after Cumberland County, England. Carlisle is named for a town in that English county, and the old county jail is a small replica of the Castle of Carlisle.

The courthouse is located at Center Square in the heart of the county seat. It is an 1846 brick structure with an imposing sandstone quatrastyle portico, with modified Corinthian capitals and an impressive bell-and-clock tower. The elegantly modeled

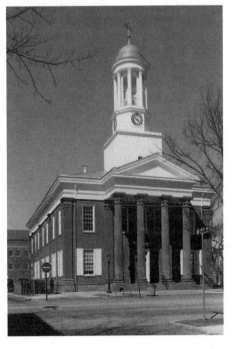

capitals are worth a close look and reflect its local artisan origin. The artisans were Daniel E. Witt, a carpenter, and Samuel Bryan, Jr., who was probably the designer, as he built other courthouses later. While this one conforms to the prevailing temple of justice Classical style of its time, it also has Georgian elements. Distinctive touches in addition to the capitals include the pilasters along the sides and at the front corner, as well as interior elements. While the designer may have seen pictures of Classical renderings, he may not have seen an actual building after which to model this one. The large twelve-over-twelve windows ensure good internal lighting. Note the cannonball ding on the front column, dating from the battle of Gettysburg and marked for the benefit of visitors. The tower consists of an octagonal clock-face tier over a square base and an open belfry in which you can see the bell. The column capitals from the main building front are repeated on the tower. The bell-shaped roof has a finial and weathervane.

Inside, the vaulted central hall of the first floor is a Witt-Bryan feature, but the stair banisters, interior decor, and second-story courtroom date from 1880. Most of the work on the building since that date, including the 1991 work supervised by Crabtree, Rohrbaugh and Associates, has been confined to systems. Thus, the courtroom is basically late nineteenth century, as are the furnishings. The room's distinctive features include the rounded corners, restrained ceiling coffering, old pews, witness box, and rails. Other than painting, the only things touched in 1991 were the light fixtures. It appears they were stripped to bare metal, revealing the iron, which was probably bronze or brass plated originally. The ornate hot-air register grates are of a rare design and must date from 1880, as steam heat radiators were installed in 1894 and removed in 1991.

The old fortresslike jail a block east on High Street (1854, Myers and Gutshall, architects) is now an office, but the interior is largely intact, including the cells, which are used as storage bins. The Center Square is pleasant, well marked with plaques, and features historic churches. Among the memorials is one honoring Jim Thorpe, the famous athlete, who attended Carlisle Indian School.

The present courthouse (1961), across the street from the 1846 structure, was designed by the firm of Lawrie and Green, who twenty years earlier had designed the elaborate Dauphin County structure. This Cumberland County building is but a faint copy of that one. It does make an effort to echo some style features of the old courthouse opposite, particularly the columns. As at Harrisburg, the courtrooms prominently feature wise aphorisms behind the judges' benches.

There is a surviving old stone Cumberland County courthouse in Shippensburg, the seat before Carlisle.

DAUPHIN
County Seat: Harrisburg

The unusual name can be understood by looking at the date of the county's creation—1785. One of the first to be created after American independence, it was named for the title of Louis XVI of France, who had given aid to the colonists in their struggle. The seat is named for John Harris, the founder of the town.

The courthouse is at Front Street and Market Street and overlooks the broad Susquehanna River. It was built in the unusual years of 1941–43 (Lawrie and Green, architects; Paul Cret, advisory consultant) and represents one of the last of the monumental, decorated courthouses, a must-see for any courthouse fan. This building likely has more words carved in stone than any other courthouse in the nation, though I know of no records kept on the subject. It is a showcase for marble, wood, and terrazzo and is loaded with iconography rendered in these and other materials, including etched glass.

The site was selected after a long controversy in which the cost of land assembly was one issue. That may explain its cramped lot, but because it fronts on the river-edge park, there is less sense of crowding. The architects pur-

posely designed the stepped arrangement of the building so that any future adjoining skyscrapers would be set back from its windows. They called its style Modern Classic, which is a key to their perspective, but in the language of this guide, it is Art Moderne. The massive square columns on Front Street bespeak of the Classical connection, but the lines of the building are severely modern, with only the carved county seal breaking the flat surface. The seal is also carved in the granite front steps, as is a portrayal of the older courthouse that this one replaced. The names carved in the marble between the lower-floor windows are those of the Dauphin County townships and boroughs. Most of the exterior lettering was done at the Georgia quarry, and sidewalk superintendents puzzled over the meaning of the alphabetic blocks as they were piled around the building site. The

seal, the male youth statue in front, and other sculptures on the building were designed by nationally renowned sculptor C. Paul Jennewein, whose work can be found on the U.S. Supreme Court building; Radio City, New York; and the polychrome tympanum of the Philadelphia Art Museum.

There is a lot of iconography to cover on this building, but as much of it is labeled, it is not necessary to detail every item here. Starting on the Front Street or fountain side, the Jennewein statue of the young man symbolizes the triumph of law over the powers of evil and injustice; thus he clutches a sheaf of arrows while stomping upon a monster. The three bronze figures over the door are, left to right, clearing the land, a settler couple, and reaping the harvest. The window etching above must be read from inside. The Market Street entrance has a more elaborate trinity treatment, with figures representing Mercy (man holding lamb), Justice (book of laws), and Wisdom (owl). The symbols below elaborate on legal themes (the elephant of India symbolizes mercy, not the GOP). To the side of the steps, the county name is carved in beautiful contemporary calligraphy.

The use of marble and wood in the interior is impressive. I was curious about how all this Italian marble could be obtained during the war, but I found no mention of the problem in the news accounts that chronicled the building progress. It must have been from stock accumulated during the low-construction Depression years. The steel framework was completed three days after Pearl Harbor. Metal was a war material, and there was limited amount available for civilian use, but war priorities only adversely affected the furnishing of the completed building and forced substituting wood for metal shelving and furnishings. The following lists identify some of the principal decorative materials.

Stone

Market Street lobby	Red Numidian marble
Front Street lobby	Fiorito rosso (flowery red) marble
First-floor corridors	Fiorito rosso marble
Second-floor corridor	Montenelle marble
Third-floor corridor	Montenelle and rouge ionazo marble
Fifth-floor corridor	Golden Morocco marble
Courtroom 1 (bench)	Escalette (fr.), Daroa vein marble
Courtroom 3	Relante marble (fr.)
Orphans' courtroom	Fiorito rosso

Woods

Third floor, west-side offices	Paldoa and mahogany paneling
Third floor, east-side offices	Figured gum
Fifth-floor lobby	Comb grain oak
Grand jury room	Brazilian rosewood
Commissioners hearing room	Brazilian rosewood (furniture oak, walnut, ebony)
Courtroom 1	Crotch mahogany and blister maple
Courtroom 2	Burl and claro walnut
Courtroom 3	Quartered white oak
Courtroom 4	Native white pine and redwood burl
Courtroom 5	Brazilian rosewood and tamo (front)
Courtroom 6	Blistered maple, gum, and redwood burl (front)
Orphans' courtroom	Redwood burl and tamo

The woods tend to be special subtypes of their species and therefore more expensive. Crotch mahogany is made from the uppermost part of the tree, where the branching alters the grain. Figured gum results from locally occurring mineral deposits, which give some texture to a wood that normally has little, and burls have unusual graining. Tamo is the Japanese word for a species of ash, *Fraxinus mandshurica.*

The first-story terrazzo floors have interesting symbolic depictions of occupations found in the county. The one for finance seems to have depicted the business cycle. The Front Street foyer floor has a huge county map, complete with a green Susquehanna River. The golden boatman above the carved history is John Harris. A commemorative quilt decorates the wall. The striking glass etchings on the first and fifth floors are by New York artist Henry Tyler, who spent nine months in the area researching the material. The wood carving in the walls outside the law library represent the major systems of law throughout history.

One of the buildings torn down on the courthouse site housed the Dauphin County Historical Society. The society was moved several blocks south on Front Street and now occupies a house started by John Harris, later much enlarged. On the grounds are the bell and cornerstone from the courthouse previous to the present one.

DELAWARE
County Seat: Media

The place name Delaware is generally understood to be after Baron De La Warr, but somewhere along the line, an Indian tribe received the name. The nation's seven Delaware Counties variously attribute their names to the man, the state, the river, and the Indian tribe. In the case of Delaware County, Pennsylvania, created in 1789, at least three of these have been cited as the source of the name. Let's just say the name Delaware was in common use in this region when the county was formed out of Chester County.

Delaware County is largely suburban, and many of the oldest Philadelphia suburbs are located here, as streetcar lines opened up this area in the 1870s. The county seat was originally Chester (on the Delaware) but was moved to the more centrally located Media in 1849. A courthouse was built in the next few years. Because of population growth and the expansion in the scope of county duties, the courthouse has been added on to many times and surrounded by a number of annexes. There is a plaque on the front of the present building stating that it was built in 1851 and added on to in 1871, 1888, 1913, and 1930. None of the first three constructions are now visible to the observer, but ostensibly, some of the brick and mortar from them is embedded in the present building. The 1851

building was a temple of justice designed by Samuel Sloan and bore a resemblance to the Lancaster County courthouse. It acquired two wings before the end of the century. The courthouse you now see began in 1913. Technically a renovation, it completely restructured the existing building, removed the old portico and tower, and created the present central facade. It also converted the building from two to three stories and extended the wings so that in addition to the central part, a three-bay and a four-bay section were added on either side. The 1930 rebuilding (Clarence W. Brazier, architect) added two more three-bay sections, with the twelve-column arcades at the ends. At this time, the interior was extensively altered, particularly to the rear; many courtrooms were added; and a new law library was built atop the central section behind the arched window emanation rising above the old pediment. In the central section, the six Ionic columns, the cornice with its Latin motto, the entablature with the historical statement, the pediment with a clock surrounded by justice symbols, the corner urns, and the ornamentation along the sloped top of the pediment all date from 1913. The massive bronze lights on either side of the entrance also come from this time.

Inside, six courtrooms on the second floor have viewer interest. The large courtroom 1 is the only two-story space and remains essentially as it was built in 1913. The others were created in 1930 and were decorated to reflect various earlier American styles. Courtroom 2 is in the Chippendale style of 1760; courtroom 3, Adams style of 1880; courtroom 4, Wedgewood and Hepplewhite of 1780; courtroom 5, Early Georgian of 1740; and courtroom 6, the Revolutionary War period. The decorative styles have been maintained, but the present colors differ somewhat from the description published in 1930.

There are four newer brick structures to the rear of the courthouse, which house many of the administrative offices and lesser county courts. There is also a multicultural Heritage Plaza.

The oldest courthouse in America still standing is in the city of Chester in this county. For those interested in early courthouses, this is an absolute must to visit. It is in the heart of the business district on what is now called Avenue of the States. Built in 1724 as the Chester County courthouse, it continued to serve that purpose until the seat was moved to West Chester in 1786. Three years later, the county split when Delaware County was created, and this building became the Delaware County courthouse until the seat was moved to Media in 1851. It is an example of indigenous American architecture. The front and east sides of the courthouse are of hewn stone, and the other two sides are rubble. The difference reflects the labor cost of cutting stones with 1724 technology. The Quaker imprint on the building can be seen in the two front doors, one for males and one for females. The hexagonal bay was added about twenty-five years later, and a door was added for the sole use of the judge. When you go inside (find the bell for admission), you will find the whole first floor is devoted to a courtroom, a typical arrangement

Old Chester County courthouse. COURTESY PENNSYLVANIA HISTORICAL AND MUSEUM COMMISSION.

for Colonial courthouses. Note that the judge's bench is in the apselike addition with the Georgian windows and adjacent to the added entrance. The blue paint was based on the oldest samples found embedded in the wood and is intended to be the original color. The upstairs, which is now being used for offices, was originally for jury rooms and court-related business.

ELK
County Seat: Ridgway

An early account written by a surveyor described seeing a large herd of elk in the area now embraced by this county. The herd still existed, though in diminished numbers, when the county was formed in 1843. While the county founders memorialized this noble animal with its name at the founding, a few years later, in 1857, the last elk in the county was killed. Animal species preservation was not yet a blip on the horizon of political agendas. Jacob Ridgway was a Philadelphia Quaker merchant who once purchased most of the land in the county and much, much more in 1817. He later commissioned the creation of his namesake town. Elk County's economy has been largely based on extraction, with timber, coal, oil, gas, and clay each playing a role at some time in its history.

The courthouse is an attractive red brick structure with sandstone accents. Like the one at Warren, it is a combination of Second Empire and Tuscan Villa styles. The similarity is not accidental. In 1872, after looking at the courthouses of Clarion, Forest, Venango, and Warren, Elk County commissioners hired J. H. Marston, who was the building contractor for the Beebe-designed Warren County courthouse, to copy that building and build them a smaller version. No recognition or credit was given to Beebe. It is not identical in that here the clock faces are in the mansard base

of the tower, with an open belfry above, whereas the Warren building essentially has the reverse. Both towers were originally topped by a statue of Lady Justice, but the one here was destroyed by lightening in the 1930s and replaced by a weathervane. This courthouse has finials at the corners of the tower base, whereas Warren's does not.

A description of the exterior reads much like that of Warren. It is a red brick building with stone accents, particularly quoins at the angles. It is six bays wide across the front, with the two central bays brought forward. There are double arched entrances in a rusticated surround. A small bas-relief of an elk on a plaque in the shape of the county has been mounted between the second-story windows. The central bays rise to a roof-level pediment with a roundel. First-story windows are segmentally arched, with drip moldings, and the upper windows have full arches. Decorative features include a belt course between the floors, stone belts at the spring line of the window hood moldings, a cornice with console-shaped modillions and brackets at intervals, and corner mansard pavilions with dormers. Alternate pairs of the ten bays along the side are extended, and the central pair rises to a pediment. There is a 1970 addition to the rear.

The interior has been completely modernized, probably in 1969. The sheriff's house with jail (altered) was added in 1884. The grounds are nicely cared for and contain a bandstand and memorials. The first major tree planting took place in 1861 to mark the departure of the famous Bucktail Regiment, whose experienced deer-hunting members became devastating sharpshooters. There may be surviving trees from that planting, but I could not verify this. A back section of the Bogart Hotel, in the next block, contains part of the old courthouse that preceded this one, but it is largely buried under subsequent alterations.

ERIE
County Seat: Erie

Maps that purport to show the original boundaries of Pennsylvania indicate that much of what is now Erie County, an area later called the Erie Triangle, was not included in the state. (Those maps are retrospective creations and do not date from 1789.) The reason for this is that when the latitude of the western boundary and longitude of the northern state boundary were established, no one knew where the two lines met in real terrestrial space. At the time, a major question was whether the converging latitude and longitude would give Pennsylvania a port on Lake Erie. Pennsylvania officials assumed that to be the case, but they were wrong, as the intersecting point barely reached the lake. No less than five states claimed what was later called the Erie Triangle, but under the terms of the Constitution, disputed western lands were ceded to the new national government. Pennsylvania was very powerful in the new Union, and it was eventually allowed to purchase the disputed parcel. However, the purchase was made without certain knowledge of whether the designated eastern latitudinal boundary of the triangle would give them a natural lake port. There was a sigh of relief when the surveyors located the boundary and Presque Isle was found to be within the purchased territory. The Congressional act that established the price of the sale to Pennsylvania did not define the species of payment. The crafty Pennsylvanians succeeded in settling their obligation in nearly worthless continental bonds, rather than gold or silver. So the purchase came nearly without cost. The county, established in 1800, is officially named after an Indian tribe, but given the 1792 purchase, it should have been after the lake.

The courthouse is located on 6th Street (West Alternate Route 5) at Peach Street and Park Street. It is just down the street from Perry Park, which was originally the courthouse square. It is a unique "double-barreled" structure, composed of two parallel, nearly identical buildings connected at the rear. The older portion (1855) is on the left. The design is probably that of Thomas U. Walter (see Chester County). There is correspondence that he sent them a plan, and there is proof that he was paid $50 for one, but what is missing is documentation that the plan was actually followed. It is Classical Corinthian, by the book, and certainly in a style with which Walter was familiar. A rear addition was added in 1889. In 1894, the tall bell tower was removed as it was felt that the tower was incompatible with a Classical temple design. True enough, but such es-

thetic purity seems a surprising reason to tear it off. Incidentally, the tower had a striking resemblance to the Walter-designed one on the Chester County courthouse, adding credence to his paternity of the original building. In 1929, when the building was enlarged, architect Walter T. Monahan simply built a look-alike parallel annex and connected it at the rear.

Each side has a classical hexastyle Corinthian portico across the whole front. The column capitals are also Classical Corinthian and without the embellishments sometimes added by later architects. There is a wide entablature and a substantial cornice with modillions and dentils. The large entrance has a grilled transom and a pediment supported by substantial consoles. Monahan's addition only looks like the earlier one; it is not a clone. If you look at the sides of the two "barrels," note that Monahan inserted a third floor. A balustraded walk connects the front of the two buildings, and there is a singularly barren interior court.

The interior is very plain, and with the present single security entrance, the Monahan plan creates a very awkward interior circulation system. However, persevere until you see the two courtrooms. Monahan's 1929 courtroom is a straightforward Classical Revival rendition probably inspired by the exterior. There are broken pediments over the doors, wood-paneled wainscot, strapwork around the top of the high room, and a very imposing high bench for the relatively small courtroom. The older courtroom (slated for restoration at this writing) is a more interesting space. While Monahan crowded his courtroom on one side of a central hallway, the nineteenth-century one is as wide as the building. It has five windows on each side, Corinthian pilasters, and furniture in the period style, using paint with naturally finished rails and backs. In 1873, an effort was made to improve acoustics by redoing the ceiling and creating the niche or alcove behind the bench. The audience seats look turn-of-the-century, with cast-iron frames and wire hat racks underneath the seats.

Nearby Perry Square is really a courthouse square, as that was its use prior to 1855. It was originally called the Diamond (see Introduction) but received Perry's name on the centennial of the Battle of Lake Erie. It has been shaved, sliced, and reconfigured, but it retains the traditional court-house ground function of a place to memorialize local heroes. The Civil War monument is one of the early ones, and its history along with the one in Wayne County shows that the monument movement was slow to gain politically correct status. When the Erie County proposal was first made, there were objections to spending $10,000 in public funds. Consequently, a women's committee raised the money (compare with the experience in Wayne County) to construct the 1872 soldiers and sailors statue. Its sculptor was Martin Milmore, a young Irish immigrant who trained in Boston and came into maturity about the time of the Civil War. One might say he wrote the book on this style of monument, because his designs were much copied. His soldiers and sailors monument on the Boston Commons done two years after this is supposedly his best, so this Erie statue was a practice run. Milmore died at the early age of thirty-nine, but he was highly prolific and created many portrait and memorial statues. He was in turn memorialized by a famous sculpture called *Death and the Young Sculptor,* executed by Daniel Chester French and shown at the Centennial Exposition of 1876 in Philadelphia.

Oliver Hazard Perry, for whom the square is named, used Erie as his base of operations for his historic naval victory over the British in the War of 1812. Strategically, the victory was probably not very important in af-fecting the outcome of the war, but it did wonders for American pride, and the admiral became an instant hero. (My grandfather was named for him, and both my father and I also bore the Oliver Perry.) The admiral's statue is a replica of the one in Newport, Rhode Island, by William Green Turner, showing him stepping aboard his flagship, *Niagara.*

Other persons memorialized in the square include Anthony Wayne, whose statue was erected by the Daughters of the Revolution in 1902. He tragically died here (at Presque Isle) after his victorious campaign, which took him eventually to Detroit. He died of an illness while on his way back to Philadelphia to marry his beautiful betrothed, Molly Vining. The diag-nosis was gout, for which the standard treatment of the day was whiskey, and after ten days of suffering and delirium, he was bled. Knowing he was dying, one of his last words was a request to be buried at the base of the flagpole on a local hill here. In 1809, his family and friends wanted to move his grave to his eastern Pennsylvania home, and his son made the arduous journey to retrieve the remains. His plan was to carry the remains back in a set of containers on horseback, but when the body was exhumed, it was remarkably well preserved, presenting a transportation problem. The unususal solution was to separate the bones from the muscle and viscera. The son took the bones east, and the soft remains were returned to the old grave; thus Erie can still claim *one* of the burial sites of Anthony Wayne.

There is a story behind the unusual Eben Brewer statue, with its cryptic message from postal workers. Brewer was a successful newspaper manager who had studied the German *Feldpost* during travels in Europe. When the Spanish-American War broke out, he volunteered to organize a mail delivery system for the troops modeled on the German system. He did so very successfully, with a minimum of help. He then saw the need for care of wounded soldiers and threw himself energetically into that task, working night and day until he died of exhaustion. The postal workers of America recognized a hero from their ranks and erected this statue.

The Thomas Alva Edison illuminated fountain memorialized the fiftieth anniversary of the Edison light bulb and was designed by General Electric. It was refurbished with Community Development Block Grant funds in 1988.

Across from the courthouse is the Strong Mansion (now a part of Gannon College), which is worth a look (obtain a brochure from the receptionist). The Ionic structure next to the courthouse is the Erie Club (1849), former residence of Gen. Charles Reed, grandson of the first settler, who became extremely wealthy and built this house for his bride. The small Doric building next to it is actually the front of the bowling alley that is part of the Erie Club. It completes the trinity of fluted columns—Corinthian, Ionic, and Doric—on this corner. The 1937 U.S. Post Office and federal courthouse south of the square at State Street contains two WPA aluminum sculptures by Henry Kreis, portraying very properly clad male and female youths. They are just outside the courtrooms, and young lawyers reputedly touch the statues for good luck as they enter to argue cases. A visit here will give you an opportunity to see the 1937 style of federal courtrooms. Across the square to the north on State Street is the famous early U.S. Customs House.

FAYETTE
County Seat: Uniontown

Fayette County is coal country. Coal was identified here very early, being observed by no less a person than George Washington during the French and Indian War. In that war, the Virginia army built a road into this area, which later became the Cumberland Road and still later the National Road. Albert Gallatin was appointed by Jefferson to oversee the construction of this latter endeavor, and he is responsible for routing it through Uniontown, an act that secured the town's future. Union (town) was founded on July 4, 1776, and thus is appropriately named. Uniontown was a center of the Whiskey Rebellion, thus prompting another visit by then President George Washington as far west as Bedford. His appointee, Gen. Harry Lee, led the military force that brought home the principle of federal supremacy under the new Constitution to southwestern Pennsylvania, including this area. Established in 1783, the county is named for the French patriot who had joined the American cause. Lafayette, by way of appreciation, honored the county with a visit here in 1825 during his famous tour.

The courthouse, located at Main Street and Court Street, is a gray, quarry-dressed, sandstone, Richardsonian Romanesque structure (1890–92, E. M. Butz [see Clarion County] and William Kaufman [see Westmoreland County], architects). The Richardsonian model in nearby Pittsburgh is reflected in the building's surface texture, the 188-foot square tower, arcaded windows, arched entryways, and stone foliage carvings. The "bridge of sighs" to the rear, added in 1902, is a direct copy of Richardson's Allegheny one. Architects during this period were quite willing to change exterior styles to fit current tastes, as can be seen by looking at the other courthouses designed by these two men. No two sides of the building are the same, which is

rather unusual, so the exterior examination involves a walk around the building, beginning with the front.

The south facade of the building has three differing planes in relationship to the street, plus a large, protruding bay window. The central section has an off-center-right arched entrance and two windows to the left on the first story. The entrance arch has prominent voussoirs and stone carving on both the archivolt and pilaster capitals. On the second story, there is a characteristic Richardsonian three-window arcade, which originally lighted a large courtroom. There is a smaller similar arcade at the third story, then two very narrow slit windows and decorated stonework, and a finial at the gable apex. There is also carved stonework at the corners of the gable. The right side of the facade consists of two bays of double windows, interrupted on the first floor by the protruding bay window, which is capped by a balustrade. The left building side is a single bay of paired rectangular windows. All the third-story window pairs are separated by a mullion column with carved capital. There are two stone dormers in the steep roof. The left side of the tower is flush with the left side of the building and rises over a side entrance. This left side of the building is on a single plane except for the rear round tower. The fenestration pattern reflects the stories on the main building and the stairsteps on the tower. The tower is a single square shaft pierced by pairs of narrow rectangular windows and the clock faces. The belfry tier has an open three-arch arcade, with balustrades and four corner turrets, which rises to conical caps with finials. There are stone leaf decorated cornices on the turrets and tower. On the north rear side of the building, the central bays protrude. The three large, arched, second-story windows light a courtroom. The original west side of the building is obscured by the attached annex.

You will probably enter the building at the annex in order to pass through security, but let us begin the interior observations just inside the south entrance of the Romanesque building. The most striking feature of the foyer there is an artificially illuminated stained-glass skylight. The floors and wainscot are marble, with a mosaic band separating them (probably a Kaufman touch). The ornate iron stairs have a marble handrail instead of the usual wood or metal. On the second floor, the large, multistory central space was probably originally illuminated by a skylight, but this was not documented. The covering over the first-floor skylight is recent, suggesting that Butz and Kaufman envisioned some natural, overhead light reaching the first floor as one entered the building. The four oval paintings represent the county's principle economic bases: mining, coke burning, manufacturing, and agriculture, the first two being very important when this building was constructed. Courtroom 1, opening to the rear off this second-floor lobby, still has some of its original look. Its chief features are ten stained-glass windows, Italian marble wainscoting, and an ornate ceiling. Decorative painted designs carry out the round arching theme. The

walnut judge's bench is truly magnificent and worth a close look when court is not in session. It probably dates from 1902, when there was some remodeling of the second floor to facilitate access to the "bridge of sighs." More recently, the front courtroom, which originally matched courtroom 1, has been split in half horizontally. Spaces once viewed as monumental are now viewed by some as wasted.

The 1927–28 annex (Emil R. Johnson and Clarence F. Wilson, architects) is described as Spanish Renaissance, a unique style for Pennsylvania courthouses. Its exterior is a striking contrast to the 1890 building. The two bas-reliefs refer to agriculture and mining. The west exterior of the building is also finished and should be examined. The interior is tastefully simple, including its courtroom 2. An opalescent glass skylight covers the monumental space on the second floor. Note the large scales in a glass case on the main floor, a reminder that at one time weights and measures were overseen at the county level. The 1902 jail matches the older courthouse in style, but its stone was from a different source. Even the minor ancillary buildings are built in quarry-faced stone, and in a fashion that gives continuity to the county complex, except for the 1927 annex.

The rather shabby building across the street from the courthouse was built in 1832 and 1859 as a tavern and hotel. The little brick building at Main Street and Court Street dates from 1832 and has usually housed law offices. While there is little ground around the courthouse, a shady park can be found one block away at South and Jefferson.

The courthouse which preceded the present Romanesque one was topped by a wooden statue of Lafayette. It was sculpted in 1847 by David Gilmour Blythe, who went on to become a genre painter of some note doing urban scenes of Pittsburgh and later Civil War material. For many years the eight-foot statue was on display in the first-floor lobby of the Romanesque building, but it is now on loan to the Hall of Freedom, at Main and Arch Streets a few blocks west. It is a remarkable piece of folk art and is worth taking a few minutes to view.

FOREST
County Seat: Tionesta

A 1924 travel guide says of Forest County that the "atmosphere is fragrant with health-giving ozone, strengthening the weak and restoring those affected by lung trouble." Seventy years may have altered the medical judgments in that sentence, but the general ambience of the place remains the same. When Forest County was formed in 1846, it was virtually unbroken primeval forest, hence the name chosen by county founder Cyrus Blood. The primeval part has long since been cut, but forested it remains. Tionesta (pronounced with an accented long *i*) is a very small county seat in a sparsely populated county.

The courthouse (1870, Keene Vaughn, architect) is a simple brick building with some stone accents, both materials from local sources. It has few decorative elements: a Palladian window above the entrance, a simulated pediment with a small lunette, a cornice with dentils, a few cornice brackets, and segmented hoods over the second-story windows. It originally was a little less plain, in that there was a bell tower (the bell is now in the yard). The interior is modernized. The courtroom walls originally had paintings of Justice and Liberty, executed by an itinerant German artist. The 1895 jail and sheriff's house to the north are now used for offices.

The various adornments and memorials around the courthouse yard have a kind of amateur appearance that is very much in keeping with the locale. Volunteers made the county sign and the German World War I

cannon mount. The millstone under the cannon reputedly came from France and was of a type that was highly regarded for its quality. One monument memorializes a 1985 tornado that was extremely destructive of life and property in the county. A memorial for county veterans is a simple list of American wars, from the Revolution through Vietnam. The pessimists who designed the stone left room for additional entries.

FRANKLIN
County Seat: Chambersburg

Twenty-four of the nation's twenty-five Franklin Counties were named for Benjamin Franklin (1706–90), and this one, created in 1784, was the second to bear his name.

The Greek Revival courthouse is located to the northeast of the fountain-filled circle at the center of the town. The most distinctive feature of the courthouse is the statue of the county's namesake that rides atop the green dome. The plaques on this building say that it was rebuilt in 1864 (S. Hutton, architect), but the "re" part can be easily misunderstood. McCausland's raiders (see below) destroyed the courthouse, leaving only fragments of several walls standing. Some of the remains from this building were reused in

1864, primarily column parts. It is in that sense that it was rebuilt. The building that was destroyed had a second Classical portico fronting on Lincoln Street, but because some capitals were broken, the restoration only had enough material for the front portico. Six massive salvaged Ionic columns now front the present courthouse. The columns support a pediment with the county seal in the tympanum. Both the present statue and the seal are modern replacements of the original wooden ones, which are now restored and safely displayed inside the building. The tower has a stepped base supporting the clock-face tier, which is square with beveled corners. Two arched windows are behind a balcony with spindle balustrades on four sides and a bracketed cornice. There are four finials at the transition to the ribbed copper dome that supports the

statue of Franklin. Six chimneys project above the roof, remnants of an earlier heating system. The rear three bays are 1902 additions and closely match the rest of the building. Note that the water table switches from white to brown stone, and the wall panels are different.

Inside, the first floor has the center hall style, with doorways to the offices of the traditional elected county officials on either side. The second-floor courtroom, entered through the new building, occupies its original space, but it is difficult to tell how much is original. The rear wall of the 1865 building was about where the judge's bench is now located. The stained-glass window behind the bench probably was installed in 1902. The judge's bench dates from the 1960s. The ceiling is modern, though the coffered arrangement and other basic design elements are likely from the 1902 renovation. There are few records of building changes extant, unless they are in private possession.

The 1979 annex to the east is by Lawrie and Green, Maekler and Hull. The first two are familiar names in courthouse architecture in the center of the state, but this is one of their postwar buildings, and nothing here resembles the Dauphin County structure. There is an 1818 brick Georgian jail one block away on King Street, which now houses the County Historical Society. Note that the building has a key motif on the weathervane, a common nineteenth-century touch.

McCausland's raid was a minor footnote to the Civil War but a major event in the life of Chambersburg. The incident stemmed from the activities of Union general David Hunter, who was in charge of the West Virginia army and conducted raids into the Shenandoah Valley, where he was highly destructive of property. Confederate general Jubal Early was in charge of the area, and he sent John McCausland on a retaliatory raid on Chambersburg. He was instructed to demand $500,000 in currency or $100,000 in gold to spare the town. When the local citizens did not raise the money, he burned the downtown. As all this took place in a day, it would appear that Early had intended on the burning in the first place. Union soldiers pursued and killed or captured many of the raiders, though not McCausland. McCausland did not surrender at Appomattox but went abroad a couple years before returning to the States. Perhaps he feared that people from these parts might make things a little warm for him.

FULTON
County Seat: McConnellsburg

Seven of the eight Fulton Counties in the nation, including this one, were named after Robert Fulton, who built the first commercially successful steamboat. The last county so named was in 1853, nearly a half century after the *Clermont* introduced steam transportation to our waterways. That says something about the significance of transportation technology in developing this large county. Paradoxically, steamboat transportation has practically nothing to do with this county, which was formed in 1850. The county was supposed to have been named Liberty, but in one of those obscure committee horse trades, a member of the legislature from Lancaster County got to choose the name.

McConnellsburg is a very small town, and it became the county seat through good, old-fashioned market principles. This town was willing to pay more ($1,300) than any of the others toward the cost of building the courthouse. The town's existence is a product of land transport, not canals, as the National Road (Lincoln Highway) is its main street. This explains the age of some of the buildings on this street. The courthouse is located one block off the National Road, but you will have no problem finding it in this

very small town. It is a simple, two-
story, 1851 Greek Revival brick building with a Doric portico. Above the
simple portico is an equally simple
tower, which consists of a square base,
open belfry with columns, domed
roof, finial ball, and weathervane.
Some of the tower's simplicity probably results from economizing measures taken when replacing original
parts, and the clock faces, which are
low on the base, look as if they were
installed as an afterthought. Jacob
Stoner, a local artisan, was the builder.
His work retains a quiet dignity after
a century and a half of use. The interior has been modernized. There is an
adjacent small park and band shell.
Across the street, at 204 North Second Street, is a former hotel built at
the same time as the courthouse.

The courthouse here survived
McCausland's raid because the Rebels
seemed more interested in looting
stores than in more vengeful pursuits,
such as burning a courthouse. Mc-
Connellsburg got off relatively easy
compared with Chambersburg.

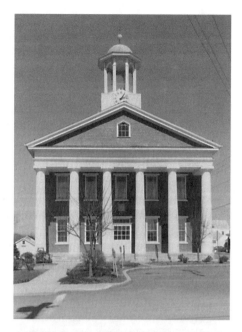

GREENE
County Seat: Waynesburg

The land that is now Greene County was at one time claimed by Virginia. Indeed, prior to the Revolutionary War, the troops of Governor Dinsmore of Virginia occupied Pittsburgh, which he also claimed as part of his state. In 1779, representatives of the two now self-proclaimed independent states established their mutual border and thereby fixed what were to become in 1796 Greene County's southern and western boundaries. Two of Washington's leading generals were honored as namesakes here, the county being named for Nathaniel Greene, and the town created to become the county seat for Anthony Wayne.

The 1852 brick and wood courthouse is typical of the antebellum "temples of justice." Being one of the later temples, however, it has a fancier order, Corinthian. A portico of stuccoed columns with iron capitals covers the entire front. The courthouse was a copy of the Fayette County courthouse of that time, whose builders, Samuel and John Bryan of Uniontown, were hired to construct it here. The portico is wooden and does not have all the embellishments of a stone one, such as at Erie, another Corinthian tem-

ple built at about this time. The tower has a square base, a slant-sided octagonal platform that supports an octagonal clock tier, a round belfry with Doric detached columns, a denticulated cornice, and a hemispherical dome. On the dome is a wood statue of General Greene, who has a sword in scabbard and is doffing a three-cornered hat.

When the courthouse was built, David Blythe, who sculpted the Lafayette statue for Fayette County, was invited to make one of Greene for this Bryan courthouse. However, his price of $300 was deemed too high by the Greene County commissioners. They found a local woodworker named Bradley Mahanna, who agreed to make one for $100.

Using a sketch of Greene created by a German clock repairman, he carved a statue out of a nine-foot yellow poplar (tulip tree) log. A 1925 fire damaged the roof, cupola, and statue, and only a few pieces of the statue survived. Local artisans took up the task of replacing it, using a drawing made by John F. Pauley and the remnants as their guide. According to a local history account, the replacement was made of laminated yellow poplar, with walnut eyeballs, a copper hat, and metal rods running up through the legs to secure it to the roof. In 1998, during the most recent renovation of the building, the wood statue was found to be badly deteriorated, and so again using laminated yellow poplar, local artisan Miles Davin made

a copy of the previous statue, with minor changes. In addition to paint, this one has some copper sheathing to protect it from rain.

There have been a number of additions to the 1852 structure. A freestanding Victorian sheriff's house and jail built to the rear was eventually joined with the courthouse. Its facade can still be seen facing the side street. Extensions were also made to the rear between 1914 and 1921. The interior of the entire complex was largely gutted and rebuilt in 1998, but some of the original interior spaces of the old courthouse survive. Upon entering, you see the original central hallway with its 1914 tile floor. The original double curved stairs lead to the courtroom above, which occupies its original space. In the courtroom, the window treatment and canopy over the judge's bench probably date to 1852, but most of the furnishings are from 1913. Most of the downstairs is modern, but here and there are remnants of the past, including the old metal window shutters.

The courthouse grounds are small and unadorned. The county Civil War monument is in a park elsewhere in the town. The county has wisely not tried to add more additions to the old courthouse and has expanded its offices along the main street, including a nondescript new building in 1977. The first Greene County courthouse, built of hewn logs, is located a short distance away on Green Street and awaits restoration.

HUNTINGTON
County Seat: Huntington

This is one of two counties in the state named after a woman, in this case Selina Hastings, countess of Huntington. William Smith, provost of the University of Pennsylvania and owner of extensive land in this area, founded the town. Then, as now, college heads were in the business of raising money. During a fund-raising trip to England in 1767, the countess was the most generous donor, and so he subsequently honored her by naming his new town for her, and eventually the county, created in 1787, took the same name.

You should have no trouble finding the courthouse, as its tower with its odd, hemispherical ornament rides well above all other buildings of the town. The basic building is an 1883 structure designed by M. E. Beebe, a prominent Buffalo architect who designed numerous courthouses, including others in Pennsylvania (Cambria and Warren). He called this one French Renaissance, which in this guide is called Second Empire. However, the fenestration is very much in the Tuscan Villa style. Beebe favored lofty bell-and-clock towers, but evidently he was not very good at constructing them. In

any case, the one here and at Cambria did not last, though his earlier one at Warren has survived. The present one is a 1930 replacement that uses lighter materials and has a different relationship with the roofline. No explanation was found as to why the odd hemisphere was chosen to top the tower. One wonders whether someone with a sly sense of humor had a hand in it, but economy was more likely the explanation. The top was painted blue at one time, leading to local bubble gum jokes.

The attractive part of the original building begins with the massive front doors that are hung in archways with keystones. At the second floor over the entrance, there are large, double, rectangular windows with transoms framed by pilasters, above which is a segmental arch pediment. The bays on either side of the central pavilion at the second-story level have smaller rectangular windows with portholes above them. Most other windows have stone arched hoods with a connecting course at the spring line in the Italianate style. There is a stone belt course between the stories.

Inside, there are some interesting things to see, but modernization has taken its toll. Note the brass push plates on the inner entrance doors. In the foyer are two decorated pillars placed there to support the original tower. The first-floor hallway is mostly original. A bicentennial quilt hangs on the wall. The upstairs courtroom is a 1970s disaster. The old courtroom has been shrunk, robbed of its windows, and hidden in modern paneling. Gone are the curved cove around the ceiling, decorated columns, and huge chandelier, but some fine original jury chairs, a walnut bench, rails, and the original marbleized slate fireplace are still to be seen. A fire gutted the south wing in 1992, but it has been sensitively restored. (The fire broke out at the very moment the jury was announcing its verdict on a case involving a minister accused of an illicit relationship with a church member.)

There originally was a standing stone on the town site that was considered sacred by the Indians, who by tradition held councils around it. When they sold the land to white men, the Indians packed up their sacred rock and took it with them. A fort located here was called Standing Stone, and several memorial stone replicas have commemorated the Indian tradition. The latest replica is in a small park dedicated to William Smith, just north of the courthouse on William Smith Street. There is a dedicatory plaque to Smith at the other end of the park strip.

INDIANA
County Seat: Indiana

Indiana county was created in 1803. Views differ on the origin of the county name. One source cites Indiana Territory, and another refers simply to Indians.

The building at Sixth Street and Philadelphia Street that looks like a courthouse is in fact the former courthouse but is now a bank office. The present courthouse is down the street. Built in 1968–70, it was designed by Lawrie and Green, a firm that was turning out very generic modern government buildings at the time, with practically no distinguishing features. There is little to remind one of the impressive Dauphin County creation that was the first courthouse designed by this firm. One assumes they were designing what their clients wanted. This one has vague Classical symbolism, such as the rather gawky, high-pocketed, square-columned portico. The building has a smattering of interior marble and a paucity of monumental space. The first-floor and fourth-floor courtrooms might be styled "a little dignity on the cheap."

There is a statue of hometown boy Jimmy Stewart on the front lawn and a museum dedicated to him next door.

The handsome former courthouse was and is the major architectural feature of the downtown, so let us turn our attention to it. The clock tower,

which can be seen for miles around, has long been the main visual symbol for the community. Designed in 1869 by James W. Drum (see Jefferson County), in what he termed Modern Renaissance but is called Second Empire in this guide, it is less flamboyant than most others built in this style. In the 1960s, historic preservation was not yet good politics in many counties, and penurious attitudes dictated that maintaining old public buildings was the accepted thing to do. When the National Bank of the Commonwealth offered to lease and restore this national registered building for their use, some of the county commissioners must have felt this meant relief for their headache. The bank renovation is in progress, and in 1998 that meant shoring up the famous clock tower, which had begun to list precariously.

The building is brick with stone accents, which include quoins, pilasters, a belt course, and a rusticated area on the first floor around the entrance. The central part of the building, consisting of five bays, is the main architectural statement. Above the first floor there are five prominent two-story, twenty-four-over-twenty-four windows with arched heads, separated by fluted columns with iron Corinthian capitals. This speaks of a well-lighted, two-story space with cross ventilation and is where the courtroom is located. Above, there is a pediment with block modillions and a denticulated cornice. The outer two bays on either end are set off by brick pilasters, with the first-story windows arched with keystones and the second- and third-story windows rectangular with pediments. The concave mansard roof is pierced with two double window dormers on each side. The tower has a square base, upon which rests a square belfry tier with two arched louvers and one window on each side, separated by freestanding columns and an extra column at each corner. The clock faces are dormers in the cap, which is topped by a crested crow's nest. The building grounds have an iron perimeter fence with substantial stone posts. This former courthouse is connected by a "bridge of sighs" to its former jail to the rear and a fine Victorian (1888) sheriff's house, which fronts on the street to the right.

Former Indiana County courthouse.

The bank has restored the exterior of both buildings and renovated the interior courthouse basement, the first floor, the north part of the second floor, the jail, and the sheriff's house, all of which now house private offices. You can visit the bank first floor, where there is a display about the renovation. Saturday public tours of the building are conducted during Christmas season, at which time the building is decorated. The old courtroom was a colossal space, with one of those impressive northern Pennsylvania wooden ceilings. When I inspected the building, this space was filled with scaffolding to support the righting of the clock tower. Plans to restore the room were not complete.

The Indiana downtown had a 1980s rejuvenation, with the help of the Pennsylvania Main Street Program. War memorials can be seen at Memorial Park, which is down South 6th Street from the old courthouses.

JEFFERSON
County Seat: Brookville

When Jefferson County was formed in 1804, its namesake was the sitting president, who was very popular in Pennsylvania at the time. It was created along with twenty others at a time when the state was trying to encourage settlements in the west. The population was not large enough to organize a county government, however. Indeed, it was nearly twenty-five years before that happened, and even then it was set up by the state legislature using nonlocal people to perform such tasks as choosing the site of the county seat. The largest existing settlement, Punxsutawney (named after a vicious local gnat, not the groundhog), was rejected as not being centrally located within the county.

The courthouse, at Pickering Street and Main Street, stands on a sloping lot so that in front the basement is above ground, exaggerating the height of the building. It is a red-painted brick structure built in 1869 and designed by J. W. Drum, who also designed the Indiana County courthouse at this time in a different style. The one here inclines toward the Italianate, featuring prominent brackets and arched windows. The front and sides of the structure have Doric pilasters and round-topped windows set in recessed arches in the brickwork. There are five bays across the front. The outer ones are blind and the central three are within a pavilion over

the entrance. The pavilion has a pediment with modillions of alternating size and a lunette with garlands. The front entrance, reached by a set of 1927 curved stone steps with wrought-iron railings, has a semicircular transom and is aligned with the windows on either side of it. The clock-and-bell tower has a square base. The clock faces above are set off by square Doric pilasters and a simple pediment, plus additional pilasters at the four angles. The next tier is a railed octagonal open belfry, with segmental arch pediments on each face above the cornice, topped by a red roof cap and finial. The building is now L-shaped, with a 1927 (Emmett E. Bailey, architect) addition set perpendicular with the Drum structure. The older part of the building is two stories high, while the addition is three, reflecting the lower ceiling heights. At the left of the addition there is a closed entrance with a prominent arched hood.

The interior is marble throughout the foyer and halls, with classical Ionic pilasters and a frieze with triglyph, metope, and guttae, decorations that evidently date from the 1927 remake. The ample second-floor courtroom carries out the Classical motif, with fluted wooden Ionic pilasters between the windows and a cross-beamed ceiling with bosses in alternative squares. The lofty space is lighted by ample nineteen-over-twelve double-hung windows. As they are metal, they also were probably the work of Bailey's renovation. The doorways have pediments, and the main entrance is more elaborate, having a broken pediment and an imbricated glass transom.

Inside the foyer is a slice of an old elm tree that was grown from a slip of the tree under which Washington took his oath to lead the troops in the Revolutionary War (see the explanatory plaque), and there is a display case of local products along the central hall.

JUNIATA
County Seat: Mifflintown

Juniata is derived from an Indian term and was the name given to a local river before this county was created in 1831. For the origin of Mifflintown, see Mifflin County. If you look at a county map of Pennsylvania, you will note that the counties in this part of the state look like bacon strips running diagonally in a northeast-southwest direction. The boundaries reflect the mountain topography. It is easier to travel the valleys that correspond to the long dimension of these counties than to take a northwest-southeast route, which would cut across ridges. When Mifflin County was formed, it included what

is now Juniata County. At that time, the big issue was whether the seat would be north or south of a narrows where the Juniata River cut through a central ridge. The result was the choice of Lewistown, which is north of the ridge. There ensued a forty-year fight by the losers of that battle, until Juniata County was created and the south-of-the-ridge folks finally gained a more accessible county seat.

The Classical Revival courthouse is located on its own sloping square in the middle of Main Street in this small town located on the Juniata River. It was built in 1873–75 (L. M. Simon of Harrisburg, architect) and remains remarkably unchanged. For that reason alone, it is one of the stars on the courthouse circuit. A further reward for the viewer is that while it

is in a Classical Revival building, it has Victorian pizzazz. This gives it a distinctive look among the state's courthouses. There are entrances on all four sides, and all are still in use, which is unusual in this era of high security. The building sits on a slope, and the front elevation seems lofty, made more so by its tall, architecturally exuberant tower. There is a substantial, three-bay-wide front pavilion, which rests on three rusticated arches at the first story. At the second story, there are four tall, fluted, iron Corinthian columns with polychrome capitals, balustrades at their bases, and roof-level pediments. Behind the columns are three windows with unique three-quarter-round transoms with double circular mountings. The lower parts of these windows light the courtroom foyer, and the upper parts its balcony. The outer bays on the front have blind niches on the first story, pedimented windows on the second, and dedicatory medallions above them. One of these medallion plaques implies that this building is an enlargement of the original courthouse. However, local stories of the time talk about the razing of the old courthouse, and if there is any part of it left in the present structure, it is most likely confined to the foundation. A denticulated sheet metal cornice wraps around the entire roofline. The tower is made of wood and is essentially octagonal, including the base. The clock faces are enclosed at alternate sides and are framed by inverted consoles with pediments above. The taller belfry tier has piers and balustrades for its lower part, arched openings resting on the piers, and pilasters at the angles. This tier has a denticulated cornice with small pediments above it on

alternate sides. The metal roof is in the form of an octagonal cap supporting a large finial and weathervane. The building has nine bays on the sides,
each bay separated by pilasters, with two exceptions.

When you enter, you know you are in a nineteenth-century building.
The interior is not spectacular, but it is surprisingly original. The courtroom
occupies its original space and retains enough of its original look to make it
interesting. The ceiling has been replaced, but the old solid interior shutters
are there and in use. It's a courtroom that is nearly self-explanatory.

Behind the courthouse are an 1833 sheriff's house and 1979 jail with
a new wall that nicely matches the old yellow stone.

LACKAWANNA
County Seat: Scranton

Lackawanna, established in 1878, was the last county formed in Pennsylvania and is named after the anthracite coal basin for which the area was
renowned. Scranton takes its name from the ironmaking family that pio-
neered the use of anthracite here for steelmaking. Both industries have long
since lost their importance, although they had everything to do with the
creation of the county and the courthouse.

The courthouse occupies a Shelbyville square bounded by Washington
Street, Adams Street, Linden Street, and Mulberry Street. In the strictest
sense, it does not qualify for that designation, because the square was not
part of the original city plan. The courthouse site was previously an old bog
that was used as a dumping ground for ashes and mine tailings and had been
bypassed in the city development. When Scranton was designated as the seat
of the new county, an iron company and a coal company that owned this site
donated it for "city, county and federal building[s] and a park." By building
the new courthouse in the middle of the square, the county preempted city
and federal use. Once the courthouse was there, it reshaped the downtown.
The present structure is the original courthouse (1884, I. G. Perry, of Bing-
hamton, New York, architect) and is Romanesque Revival in style. Construction problems were created by the history of the site, and in places thirty-
foot foundations were necessary to find firm ground.

The courthouse is constructed of attractive local, quarry-dressed stone
with Onondaga limestone trim. On a clear day, with the sun rays at the
proper angle, the yellow stone surface can be stunning. The building is
much more complicated than it appears on first glance. At least seven dif-

ferent vertical planes move backward and forward across the facade. Starting at the far left, this section has a turret to the left and a partial double-curved gable above. There are flaring buttresses below the water table at its base, and here, unlike most buildings, the foundation stone is the same as that of the main walls of the building. The turret begins about three-quarters up the first story and is divided into three tiers separated by two bands of corbeled stonework; each tier has distinct windows. The balance of this section has three rectangular windows on each story, under blind arches on the first, with segmental arches on the second and full arches on the third. There are two arched louvers in the gable, as is the case with the others as well, but each gable differs in its decorations, using urns and finials. The curved coping that outlines the gables is technically called a fractable.

The next section to the right recedes and has four bays, with the left one somewhat separated. The windows of the right three bays are rectangular, with blind arches above on the first story and under a single semielliptical blind arch on the second.

The next section has three bays and is associated with the front entrance. It has had replacements made to the steps, doors, and pilaster capitals—for modernization purposes in the first two cases, and because of severe air pollution erosion in the third. Three tall arches framed by pilasters form the outer entrance. There is an open arched porch at the second story with a balustraded balcony. The second-story windows are arched, and the third-story ones are rectangular.

The next vertical section to the right is the widest and is set back. On the first floor, pairs of arched windows are recessed under segmental arches. The second and third stories have large, multipaned, rectangular windows. The gable has arched louvers and only covers two bays. The right angle of this section is a pier with a flaring bottom.

The next section recedes in two vertical steps and has a fenestration pattern similar to the first section on the far left.

Finally, the tower section is forward and differs from the others in that it has windows on three sides. Above the water table, it can be divided horizontally into seven distinct levels, or tiers, defined by belt courses or other horizontal markings. The windows in the first three stories (levels) follow the pattern of the previous section, but with variations. The fourth level is a recessed blind arch and is the beginning of the tower where the features are repeated on all sides. The next level has three segmental arched windows with small blind arches above, which encroach into the next level— the large belfry level composed of prominent arched openings with louvers at the top and prominent iron balconies below. The angles here have ashlar ornamentation. This stage has blind arches at the top. The clock faces are set in vertical planes, with gable tops that sit like thin dormers in the pyramidal green tile roof. Originally this pyramid was much steeper and about three times the present one's height (altered in the late 1920s).

The interior changes, which evidently began in the 1960s, are one of the worst examples of courthouse modernization. The original grand entrance doors are gone. The grand stairway is also gone, along with all the other principal interior embellishments. All that remains are the marble floors and a few fragments of the original decor in the south corridors of the first and second floors. Two of the courtrooms appear to have retained some of their original materials, however. Courtroom 3 is the former law library and is a fairly sensitive conversion.

The square holds many interests, beginning with the statues or memorials on the four corners, which commemorate Columbus, Pulaski, Washington, and Sheridan. Why the choice of these men? The earliest memorial was erected in 1892 for Columbus with funds raised by the local Italian community in recognition of the four hundredth anniversary of the great voyage. A local patriotic group matched that effort by balancing the block with a statue of Washington. The Civil War generals are represented by Sheridan because the local Ancient Order of Hibernians raised the funds for the 1910 memorial. The fourth corner is also the result of an ethnic-group effort, and in this case the Polish community memorialized Pulaski in 1973. Ethnicity has clearly been very much a part of county politics. The very tall soldiers and sailors monument topped by the bronze allegorical Goddess of Victory was erected in 1900, and according to one account, it has a massive piece of coal as a foundation.

There is a novel statue and memorial for labor leader John Mitchell, who is credited to be the father of the eight-hour day. It is novel in that one rarely sees a labor memorial on a courthouse square, particularly at this early date. The monument was dedicated in 1924, and most of the major luminaries of the labor movement were present, including Samuel Gompers, William Green, John L. Lewis, A. Philip Randolph, as well as other dignitaries, such as Wilson's secretary of labor, Thomas Kennedy, and Governor Pinchot. The bas-relief on the back portrays a scene rich in messages. The sculptor, Charles Keck, was renowned and had carved scores of significant statues and monuments all over the country. Here he portrays a coal miner family that includes the parents, five children, and two pets gathered around the kitchen table. The father is in a laborer's outfit, with jacket over a chair laden with a miner's hat, water tin, and lunch pail. He is embraced by the second-oldest son, who is dressed in knickers, shirt, and tie, a student's garb, suggesting an aspiration for the next generation. However, the oldest son is standing and reaching for his lunch pail, with his shirt fully buttoned to his neck, which will keep out the coal dust. His labor in the mines is obviously essential to support the family and perhaps to free his younger siblings from a similar life. The kitchen door is open, and the colliery is in plain view, showing the proximity of home and work in a mining town. A kerosene lamp is on the table and an alarm clock on the mantle; these workers were punctual. The wife, with her hair in a casual bun, is supported by the eldest daughter and holds a baby. Her garment includes an apron, and she appears ready for domestic chores. Keck arranged his figures in a classic triangular layout.

A brochure is available on the buildings around the square, but for a quick overview, here are a few identifications. Starting opposite the statue of George is a 1930 Art Deco post office (James Whetmore, architect) with in-

teresting tilework. (At this writing, it was being yoked by an atrium with a new annex to its left.) Swinging to the right across Linden Street in the middle of the block is the 1896 Beaux-Arts Scranton Electric Building (Lansing Holden, architect), with an appropriate lighted sign and ornate copper roof. At 200 Adams Street is the present Lackawanna County Administration Building. This 1923 building originally was a furniture store, which explains terra-cotta tilework depicting furnituremaking on the band above the first story. Across Spruce Street is the 1916 Gothic Scranton Life Building (Edward Langley, architect), and at 436 Spruce Street is the 1896 Romanesque Brooks Building (Lansing Holden, architect), with its Chicago-style decorative masonry work. The square provides a fine sampling of turn-of-the-century American architectural styles.

LANCASTER
County Seat: Lancaster

Lancaster, the fourth-oldest county in the state, was created in 1728 by the division of Chester County, and when created extended to the western boundary of the state. It was named for Lancastershire, England, the native county of one of the three men appointed by the governor to set up this first new county after the original three. Initial settlement of Lancaster County was by Swiss and Pallatinate Mennonites, French Huguenots, English Quakers, Welsh Episcopalians, and Scotch-Irish Presbyterians. Today the county is primarily associated with one group, now often called the Pennsylvania Dutch. Most members of the early German sects were farmers, and their descendants to this day tend the rich farmlands and have made Lancaster County practically a quality brand name for agricultural products. The nineteenth-century Lancaster residents were also good craftsmen, creating quality farm equipment, including the famed Conestoga wagon, named for a county river. Lancaster city has the distinction of having served as the nation's capital, state capital, and county seat. It was the nation's capital for but a day, as the Continental Congress moved on to York to be farther from the British forces. President James Buchanan was a native of Lancaster, and his home, Wheatland, is one of the many local points of interest. The central area of the city, with its quaint Colonial street names (King, Queen, Prince, and Duke, as well as Strawberry, Orange, Lemon, and Lime), is a delight to walk around. It is lovingly cared for, and its streets are steeped in history.

The oldest part of the present courthouse was designed by Samuel Sloan, one of the most renowned architects of his day. In addition to being an architect, he was also an author and publisher of books on architecture, occupations to which he turned again and again when building commissions were slow. He was largely responsible for founding *The Architectural Review,* America's first periodical devoted to a serious treatment of its subject. He looked upon himself as a craftsman who solved problems. To him, architecture created a convenient building environment for clients. He was not wedded to any particular style and moved easily from one mode to another as they became fashionable. He designed many hospitals, particularly for the mentally ill, as well as churches, schools, commercial buildings, and county courthouses. He would work out a solution for a type of building, and then he would sell the Sloan idea over and over. He was a voluble and sometimes irascible man and went through a number of partners, one of whom was Addison Hutton (see Bucks and Venango Counties). Sloan designed at least eight county courthouses, six of which were in New Jersey and Pennsylvania, and three of which survive (see also Clinton and Venango Counties). The Sloan courthouse is located at East King Street and North Duke Street.

The courthouse complex has no grounds, for reasons associated with site selection. Prior to the Samuel Sloan structure, there had been two previous courthouses, both located in the middle of Center Square, where the Civil War monument now stands at the intersection of King Street and Queen Street. Note how the square is formed by taking a corner out of the four adjacent blocks. The Lancaster 1729 courthouse was the first to be located in this type of town layout, hence the term Lancaster Square. The second courthouse was also built here, but when it was declared too small, it was clear that there was not enough room on this site for an enlargement.

Under the law of the time, two successive grand juries and then the court of quarter session had to declare the need for a new courthouse, and then the commissioners were charged to carry out the construction. Because the city was already built up, it was necessary to clear a lot if the new courthouse were to remain close to the center of town. Site selection proved to be a protracted and heated controversy. The courthouse location increased the value of adjacent real estate; consequently, there was much jockeying and intrigue over the location. Ten different sites were considered before three commissioners could agree, finally, to build but a block from Center Square. Close enough, one might surmise, that most lawyers would not have to move their offices. Because the new location was already occupied, the site was expensive, and only enough land was cleared to accommodate the building. There would be no courthouse square.

Politics had everything to do with all the courthouse decisions, including its construction. It would be fair to say that the resulting courthouse was a product of political patronage, which in this case speaks well for the system. It was well built, but only by Whig artisan contractors. Artisans of other parties who wanted the work pleaded their cause to no avail. The commissioners openly discussed how the contracts could be used to assure a good Whig vote in the city for the 1852 presidential election.

The county courthouse complex extends for a block along the west side of Duke Street between King Street and Orange Street, with the older half facing south. Prominently embedded in this portion is the 1854 Roman Revival Samuel Sloan courthouse. Sloan's building was large compared with other county courthouses built at that time and was clearly too large for Center Square. In looking at Sloan's building today, it is necessary to mentally remove two additions, the 1898 transverse rear portion and the two 1920 first-floor extensions on either side of the front steps. The scale of the building is further emphasized by its elevation. The basement is a full story

aboveground to the south, and then there are two stories with high ceilings (the courtroom was twenty-six feet high), plus the large dome.

The building material is basically sandstone and brick, with granite steps and foundation. Some of the stone is painted, and the brick is covered with plaster made to look like stone. The sandstone, from Cocalico, Pennsylvania, is of high quality and has stood up well to wear and erosion. Viewing the building from the front, despite the intrusion of the two 1928 additions, the facade remains impressive. At the top of the stairs is the lofty hexastyle Corinthian portico with pediment at the roof level. The first story has three rusticated archways, with fanlights over each door. The fluted columns are at the second-story level. This story features tall windows, three across the front and eleven along each side, all with prominent pediments. Sloan's most successful building prior to this commission was the Philadelphia Central High School for Boys. It used very large windows in order to provide superior daylight for the students, and this idea also was employed at the courthouse for the benefit of county employees. The sides of the building have a midway pediment at roof level. The rear, three-story, cross-gabled 1898 addition has detached columns supporting the gable on the right side, but not on the left. Actually, the architect of the addition, James Warner, designed a Romanesque rear facade, but the contractor persuaded the commissioners to instead construct one conforming to the Sloan style. They may have been persuaded by the lower price, but the decision was probably fortunate from an esthetic perspective. The copper dome contains a 1,031-pound bell, made in Philadelphia, and is topped by an unblindfolded statue of Justice. The original statue was carved from wood by William P. Balton of Philadelphia. The bronze replacement dates from 1929. The cornerstone for the building was laid with great fanfare and, as customary, contained various documents. The location of the stone became lost in the subsequent renovations and additions. Documents were also placed in one of the six metal Corinthian columns, but which one is also a mystery.

Inside the front door is Sloan's original foyer, with its row of massive squat columns with acanthus leaf capitals and ribbed lower sections. Most of the remainder of the present interior dates from 1926. It is the work of local architect C. Emlen Urban, who also designed the pair of front additions at this time. The twin stairs in the front are no longer used, and to view the main courtroom, you must now enter from the rear, so proceed down the vaulted hallway to the elevator. The courtroom that runs crosswise in relationship to the building front is the work of Urban. Sloan's main courtroom occupied nearly the entire second floor and was a much larger room than the present one. His had the crossventilation and large window illumination arrangement seen in so many nineteenth-century courtrooms. Sloan's Lancaster courthouse solution may have influenced other architects. Urban's courtroom has some interest, but it is a much darker room than was Sloan's. Note in the corner some chairs from the

original courtroom and the head of the wooden Goddess of Justice that once graced the dome.

The 1970 annex to the north (Buchart Associates, architects) is certainly above average in design for county courthouses of this decade and is well worth a look. If preserved, it will probably hold more interest for future generations.

Though there are no grounds outside, the environs of the courthouse complex contains much of interest for visitors. A half block to the right, facing the front entrance, is a small house museum for Lancaster-born twentieth-century artist Charles Demuth. It is a change of pace from most things memorialized here, the emphasis of which is on the seventeenth and eighteenth centuries. One block to the left is Center Square, with its Civil War monument where the previous courthouse stood. It is filled with plaques and is the site of a museum. Among other things, the museum contains the doorway to the Lightner House, which was demolished to make way for the Sloan courthouse. Walking guides are available for the plethora of historic sites in central Lancaster. The Lancaster County jail has a great medieval-looking, nineteenth-century facade, but it is not within walking distance.

LAWRENCE
County Seat: New Castle

Lawrence County is named after a ship, and as far as I can find, this is unique among county names. The ship was named for Capt. James Lawrence, who, while mortally wounded, uttered the famous phrase "Don't give up the ship" in the Battle of Lake Erie during the War of 1812. That phrase was later carried on the flag of Commodore Perry's ship, named for Lawrence. Lawrence is one of the late Pennsylvania counties, established in 1849, and its proximity to the site of that famous naval battle has something to do with the name choice. The origin of New Castle is associated with John Steward, an early iron mill operator from New Castle, Delaware, who laid out the town and evidently named it for Newcastle upon Tyne, not his native American town. New Castle, Pennsylvania, was destined to become a substantial manufacturing center, at one time a major center of steel, cement, clay products, and metallurgy. Today it has a kind of "gritty city" appearance.

Being a city bisected by two rivers and in a valley floor, it does not have a conventional layout. The courthouse is not easy to find, because it is not where one would expect it to be, in the central business district, but instead on one of the hills of New Castle. The story of its location is classic Americana. There was support for four different locations, and the commissioners hit upon the novel idea of an auction. The courthouse was located on the site whose supporters raised the most money toward the cost of its construction. The city lucked out, because the winning site is an attractive one. A good way to spot it is by taking Business Route 422 going east leaving the downtown. Look up to the left. It's an impressive sight, being pure white, with six large Ionic columns beneath a pediment, a true temple of justice on a hill. (It is not the building on the hill with the big houses in the other direction; that is the Scottish Rite Cathedral.)

The courthouse is the original one built in 1852, but there have been many additions and subtractions, the most tragic of which sheared off its bell tower in the 1950s. Insensitivity to historic preservation appears to be the prevailing attitude of the county commissioners here. Once they removed the tower, there was a serious, but short-lived, proposal to replace it with one in gold-colored aluminum. Despite promises of restoration, the subsequent renovations and additions have managed to obliterate just about all vestiges of the last century except for the Ionic facade. Even that has been ruined by the awkward addition to the right. The courthouse, with its white coat of paint, still manages to look imposing, but what a stunner it would be if the original profile had been kept. The grounds are neat and filled with parking lots.

An interesting footnote on the 1852 building is that the masonry contract was awarded to a sixteen-year-old black man, P. Ross Perry. Perry went on to become a prominent contractor (with many white employees) in the region, constructing many significant buildings in New Castle, Youngstown (the original courthouse), Oil City, Mercer, Warren, and Poland. He headed his company for fifty years, and then remained active until his death in 1917 at age eighty-two.

All the plaques and memorials that usually surround the courthouse are in the struggling downtown area at Kennedy Square, which features a fountain flowing with colored blue water. The county historical society is located on North Hill (Jefferson Street) in the stunning former residence of one-time tin-plate tycoon George Greer. They sell small souvenir replicas of the courthouse as originally built and serve as caretakers of old courthouse records.

LEBANON
County Seat: Lebanon

The biblical name was evidently suggested by the presence of cedar trees in the area when the county was settled. It speaks to the faith of those who formed the first local government in 1813.

The courthouse (combined county-city building) is a modern (1960, William Lynch Murray, architect) building located on South 8th Street at the edge of town. From a citizen-service perspective, this building makes a lot of sense and probably serves its purpose very well. From the standpoint of visual interest, it is near the stylistic low point in courthouse architecture. It is a buff brick building, with an aluminum decorative screen and modern pink Georgia granite square columns on the front facade. The foyer is the only monumental space, and it features a large marble wall with an overly long carved text about county history. The halls are marble in the front section and tile for the rest. The courtrooms are modern and functional, with two-story spaces that afford them some dignity. Courtroom 1 exhibits a little extra effort. The building states very volubly, "Watch those taxpayers dollars!" The golden statue of Lady Justice from the old 1818 courthouse, demolished when this one was built, now resides in the foyer.

For a more interesting courthouse experience in Lebanon, go to 924 Cumberland Street, which was the courthouse from 1813 to 1818 and is now the county historical society museum and library. Among the many

artifacts in the museum are a scale model of the 1818 courthouse and the head of the wooden Lady Justice statue that once graced its tower before being replaced by the gold gilded zinc one now in the foyer of the 1960 building. To the best of my knowledge, this is the oldest courthouse Lady Justice icon in the state.

LEHIGH
County Seat: Allentown

Though it neither looks nor sounds like it, Lehigh is of Indian language derivation. The William Allen family was the first owner of the land in this area, receiving it directly from friend William Penn. Lehigh County was formed in 1812.

The courthouses are east on Hamilton Street (the main street) a few blocks beyond the Civil War monument. Here you will find a civic center comprising several county courthouses, city hall, the post office, a new federal building, and an art museum.

The old courthouse is a complicated composite built in four stages, beginning in 1814, which means part of this structure is the original first courthouse. What you see from the front, however, is largely the Italianate addition of 1864. The original 1814 courthouse was of Federal design with

a Federal cupola. There is a record that Benjamin Latrobe was brought in as a consultant at the preliminary design stage, but what was actually built had nothing to do with him; he did not get the commission. Instead, the building commission sent one of its members to Williamsport and simply copied that courthouse (now demolished). The concern for economy was reflected in what they constructed. The front and east sides of the courthouse, the sides that would show to the public, were coursed gray limestone laid in ashlar style, and the north and west were coursed rubble. Most of these 1814 outer walls are still in place and can be seen, except for most of the front. Here a section was leveled and the present pavilion inserted in 1864, but with the same material and wall alignment. The outer two bays on the south front remain from 1814. The 1864 construction installed the prominent Palladian window on the second floor and introduced new Italianate-style features, including the bracketed eaves, the balcony (which then had an open balustrade), the slate roof, and that exuberant tower. The door design also probably dates from this time, but the present doors are copies. The half-daisy fanlights above them add to the attractiveness of the new facade. The roof was reshaped when the new tower was added, producing the east and west gable ends. The tower rests on a square base with slightly sloping sides and a parapet (altered from the original) at the base of the belfry tier that has Palladian louvered openings on each side. Above are bracketed eaves with segmental arch center sections. The clock faces on the next tier are now blind, something that occurred sometime between 1890 and 1898 judging by pictures in the county historical society library. The octagonal cap supports a finial with a banneret weathervane that may have been transferred from the Federal cupola. The 1864 expansion transformed the building to a cruciform ground plan by adding to the coursed rubble section that is now the narrow waist of the building. This 1864 transformation was designed and directed by Eber Culver, a carpenter from Williamsport, a manufacturer of plane mill supplies who designed buildings on the side. His role here qualifies him to be given the title of the architect. A small 1880 section of orange brick was added on the west side and is not visible from the street. You can see it by following the path to the small geological garden display on the left side of the building.

When the 1914 addition to the rear was added, the intention was to gradually replace the older front sections. Note that the north facade of this addition looks like it was designed as a courthouse front, with the name prominently carved in stone. This explains why the three-story Beaux-Arts structure designed by local architect Henry Anderson makes no attempt to be integrated with the older portion. It is indeed a shocking contrast in design. Evidently, the local response at the time to his design was quite negative, so Anderson's replacement scheme was aborted. The result is that his addition remains but a fourth appendage to this strange amalgam of a building.

The building is presently used for a variety of functions, including a museum on the Hamilton Street side first-floor front; however, much of the 1864 interior courthouse arrangement remains. A spacious front hall has pillars supporting a high ceiling and two curved stairs leading to the courtroom foyer. The courtroom is in the old 1814 portion and in some respects might be considered the oldest Pennsylvania county courtroom in continuous use, though how much of what you see dates from that time is another question. The room is lighted on either side by four large windows, which are topped by ornate broken pediments. The audience section is banked for good viewing, and there is a balcony for added spectator

space. The massive judges' bench is backed by a Corinthian order *in antis*. Other interior spaces of interest are the old second-floor law library (now occupied by the County Historical Society Library) in the 1880 addition and the large, lavishly decorated courtroom in the 1914 addition. The courtroom features lots of yellow and pink marble, elaborate coffered plaster ceiling, and massive copper chandeliers hanging from very unusual plaster escutcheons. It matches the exterior in taste.

Across the street, behind a radiant-heated plaza with planters, is the new 1965 courthouse (Wolf and Hahn, of Allentown, architects), which is modern and functional and, esthetically, a little above average for county buildings of this decade. It is faced with sunset red granite from Texas and charcoal gray from Minnesota. The Charles Rudy bas-relief on the left facade portrays a judge backed by citizens. The lobby is done in an Italian marble called loredo chiaro. A distinctive feature of the interior building layout is the placement of the hallways that are along the front of the building at the upper floors. The natural lighting is extended to the offices the hall serves. One wonders whether the architects were inspired by the well-lighted front areas of the old courthouse. The main courtroom (room 203) has a dignified scale.

Among other buildings in the civic center, note the trendy Postmodern Federal courthouse (Roger W. Johnson, architect) and the James Whetmore Art Deco post office. The latter is worth examining for its decorative features, unusual building materials in the lobby, and ten murals of public art painted for the New Deal mural program by noted artist Gifford Beal (1879–1956). They portray county scenes, some of which were suggested by local organizations, including the Engineer's Club of the Lehigh Valley. The murals cover the following subjects: Pennsylvania German riflemen (local history vaunts that local citizen skill in gun manufacturing and marksmanship made a major contribution to the successful Revolutionary War effort); Trout Hall, the home of James Allen, son of William (showing two sets of figures, including fishermen returning from the Little Lehigh with their catch); departure of the Jordan Rifles (local Civil War volunteers leaving for Washington, viewed by citizens); the Walking Purchase (showing participant Indians and colonists in that infamous bargain); transportation (canal boats in the background and brawny canal men in left foreground); the Liberty Bell brought to Allentown; the iron industry (mills and trains); Lehigh County cement industry (showing the infamous air pollution before the days of stack scrubbers); Kimmit's Lock (local canal); and barn symbols (farmer in foreground and barn behind). Beal was one of the more significant artists in the mural program. His works are in the collections of several notable art museums.

LUZERNE

County Seat: Wilkes-Barre

Luzerne County was formed in 1786 out of land previously claimed by Connecticut. Connecticut settlers continued to be unhappy after the dispute was settled in favor of Pennsylvania and agitated for a new state. Luzerne County was created just four years after the settlement and was intended to draw them closer to Pennsylvania by providing them with a local government. The names of both the county and the seat are memorials to European friends of the new nation during its independence struggles. Anne Caesar, chevalier de la Luzerne, was minister from France during the late war years, and Jack Wilkes and Isaac Barre were British citizens who had espoused the colonist cause during the Stamp Act furor. Citizens in this area suffered badly during the Revolutionary War. A superior force of English and Indians defeated the Wyoming Valley militia, made up of old men and young boys. Following the battle, there was a gruesome massacre and destruction of all houses, and most women and children died of starvation and exposure. Some of these events are memorialized in the courthouse.

The courthouse is a remarkable building, made even more so given the story of its construction. The proposal for a new courthouse was first made in 1894. Elijah E. Myers (nationally renowned designer of three state capitals) was appointed architect, and he produced a design. Lawsuits and countersuits developed, as local groups fought over both whether and where to build. Myers dropped out and sued the county for fees. (The case was eventually settled in 1924, years after his death.) After about ten years of legal wrangling, an architectural competition was held, and the winner, F. J. Osterling, designed a building to be located where the old courthouse stood on Public Square in the center of Wilkes-Barre. After Osterling completed a design, the county decided to locate it on the Commons at its present location and to limit spending to about a half million dollars. In an unusual strategy to abide by this figure, the dome and internal furnishings were not included in the first invitation for bids.

Nevertheless, the low bid came in overbudget, and then this bidder reneged, claiming the cost of stone had gone up. Despite increased costs, the cornerstone was laid in 1906. Soon Osterling quit as a result of a fight over cost controls with the replacement contractor, and so a third architectural firm came into the picture. This was McCormick and French, a local firm, who followed Osterling's basic plan for the structure but supplied the design for the elaborate interior themselves. External consultants criticized the in-

terior plan as being overly elaborate and too expensive, but a local stone contractor, Carlucci Stone Company, offered a surprisingly low bid for all of the decorative interior work. While the final cost of the building was quadruple the original intention, there is little doubt that all the money went into the building. Given the scale of the structure, it is fortunate that the commissioners moved the site from Public Square to the present one.

The courthouse is a Beaux-Arts sandstone structure, built in a cruciform pattern with three sides having a five-bay pavilion with Corinthian columns and a rusticated first floor. While the pavilion facades are identical, the southern one, facing the garden, is the building front, as it has the inside foyer. The pavilion pediments have acroteria at the peaks and corners, and a large cartouche on the tympanums. The first story is rusticated with arched windows and entrances. The second-story windows have pediments, and the third-story windows are undecorated. Certainly one of the most unusual features of Osterling's design is the terra-cotta central dome with its four satellites. Note the four pedimented extensions around the dome with stained-glass windows. These provide the light for the great rotunda inside. There is a parapet around the roof perimeter, which originally had large eagle statues at the corners, and a second parapet around the side base of the dome. The cornice has dentils and modillions.

The interior is so elaborately decorated and has so much artwork that there is not enough space to cover it all in this guide. A pair of opera glasses will be helpful in scanning the dome.

The first-floor interior consists of a central space that is the floor of the central rotunda, and a circular perimeter corridor with a mosaic ceiling filled with small portraits and lunette paintings portraying scenes from local history and commerce. These were crudely retouched after a damaging flood. The foyer, which was intended to be the front reception area, breaks the corridor to the south. McCormick and French certainly did not skimp on the marble, and nothing they did was simple. For example, on the massive marble stairs, note the classical band around the newel posts (surmounted by monumental bronze lamps), the slots in the stair rail filled with bronze decorations, and the arch spandrels with two round insets of a different color stone. They never missed an opportunity to add a decorative twist. The walls of the corridors to the north and east entrances are marble to the ceiling, but with changing planes. Even the base moldings are of two different colors of marble. The floor is not the usual diaper pattern, but rather has complex circles and squares in a field. The center of the rotunda floor and the stair landing have brass inlays. The walls on the first-floor rotunda are rusticated, reflecting the exterior surface. The doorframes on all floors are marble, some elaborate, except at the intersection of the north and east sections, where the office entrance is elaborate bronze. The

banisters of the secondary corner iron stairs are polished brass where one would normally find wood.

There are five courtrooms, with murals painted by five different muralists. Most of these men were very well known. Edward Howland Blashfield, Kenyon Cox, and Will Hicock Low were associated with the decoration of buildings at the World's Fair of 1893, which launched the Beaux-Arts style into popularity for Americans. These men worked together on a number of public buildings, including the county courthouses at Newark and Jersey City, New Jersey. William Thomas Smedley had local connections. One source indicates that he was retained by McCormick and French and, upon seeing the scale of the building, suggested that the more famous muralist be called in.

The former orphan's court on the second floor has a mural by Charles Lewis Hinton, entitled *Symbols of Life,* evidently the only one he ever painted, depicting Justice with her mirror and sword, beside her a child holding the tablets. There is a family group on either side. This small courtroom has curved church bench seats for the audience, a marble judge's bench, a florid marble column, white marble walls, and mahogany woodwork.

The four courtrooms on the third floor have numbers assigned according to the seniority of the sitting judge. They are of nearly identical design, with wood paneling, wooden pilasters, and attached columns on the walls. The unusual benches for the audience have fasces carved along the ridge of the seat backs. Over the entrances, there are painted seals of the county and the various courts. Each courtroom has a different mural, the title of which is on a rear wall plaque.

The iconography of the murals is as follows. Smedley's *The Awakening of the Commonwealth* shows the Commonwealth clad as a female figure seated before a keystone, holding a cloak of darkness as the day dawns behind her. She has the morning star in her hair, and her hand is on a fasces. At her feet are figures representing the two principle industries of the state, coal mining and ironmaking. To the right, a boy and girl (the future) gaze at the group of notable Pennsylvanians who represent their heritage. On the left front row are artist Benjamin West, General Dickinson, Declaration of Independence signer George Clymer, and James Wilson, who was the lawyer for Pennsylvania in the dispute over land with Connecticut. On the right are twice governor Thomas McKean, Bishop White, Benjamin Franklin (flying kite), Charles Thompson, Anthony Wayne, financier Robert Morris, and inventor Robert Fulton.

Cox's *The Judicial Virtues* portrays the virtues that should hold in court. In the middle is a large figure of Rectitude with builder's triangle and plumb bob. She is flanked by naked boys, who hold tablets with words that in English mean "Let justice be done, though the heavens fall." On the right, Learning consults books, while Wisdom (mirror) bids, "Know thyself." On the left are armed Courage and Moderation nearby with a bridle. This was a prize-winning effort for Mr. Cox.

Low's *Prosperity under the Law* is an allegory about the locality. In a beautiful setting, an Indian maid representing Wyoming Valley sits among the laurel, backed by the white figures Justice and Civilization. With water flowing from the vase in one hand, she beckons a miner welcome with the other. A youth representing Agriculture offers grain, accompanied by Plenty with the horn. On the miner's side is a cherubic Mercury representing transportation and commerce. It is a celebration of the naturally endowed land and the prosperity it affords.

Blashfield's *Justice* shows seated Justice (red and gold) separating the good from the bad in the coal region. Her sword deals with the bad ones, and her hand is extended to the good. Another group represents those in the middle (the unintentional wrongdoer), where a woman throw herself upon the Law and has her hand held by Mercy, and Justice looks to the balance. The American flag is at the rear.

From the third-story gallery, one can better see the allegorical paintings and stained glass. The allegorical figures on the walls are in two series. One on human traits includes Patriotism, Courage, Understanding, Fortitude, Knowledge, Conscience, Government, and Virtue. The other refers to nature, with Earth, Air, Fire, Water, Minerals, Winds, Electricity, and Steam. At some time, the round symbols in the large stained-glass windows to the east and west were switched so that the symbols for the Battle of Wyoming and the massacre of the settlers were transposed.

There are two annexes, but only the Postmodern North Building (1988, Bohlin, Powell, Larkin, Cywinski, architects) is of interest. The orphan's court on the third floor is of attractive modern design, with a stained-glass window by local Gary Smith behind the bench. It portrays a figure of Justice under a blue firmament surrounded by palm leaves.

The courthouse grounds are part of a park that runs along the bank of the Susquehanna. This usually placid river can get nasty, and the courthouse has experienced flooding. On the lawn south of the courthouse, there are a variety of memorials that are all self-explanatory except for the strange iron deer. It dates from 1866 and was originally a free addition "throw-in" by a company that built an iron fence around the previous courthouse on Public Square. Public Square (a ten-minute walk) contains a number of plaques and symbols of interest, the kind one usually finds next to the courthouse. Among these are a memorial to Dan Flood, longtime congressman of waxed mustache fame, a claim that Wilkes-Barre is the birthplace of HBO, and an abstract sculpture entitled *No Place Like Home.*

LYCOMING
County Seat: Williamsport

Lycoming, a very English-sounding word, is actually derived from an Indian word meaning "gravel-bedded creek." Lycoming County was formed in 1795.

Until modern times, there was an 1860 Samuel Sloan courthouse here similar to the one in Lock Haven, but with a single tower. Some time in the 1950s, the county commissioners set on the fateful course of razing it in order to build a modern replacement. Though there were some protests about tearing down a Sloan building, the preservation movement was too much in its infancy, and the local newspaper apparently supported the modernizing move. The result is the 1970 courthouse (Wagner, Hartman, architects) which provides functional space but does little to enhance the interest of downtown Williamsport. It is a brown brick building of modern construction surrounded by a native stone wall and landscaping.

Remnants of the Sloan building may be observed here and there. The corner fountain has a tower where the old bell hangs, silent. At the side of the building is what a plaque purports to be the old building's weathervane but is in reality a replica, the original one being in the county museum. The museum also has the Sloan courthouse cornerstone. When the old courthouse was sold, its contents were auctioned for a paltry $4,500. The

courtroom chandelier and rail were purchased by Charley's Caboose, a local watering place in the converted old railway station. The old witness stand and other furnishings eventually found their way into another restaurant, Peter Hebric House, where they may now be seen. In an attempt to remove three statues that were in a niche above the judge's bench, they were dropped and broke into 150 pieces. A local volunteer patiently reassembled them, and they now occupy a niche on the second floor of the new courthouse. Observing the historic courthouse in this town turns into an archeological experience.

The building that looks like it ought to be the courthouse is the former city hall. It is an 1894 Richardsonian Romanesque building (Culver and Hudson, architects) on the National Registry, featuring a low sprung arched entryway. At least, when the city government decided to move out of its historic building, it did not tear it down. It is occupied by the Chamber of Commerce and is, architecturally, the most interesting building downtown.

McKEAN
County Seat: Smethport

Thomas McKean was the second governor of Pennsylvania and a late signer of the Declaration of Independence. His political career really began in Delaware, and he represented that state in the Continental Congress, which wrote the declaration. It was McKean who sent for Caesar Rodney, who undertook his famous ride to break the tie and bring Delaware in as a supporter of the declaration. For some reason, McKean failed to sign the document when the others did and may have done so a year later. His major law practice was in Philadelphia, and while serving as Pennsylvania chief justice, he continued to hold, simultaneously, various Delaware state offices for six years. First a Federalist, then a Jeffersonian, he was elected for the first of three three-year terms as governor in 1799. In the then turbulent political context of Pennsylvania politics, he would be called a conservative using today's terminology, upholding the law and the constitution against rural factions who chafed under the new rules. He had a tough, no-nonsense demeanor, and he would not pander to malcontents. The county that bears his name was formed in 1804. Smethport was named for Theodore de Smeth, agent for the exiled French in their dealings with the Ceres Land Company.

The courthouse is on Route 6, which goes through Main Street. It is Classical Revival, a style that is not bounded by time, so dating it presents a problem. However, something about this building says twentieth-century, partly its scale, and also the look of the wings on either side of the imposing portico. If you walk around the building, things get more confusing, because the rear annex looks nineteenth-century. This is unusual, because annexes are usually newer than the main building. Here is the reason why. McKean County built a Beebe courthouse in 1881 (see Warren, Cambria, and Huntington Counties). It was enlarged in 1914 and 1938 with rear wings, which the architects designed to match Beebe's style on the exterior. In 1940, the 1881 part burned in a destructive fire, but the newer wings were saved. (The old office vaults in the burned section proved to work perfectly, because the papers inside remained dry and unscorched.) Thomas K. Hendrix was the associate architect credited with the replacement structure you now see from the front. It is not clear why this Classical Ionic hexastyle facade was chosen for the replacement, but Classical Revival is always a safe style for public buildings. For astute observers, the clock tower is unlike those on older Classical Revival buildings, as it uses the architectural liberties more characteristic of Beaux-Arts.

If you have any doubts about its age, the front entrance is a giveaway once you open those modern bronze doors. The interior is surprisingly well appointed for a building constructed at this time; it does not look like a Depression building. The explanation is a combination of insurance money, local oil resources, and low Depression labor costs. Beyond the foyer, there is a one-story central rotunda at the crossing of halls. The marble decorations are in a modern Ionic mode. The courtroom is in wood, where the

modified Ionic theme is repeated in a pleasantly illuminated space. Back on the first floor, note the display cases on the corridor to the older rear annexes. Note that the interior of the annex is plain, twentieth-century, and very unlike its Beebe-copied exterior. While the architects matched the exterior, they built a contemporary interior.

There is a substantial county museum in the basement, which has pictures of the courthouse in its various stages of construction and destruction, as well as interesting exhibits of local history and industry.

MERCER
County Seat: Mercer

This county, established in 1800, is one of the seven American counties named for Gen. Hugh Mercer, who gave his life in the Battle of Princeton.

The courthouse is prominently situated on the center of an elevated and sloping square in the center of Mercer's business district. The square (locally called the Diamond, but not technically one) is a rare Harrisonburg type (see Introduction). The 1909 (Owsley, Boucherle and Owsley, architects) Beaux-Arts structure is a descendant of the Chicago 1893 World's Fair in form. The rectangular, brick-and-sandstone structure is similar on the north and south sides and identical on the east and west. While there are entrances on all sides, the main one is to the north, where the steps lead up to a monumental Ionic portico with the county name on the entablature.

Sandstone is used on piers that form vertical separations between some bays, on window surrounds, the entablature, and the horizontal lines of the water table and belt courses. There is a wide but restrained cornice. The five bay east and west ends have a one-story Doric portico over their entrances. The main body of the prominent tower is eight-sided. The four open sides have pairs of double Doric columns supporting an entablature. The clock faces are above the open sides and are like round, shallow dormers at the base of the dome roof. At the very top are a small lantern and finial. There was a a rooster weathervane on the top until 1929, when it was destroyed by lightening.

This is the third Mercer County courthouse, fire having destroyed the previous two. There was a great public resistance to the cost of this building, but the commissioners and, particularly, the sitting common pleas judge were determined to keep up with other counties. Westmoreland, Fayette, and Washington were particular reference points. The judge vetoed the first plan selected by the commissioners and pushed for the more ambitious proposal of the Owsley firm, with whose work he was personally familiar. (The Owsley firm was working on the even more ambitious Mahoning County, Ohio, courthouse in Youngstown at this very time.) The commissioners promised a $200,000 courthouse, but through a series of incremental shuffles, they ended up with one nearly twice as expensive.

Present-day Mercerians should thank them for their devious maneuvers, because the courthouse is the town's main architectural attraction.

The interior consists of wide, marble-clad halls that cross at the central rotunda, with monumental stairs to the south. Note the framed sketch of the courthouse by the younger Owsley, which was used in the firm's proposal. The stair rails are brass-plated iron with the county monogram as ornament. Most of the decorative elements remain on the hall ceilings except for the original elaborate stenciling. Console modillion brackets are used throughout the halls and the rotunda. The columns and their elaborate capitals in the rotunda are scagliola. The skylight seems small for all this space.

There are murals in the two courtrooms on the second floor and on the penditives. Of the three artists, two, Vincent Aderante and Alonzo E. Foringer, were protégés and longtime assistants to Edwin Blashfield, who was arguably the most celebrated muralist of the 1893 World's Fair. The mural entitled *Criminal Law* in courtroom 1 is by Aderante. In it, four figures representing Humanity ask for Justice under the Law guided by Mercy. Foringer's mural in courtroom 2, *Civil Law,* portrays a lawyer pleading his case before a judge with witnesses. (Aderante returned in 1937 and removed and restored both of these canvases.) Edward Simmons's (1852–1931) paintings on the pentitives of the rotunda show four aspects of law: Guilt, Innocence, Power, and Justice. Penditives were a Blashfield specialty, but at this time he may have been engaged at the Owsley courthouse under construc-

tion at Youngstown. Simmons painted murals at the Library of Congress and the South Dakota and Minnesota state capitols.

Owsley's courtrooms proved to have acoustical problems, which explains why the walls and ceilings are not original, while most of the rest of the rooms are. There is one existing poor photograph of the original courtroom at the Mercer County Historical Society, which gives us a glimpse of a ceiling corner. It appears that the original courtroom design employed a prominent curved cove between wall and ceiling. Whether the ceiling was coffered is not clear, but most courtrooms of this period, which had skylights also, have decorative coffering.

The present stenciling probably dates from a 1930 effort to improve the acoustics by installing soundproofing tiles on the walls and ceiling.

To the south of the courthouse is the 1868 Victorian former jail (Barr and Moser, architects), shorn of its old crenellated roof line but still attractive with its Palladian window, quoins, hood moldings, flared foundation, and belt course. One block north of the Diamond on Venango Street, there are two other stops worth making. The post office has a quality WPA mural by Pittsburgh artist Lorin Thompson (one of three he painted), showing locals removing stumps the old-fashioned way. Down the street is the earlier 1818 stone jail, now a private office building. It has been variously a temperance hotel and private residence. There still are stone fireplaces, which were originally in each cell. Each has iron rods running through the chimneys, placed there to prevent prisoners' escape.

MIFFLIN
County Seat: Lewistown

Thomas Mifflin, the first governor of Pennsylvania, also served in numerous other state offices and was an officer in the Continental army. In addition to this county, several towns, townships, and other places in this state were named for him. The namesake of the county seat is much less clear, but one of the stronger cases is for William Lewis, a prominent entrepreneur in southeast Pennsylvania who had friends on the legislative committee that created the county in 1789 and designated the seat.

The presently functioning county courthouse is an uninteresting, modern Classical Revival building built in 1978 (Jon Spalding, architect). However, the previous building, which was completed in 1843 and served the county for over a century, still stands conspicuously facing Public Square. It is now used for various purposes, primarily housing activities of the Mifflin County Historical Society. The courthouse prior to the 1843 one was built in the coffeemill style and was located in the middle of Public Square, about where the Civil War Monument now stands. The square, which was laid out when the town was created in 1797, has had many names, including Diamond. Its present contours date from about 1891, when the monument was elected.

The old courthouse not only is of interest as one of the few surviving early temple of justice structures, but accounts of its use give insight into the role the county courthouse played in community life. There is no ar-

chitect of record, simply a builder, which is not unusual for the times. Its strongest visual features are the tall Ionic quatrastyle portico and the tower. The single doorway at the top of a short flight of steps has an impressive pediment and engaged pilasters. On either side are first-story windows with shutters and radiating voussoirs, and above on the second floor are three Norman windows. The roof-level pediment has an unusual indented,

shelflike space on its tympanum, but no picture shows it filled with anything, as would have been the case with the ancient models. The bell tower is rather plain, having been simplified by economizing maintenance measures. It is composed of four tiers and topped by a weathervane on its silver-colored cap. The flared base supports a square clockface tier with corner pilasters. A transitional slant-sided octagonal tier in turn supports an open belfry. In 1878, the building was extended three bays in the rear (Daniel Zeigler, architect). The original clock gave out in 1916, and the county tried to get the city of Lewistown to help pay for a replacement, claiming local citizens got the most use from it. The strategy did not work. The new clock dial was electrically illuminated, and when the first electric bill arrived, it came as a big surprise to the commissioners. The utility company finally consented to provide the electricity free. These incidents indicate how minimal the county government budget was at this time.

Inside the front door is a foyer, which continues the Ionic theme. This space provides access to the center hall and the traditional pair of curving stairs leading to the second-story courtroom. The woodwork is probably pine, as it has painted graining. The courtroom is still there but is not being used at this writing because the expense of making it handicapped accessible. Its decor and old furnishings probably date from 1878, when the courtroom was enlarged at the time the building was extended to the rear. The judge's chambers were built in 1933, and the graining was probably applied at that time. The lighting fixtures are a 1969 reproduction, but of what it is not clear.

The building was financed by conducting a lottery and issuing "shin plasters," small-denomination notes that were used as local paper currency. Their continued value depended on the county's redeeming them on schedule. They were so called because in many places where they were used, the local government defaulted, and their value went so low that they were only worth the paper they were printed on, and one use for such paper was to make shin plasters. Newspaper references and records give interesting insight into the early use of the building, which may reflect on the financing problem. Evidently, the basement level was used as rental space for whatever would command payment. This included a short-lived academy, which advertised language instruction in French, Italian, Spanish, German, Latin, Greek, and Hebrew. There are several mentions of an "oyster saloon," which was probably just a restaurant. There was one reference to use of the upstairs by a "Daguerrean artist," who perhaps needed more daylight than the basement afforded to practice his trade. Those sitting for his services were instructed to dress in black and white only. Despite the financing burdens, the building served the county well, survived reasonably intact, and provided a defining architectural symbol for this small city.

The jail erected in 1856 is down the main street in the same block with the new courthouse. Its original crenellated facade is now painted in rather gay colors.

MONROE
County Seat: Stroudsburg

Monroe County, created in 1836 and named after the president, is identified with the Poconos, longtime recreational area for Philadelphians and now, thanks to the interstates, increasingly by New Jerseyans and New Yorkers. This is, in a historical sense, a kind of return, because the New Yorkers were here first. Before Penn came to the lower Delaware, New Netherlanders made their appearance here, which explains all those place names ending in "kill," the Dutch word for stream. Stroud was an early settler, whose tombstone is in the courthouse and whose grandson, Stroud J. Hollinshead, gave land for the first courthouse.

The courthouse on 7th Street north of Main Street (1890, T. I. Lacey and Sons, architects) is a simple but attractive, mildly Romanesque structure with a design in keeping with its times. When viewing the plan, the local paper announced that "Monroe citizens will be able to point to the new structure with pride." Of quarry-faced ashlar stone construction, it features the round arch in the windows, doorway, and belfry. The stone material is one of its most interesting features. The county building committee and Lacey visited Woodbury, New Jersey, and Scranton in preparation for choosing a design. The style has similarity to that of Woodbury, but the basic stone used is the same as Scranton's, from Nickolson quarry in Lackawanna County. Accent stones were added from other sources: Euclid, Ohio, brownstone windowsills; Warsaw bluestone front steps and a string course above the entry; and granite columns. The use of colored grout further emphasizes the masonry as a design element.

The building floor plan is rectangular, with the front and rear on the small sides. The front, which faces a square, is three bays wide, the central bay being brought forward and rising to the tower. The entrance is under an arched opening, with radiating voussoirs resting on two attached granite columns with leaf capitals. Above are two-story arched windows with regular voussoirs. The tower proper begins with a section of decorative stonework, with the belfry tier having arched windows and masonry balconies. The copper roof has round sections on the sides, seemingly designed for clock faces, but the spaces were never filled. The windows on the outer front bays are also arched and have a third voussoir pattern. There are ten bays on the sides, with two cross gables. The large windows under the gables that have no horizontal midband are for lighting two-story interior spaces for two courtrooms and a law library. There are two large, stone chimneys and a flat-railed rooftop that appears to have replacement railings.

The building was enlarged in 1933 (H. T. Rinker and M. R. Kiefer, architects) with federal PWA aid, and the county specified that the building stone be from the same Lackawanna quarry. While the addition is steel frame construction, there was an effort to match the style of the existing courthouse in both exterior and interior materials. The most recent modern addition to the right included a prominent sculpture at its entryway. Its modern look did not fit local tastes and was rejected. The base is still there, presumably awaiting a more acceptable subject.

While much of the interior of the older building is modernized, you will still find the original vestibule quarry tiles, black and white Vermont marble floor tiles, and an iron stairway with unusual patterns leading to a grand courtroom 1. The courtroom is as wide as the building, illuminated by large windows on either side, has a fine balcony, and is furnished in oak, including the rail and bench. Note the iron theater seats with the wire hat racks underneath. Behind the bench is an unusual niche draped in velvet, with two doors that originally led to the offices of the judge and district attorney. The rooms to the rear and at the balcony level were originally for jurors. The first-floor halls are decorated by works donated by local artists, and there is a portrait of orchestra leader Fred Waring, a local citizen.

The square in front of the courthouse where the diminutive doughboy resides was the site of the previous courthouse. The red brick building with eyelid windows facing the square is the old 1875 jail, which was in use until the late 1980s.

MONTGOMERY
County Seat: Norristown

Most sources routinely state that the county is named after Gen. Richard Montgomery, a New York resident who died in the battle of Quebec in 1775. However, someone has raised the question of why a county filled with pacifist Quakers and Mennonites would name their county after a soldier. Montgomery was a common place name in the county, and two members of the assembly committee who set up the county in 1784 also had that name, so it may have had differing connotations for some in a position to influence the choice. Isaac Norris, for whom the seat is named, owned the land now occupied by the borough and operated a gristmill at the foot of Water Street. Unlike the other suburban Philadelphia county seats, Norristown is more working class than middle class. An old industrial mill town on the Schuylkill, it developed in a row house tradition, and its main street has never been able to develop a commercial appeal for middle-class tastes as have Media, West Chester, and Doylestown. Many of the old houses around the courthouse have been converted to law offices. Old churches and institutions are still around, providing some interest for the county seat explorer.

The first courthouse was built on what is now Public Square, where the Civil War Shaft and the Vietnam and other memorials are located at Main and Swede Streets. This structure was replaced in 1853–56 by a Classical Revival (N. LeBrun, architect) building on land that the county had bought from the University of Pennsylvania for five shillings in 1785. The county fathers admired the LeBrun building so much that when the county outgrew his structure around the turn of the century, they instructed the architect to retain the old walls and Ionic portico of six columns in the new expanded building. However, the similarity stops there, as LeBrun crowned his building with a very tall spire. The present larger structure (1902, Schermerhorn and Reinhold, architects) was poured inside the previous one but extended and crowned with the copper dome. In 1929, a parallel but connected annex was added (Rankin and Kellogg, architects). It has five stories and is about the same height as the two-story 1902 structure. A further 1968 addition includes the garage and entrance toward Main Street.

At the dedication of the 1902 structure, a commissioner assured an audience that the great expense was worth it, because anything less imposing would not satisfy the citizens. Pride was alive. This courthouse now has a front central pavilion that is five bays wide, with six Ionic columns. The bays on either side of the pavilion are at an intermediary vertical plane, and then the final three bays on either side recede farther. The walls are in rusticated stone, with only slightly beveled edges, but much of the facade is

set off with smooth ashlar pilasters with simple capitals. The casement windows are mostly quite plain, with only the middle bays on the wings having decorative pilaster mullions. The copper-covered dome sits on a platform with window lights. Atop the dome is a louvered lantern with a hemisphere cap. The clock faces are simple, round, unadorned dormers. The bell has an above-average tone. The ends of the building are five bays rising to a pediment, with the central bays having attached columns *in antis* at the first-story level.

Inside, there are a number of decorative features, including massive marble columns, great central stairs, skylights, and according to contemporary accounts, sumptuously appointed courtrooms, using Flemish oak. Courtrooms B, C, D, and F are decorated with 1950 murals painted by local artist George M. Harding. They portray local historical scenes, including one of the 1854 courthouse in courtroom D. The courtrooms carry out the Classical theme with pilasters but on the whole are rather plain, though dignified. The slat-back audience benches are attractive. Courtroom F has a circular, clear glass skylight.

Note the forbidding crenellated facade on the jail down the street behind the courthouse complex. Across from the jail, in the lobby of the attractive Art Deco U.S. Post Office, there are two WPA murals by Paul Mays portraying scenes of local industry and agriculture. It is a panorama about which the artist stated, "I wished to express the meaning of strength—the force and vitality of the working people in the valley of factories and furnaces." In the iconography of the 1930s, work was still a man's world.

MONTOUR

County Seat: Danville

Of the few counties in America named for women, more than half are for Indian females, including this one. Madam Montour was a rather mythic figure who was probably part French but was Indian by choice. She spoke French, English, and many Indian languages and was respected by those whose languages she spoke. This made her influential at conferences and in treaty negotiations, and it is most singular that Pennsylvanians should honor such a person in 1850 by choosing her name for this new county.

The small town of Danville is on the Mahoning Creek where it joins the wide Susquehanna. An early anthracite and iron town, which provided rails for the railway expansion, it now experiences quieter times. The Italianate courthouse (1871, O'Malley, architect) is located at Mill Street and Market Street at the end of the commercial strip and just before the Susquehanna River Bridge. It is a cross-gabled structure built of red brick and greenstone, both of which have unfortunately been painted variously and often. The stone does not stand up well to air pollution and requires protection, which may explain the various coatings. However, if the original finish could be restored, the building would be much more attractive. This is particularly the case for the quoins, which are brick and probably covered with white plaster from the beginning, judging by a 1905 photograph. Other than the sur-

face smearing, the exterior has been little altered. The facade is five bays wide, with the outer ones consisting of blind recessed windows. There are arches embedded in the building wall for each bay on both stories. The central three bays are forward and embrace the three arched entry doors (two now glass bricked) with transoms and rusticated surrounds, above which is a balcony with an extended central section. The second floor features three narrow arched windows, the middle one being double. The pediment above the roofline has a round window with four panes. The cornice features a decorative frieze and prominent brackets. The quoins are presently the same color as the body of the building, but that has usually not been the case in the past.

The tower has a square base featuring triple Norman windows similar in style to those on the building front. The bracketed cornice has raised semicircular sections at midpoint. The second tier is octagonal with round-topped louvered windows on alternate sides. The tower is topped with a hemisphere roof and finial.

While the exterior is large as it has always been, the interior is another story. The transgressions are proudly listed on brass plaques on the central hallway wall and took place primarily between 1969 and 1975. The only things left of the original building that show are the doorways to the row offices, and most of these have been altered.

The courthouse is located in an interesting old neighborhood with houses on the national register. Among those of particular interest is the Thomas Beaver Free Library (1888, Charles S. Wetzel, architect) southeast on Market Street. By all means, go in. Its interior somewhat makes up for the one missing in the courthouse. Note particularly the area above the circulation desk. The Beaver family fortune was made in the local iron industry, particularly in the manufacturing of sturdy ranges and stoves. A half block down Mill Street toward town is a post office with WPA art. It is an aluminum bas-relief by Jean De Marco on *Ironmaking*. One block the other way on Mill Street is a small park overlooking the Susquehanna

River. A stroll around the neighborhood will reveal many ornate iron fences, which are suggestive of the town's iron past.

Whitley's book on American architects credits the courthouse to Wetzel, the local architect who designed the Beaver Library, but other sources disagree, and I am inclined to side with them. O'Malley (whose first name is not recorded) was the builder, and there probably was no architect in the modern sense.

NORTHAMPTON
County Seat: Easton

By its English place name, one can tell that Northampton County was a Colonial creation. The creator was Thomas Penn, and the county he established in 1751 once encompassed most of northeastern Pennsylvania. The county seat, Easton, is at the confluence of several rivers, primarily the Delaware and Lehigh, which assured it an early place of importance when water was the cheapest route for transportation. This advantage was prolonged when it became the terminus of important canals. As the era of water

transport primacy has long since passed, Easton has settled into a more steady state. A large memorial column in the middle of downtown Easton, in Centre Square (which looks more like a circle), marks the site of the original courthouse, which served the county for over a hundred years. Its location conformed to the Lancaster type of town plan (described in the Introduction). Just as in Lancaster, the site proved too small to accommodate a larger replacement building.

The second courthouse, which is still in use, is on one of Easton's hills (7th Avenue and Walnut Avenue) and now is part of a complex that includes the jail. Both courthouse and jail have experienced many additions. The Classical 1860–61 courthouse

(C. Graham, architect) features a facade of monumental metal Corinthian columns and a high (155-foot) tower. The columns stand on substantial pedestals, which lessen their height and help keep them in proportion. In the five bays across the front, the upper windows are modified Norman style, with the center one larger. Classical detailing is used extensively on the cornice, with egg and dart, bead and reel moldings, as well as dentils and modillions. The tall wooden tower is in three tiers and can be examined best with binoculars. Above the octagonal base, the first tier has louvered arches with Corinthian pilasters at the angles, which are linked by blind arches. There is a denticulated cornice and pediments on alternate sides. The next tier consists of blind arches with blind roundels on alternate sides. At the top are a dome, finial, and weathervane. On three occasions, 1887, 1922, and 1933, the commissioners wanted to remove the tower rather than maintain it, and each time citizen protest saved it.

In 1887, a rear addition and west wing were added (John M. Stewart, architect). A further addition to the east was made in 1913 to accommodate the controller and register of deeds. In 1921, another west addition (Edward R. Bitting, architect) provided two more courtrooms. Viewed from the front, the 1913 and 1921 additions appear as wings that come forward parallel to the original building. Most of the administrative offices are now in the modern annex (1976, Pharo and Haas, architects), which is to the rear of all of the above. This is where you will enter the complex. Three courtrooms are worth a visit, two in the 1921 addition and the original courtroom in the old Graham building, all on the second floor. On your way to them, you will pass Easton's Liberty Bell and a series of murals, two pertaining to the reading of the Declaration of Independence at the Centre Square Courthouse and one triptych on a 1758 local Indian treaty. The county has handouts on the bell and the murals. The handsome courtroom 1 employs the Corinthian motif of the exterior. The lofty ceiling is coffered. The furniture is in naturally finished oak and exhibits Gothic touches. The no-longer-used entrance doors are notable. The jury box employs seating in three rows of four rather than the traditional two rows of six. This room and its original ancillary rear chambers probably took up the entire second floor of the original building. Courtrooms 2 and 3 are virtually identical except for color, and they are good examples of 1921 styles. Major features are the windows on three sides and the high ceilings with a curved cove.

On the grassy hillside, and linked to the courthouse complex on the east side, is a Classic nineteenth-century jail (1871, John Haviland, architect), with the typical foreboding fortress appearance the architect favored. There is an addition from 1903–5, as well as a later one.

Note the use of slate in walks and benches around the grounds. This county once had many roof tile slateries, which were in full production in the latter part of the nineteenth century. The slate shingle splitter's craft is now a dying one, and only a few operations are left, primarily supplying replacement tiles. Most slate production is now for landscaping, as you see here.

NORTHUMBERLAND
County Seat: Sunbury

The Susquehanna River divides into major branches in Northumberland County, which was formed in 1772, and the fork was a place of great strategic importance in the river transportation era. It was the site of many Indian villages and later military forts. The county seat, Sunbury, is just south of the fork on the east side of the main stem and was built on the site of an important earlier Indian town (Shamokin) and later Fort Augusta, built during the French and Indian Wars. Among the important eighteenth-century residents of Sunbury were John Lukens, surveyor general of Pennsylvania; one of its first senators, William Maclay; and Dr. Joseph Priestly. Priestly, the discoverer of "dephlogisticated air" (oxygen) had suffered in England the burning of his chapel and extensive library and laboratory by a mob objecting to his sympathetic statements about French revolutionaries.

He came to America, where he was made most welcome and was offered a professorship of chemistry by the University of Pennsylvania. Instead of Philadelphia, he chose to live at the fork of the Susquehanna, where he carried on his experiments and wrote in support of the cause of liberty everywhere. As a result of one of his letters, English poets Southey and Coleridge considered coming to join Priestly with the purpose of founding an ideal community, which was to be called Pantisocracy. It lived only in their imagination, however, and never came to Northumberland County.

Sunbury was laid out after the Philadelphia plan, though the resemblance now goes little further than street names. The courthouse faces Market Street at a point where it is divided by a park strip. The park was dedicated for public use when the town was platted. The building (1864) closely resembles the Romanesque Revival Sloan courthouses, but Sloan, strictly speaking, was not the architect. The Northumberland commissioners hired the builder of the Sloan-designed Lycoming County courthouse (demolished in 1969) to build one like it for them. He cloned it to the best of his ability but constructed it as a mirror image. Sloan, who received no fee, successfully sued the county and established for architects the right of ownership of their plans. Instead of saving money, the county ended paying more than if they had hired Sloan.

The brick and Hummelstown brownstone (both now painted) courthouse has three bays across the front, with the outer ones protruding forward

and the right one rising to the tower. Sloan's similar Clinton and Venango County courthouses have dual towers, although the Lycoming one did not. Note, however, that the left bay has the first stage of a tower above the cornice, suggesting the basic Sloan plan provided for a one- or two-tower option. The front section is the widest part of the building and has appointments that differ from the remainder of the building, primarily prominent quoins and bracketing under the eaves. The central bay starts at the ground floor, with the three doorways with rusticated brownstone surrounds, above which are three long, narrow Norman windows with slim hood moldings, a hooded roundel, and a gable that pierces the roofline. The first-floor window surrounds of the outer bays have alternating short and long blocks of brownstone. This is a variation on what is called a Gibbs window, after an earlier English architect who essentially adapted quoins as window decoration. The tower begins with a double square base decorated by panels and bracketing. A balcony stage serves as a transition to the octagonal clock-and-belfry section, where there is a repeat of the normal window theme prominent on the building front. This section has a bracketed cornice above which are the painted copper dome and a finial. The side of the building has a corbel arcade of six windows with a shallow portico at the center. The cornice on the sides is much simpler than on the facade, with dentils and modillions but no brackets. The rear section, which makes the building L-shaped, is a 1915 addition constructed in a differing but compatible style. The bell was given to the county by Simon Cameron, who seemed to have made a practice of this, and the clock was made by E. Howard of Boston and installed in 1872.

Entering the front door, note the original front stairs leads to a courtroom (the landing is no longer lighted by the triple front Norman windows because of the interior changes). The courtroom features a coffered ceiling and a rather florid Classical niche behind the bench, with a quotation by George Washington. The arrangement is similar to the late Williamsport (Lycoming County) courtroom, where statues once rested on a niche shelf much like this one. The wood wainscot and the combination of painted and finished wood on the furnishings around the bench point to the original period of this building. The last of the Molly Maguire trials took place here in 1878.

The rear stairs in the 1915 section lead to a two-story seating area, which is lighted with a skylight. Courtroom 2 in the newer ell is also a two-story space with a decorative coffered wood ceiling. The room has Classical theme decorations, including an elaborate installation topped by an entablature behind the rather plain judge's bench.

The long, narrow Cameron Park, named for the soldier on the Civil War monument, contains numerous dedications. An 1870 photograph shows the park fenced in and streetcars running along Market Street. It was paved for the first time in 1892. The 1878 C. S. Wetzel (see Montour County) jail one block east is well worth seeing.

PERRY
County Seat: New Bloomfield

This is one of the many counties named after my namesake, Commodore Oliver Hazard Perry, the hero of the Great Lakes naval battle. When the county was formed in 1820 there was an intense fight over the location of the seat. No less than four successive commissions failed to reach an agreement before one finally selected the site of the future New Bloomfield. This site at the time was George Barnett's farm. It was Barnett's willingness to donate eight acres that strongly influenced the seat selection. This not only provided a free site for the county buildings, but also allowed the county to sell off lots to help finance the launching of the new government. Barnett also donated the site of several springs to the new seat, one of which is preserved in a park down the street from the present courthouse.

The Greek Revival courthouse (Jacob Bishop, architect) is located at the town center, where Main Street and Carlisle Street intersect around a Civil War monument. A portion of the original 1826 courthouse is embedded in the existing structure, but the red brick building you see is essentially an 1868 reconstruction and enlargement. The result is an example of Eclectic architecture, a rather attractive one in this small-town setting.

The building is three bays wide, with quoins at the angles and a shallow central pavilion. The major decorative features of the facade are the second-story Norman windows. The large central window has a round hood mold-

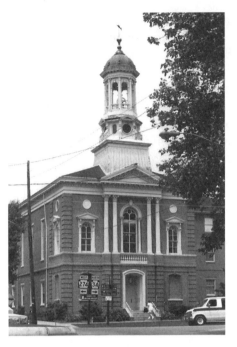

ing, while the outer ones have small pediments. There is a balustrade above the entrance, and pairs of fluted Corinthian columns support a roof-level pediment. The tower begins with a plain square base; the second tier has elaborate inverted consoles, pediments on alternate sides, and round and oval windows. The belfry tier is an arcade of modified Corinthian columns supporting a cornice with modillions. The copper dome has a finial and a fish weathervane.

The interior of the courthouse is modernized, including the main courtroom upstairs. This was the scene of a nationally publicized modern trial involving the murder of two hikers on the Appalachian Trail. Paul David Crews, a farmhand from South Carolina, was convicted by a jury that deliberated less than an hour.

The building across the street was once a hotel but has been converted to a modern office building.

PHILADELPHIA
County Seat: Philadelphia

Philadelphia County, created in 1682, is the smallest Pennsylvania county in area and the largest in population. Its county courthouse is called the city hall, because in 1854 the city and the county were combined into a single coterminous government, largely because of a law-and-order issue. Among other things, independent fire companies, many located outside of the city's borders at that time, were rioting at fire sites over who had jurisdiction for extinguishing the flames. The new enlarged city-county covered all the built-up areas and could thus impose some rules. Philadelphia City Hall has always been largely a county courthouse, though it has also housed the elected city officials. It is the most complex and complicated building covered in this guide and certainly the largest. When it was designed, it was intended to be the tallest building in the world, but it took so long to complete that the Washington Monument and Eiffel Tower surpassed it. It was the tallest occupied structure, and Philadelphians still claim it is the world's largest masonry structure.

The 1854 consolidation of the city and county came at a time when the existing city and county facilities were inadequate for growing needs. Plans were immediately laid for constructing a new combination city and county building, but the Civil War intervened, postponing any actions. The old county courthouse that the present one eventually replaced is none other than Congress Hall, which stands next to Independence Hall (see below). As it was then configured, it had many deficiencies as a court facility. The major problem was that it lacked a way to separate the judge, jury, criminally accused, and audience during court sessions. Spectators talked openly to jurors, judges had to make their way through the audience to get to the bench, and court personnel had no office space. Finally, in 1870, the decision was made again to build a new city-county building, but it was more than thirty years before it was finished. The reasons for the delay were many; they included the politics of the time and the towering ambition of the head of the building commission to do something remarkable for Philadelphia.

To give you a feel for the politics of the day, consider two early actions taken by city council in relation to the new structure. Before the building was even designed, the city council debated over what material would cover the building. The debate pitted granite against marble, and the winning white marble, which now covers city hall, just happened to be quarried by an acquaintance of the new mayor. Second was the long debate over where to build the new city hall. The major choices were between Washington Square, next to Independence Park, and Penn Square, its eventual location. The interests included merchants and land speculators, who had obvious stakes in the direction commercial expansion would take.

Completely unrelated matters are often joined in politics, and in this case, a street railway fight was linked to the location issue. The West Philadelphia Company had exclusive rights to run street railways on Market Street from river to river, and at that time Market ran directly through Penn Square, where City Hall now stands. If the new building was located on Penn Square, the tracks would have to be rerouted. The Union Company wanted to build a second Market Street line from Ninth Street to Front Street to connect lines it operated on those streets with their ferry, which docked at Front and Market, but the WPC stood in its way. The Union Company supported the Penn Square location and, by influencing city council, successfully blocked West Philadelphia's effort to build tracks around the new building. To obtain this permission, West Philadelphia had to cave in and share Market Street from Ninth to Front with its rival, the Union Company. The actual choice of the Penn Square location over Washington Square was made by a vote of the electorate, with the very active participation of all of the downtown interests.

Surprisingly, the actual construction process was remarkably free of corruption. Recognizing the realities of the political environment in the city, various local business leaders succeeded in having the state legislature create an independent building commission. The commission was appointed by the governor and was given power to fill its own vacancies, but the taxpayers of Philadelphia were still to pay the bills. Though it took several years for the commission to find its bearings, eventually Samuel C. Perkins, a corporate lawyer, assumed the chair, and his steely will was responsible for the eventual completion of the task. Given its composition and origin, the commission was the object of constant criticism by Philadelphia politicians and newspapers, both encouraged by unhappy taxpayers.

The architect for this remarkable building was John McArthur Jr. who was chosen in two competitions, one in 1860 and another in 1870, winning each time over some better-known architects, including Samuel Sloan (see Lancaster County). Though young (thirty-seven in 1860), McArthur had experience, and in the ten years between competitions, he was very active in Philadelphia, including wartime work for the quartermaster general. In looking at the City Hall today, one is impressed by its striking style, the epitome of Second Empire ornateness. McArthur was not devoted to this style and used many others in his works. He was known for the practicality of his structures as he sought to serve the needs of his clients. His city hall solved all those problems of the old courthouse mentioned above and provided very good judicial facilities for its day. The building sorted out the various Philadelphia government functions and gave them each a separate zone. Its very commodious circulation system, both vertical and horizontal, accommodated both public and employee traffic. He anticipated the large crowds that this growing city would generate. He was attentive to the work environment and supplied all offices with natural light and ventilation.

This is a very large and complicated building and is nearly impossible to cover in one visit. The Second Empire style can be compared to a musical composition that has a number of themes and then variations on those themes. This is the largest and most complicated building of this style in the country, and a full description is a formidable task. What follows will make daunting reading, and it is unlikely that anyone will want to follow it through in one visit. Treat it as a reference work. It will cover most of the major themes and will demonstrate the complexity of the decorative patterns, pointing out the functional achievements of the building, not merely its stylistic flourishes. For descriptive purposes, the building is divided into different zones, and the iconographic sculpture is treated as a separate section.

OVERVIEW
City Hall is essentially a square, donut-shaped structure with portals at the center of each side connecting the outside with the inner court. The huge tower that supports the William Penn statue rises from the court and is attached to the northern side.

Philadelphia City Hall. Photo by Greg James, Courtesy Foundation for Architecture.

EXTERIOR

Prominent features of City Hall that led to its style designation of Second Empire include the mansard roof and pavilions on both the central facades and the corners. Though all four sides are virtually identical, the building faces north, and on that side the central pavilion extends farther forward than on the other three sides. The best vantage point for viewing the exterior is to the west, where there are benches, summer shade, and space to move around without dodging automobiles. The essential modeling of the structure is the same on each side. The first, or basement, floor is above-ground and is constructed of rusticated granite. The central pavilions are each nine bays wide, with the central three forward. On either side of the central pavilions are four bays, which might be called the true sides of the building proper. Finally, there are corner pavilions. Horizontally, the main part of the building is divided into three tiers above the basement first floor, each tier being two stories high. The tiers are separated by an elaborate entablature rather than mere stringcourses. The central pavilion projects upward an additional tier.

Standing before the central bay over the portal, note that there are pairs of detached fluted columns on either side and on each tier. The stacked pairs rise to support a segmental pediment. The capitals differ on each floor, and none are standard Classical orders. Behind each pair of columns is a pair of pilasters. The arched portal has an iconographic head on the keystone and figures in the spandrels. At the second tier is an arched

window, the arch being supported by a one-story order of columns, pilasters, and entablature. Again, there is an iconographic head on the keystone and figures in the spandrels. The third tier is not so high, because the fifth and sixth floors have lower ceilings. Here there is an arcade featuring pilasters at the corners, detached columns in the middle, a keystone head, and wreaths in the spandrels. The pediment above is filled with figures.

The two bays flanking the central one are on the same vertical plane as the pilasters of the central bay. The theme of paired columns is repeated here to frame the windows; however, they are present only on the first and second tiers. The windows differ on each floor but maintain the same rhythm within the tiers. The first tier has a blind rectangular window and a roundel; the second tier, a rectangular and an oval window; and the third tier a rectangular window and a lunette. The window surrounds change with each floor. On the third tier, solitary iconographic figures sit on either side above the columns. Above the three central bays, there is a complex, two-level mansard roof, with the outer portions convex and the central and higher ones straight sided. At the center above the segmental pediment, an elaborate dormer comes out of the roof, with caryatids or telamons on either side and a pair of figures above. The convex portions of the roof on either side have roundels, and above it all is an elaborate iron cornice. Finally, there is a flagpole.

The three remaining bays of the central pavilion, which are on either side of the ones just described, employ pilasters to frame the windows, and again the capitals differ with each tier. The fifth-floor windows have segmental arched head moldings supported by consoles. The sixth- and seventh-floor windows are dormers projecting through the convex mansard roof. The window surrounds of the sixth floor are joined at the bottom. The seventh-floor windows are smaller, prominently hooded, and not aligned with the windows of the floors below.

The next four bays on either side repeat the themes of the bays just described, but with less elaboration. Here the sixth-floor windows have triangular heads rather than the segmental arch.

The corner pavilions contain freestanding octagonal staircases. The windows are aligned with those in the other bays rather than with the staircase landings, which is a more typical arrangement. This window placement strengthens the exterior horizontal lines of the building. The corner pavilions repeat the central pavilion arrangement of windows framed by pairs of two-story fluted columns; however, they rise for only two tiers. The window of the first tier has a segmentally arched head molding with the usual figural keystone. The second-tier window has a full arch and is more elaborately decorated. In addition to the keystone, there are figures in the spandrels and impost bas-reliefs on either side. The corner pavilions have straight mansard roofs. The dormers have segmentally arched pediments supported by caryatids or telamons and another statuary group above the curve. The pavilion angles have vermiculated stone quoins.

TOWER

The tower rises from the ground within the interior court but is attached to the north section of the building. It is built of stone and steel, with the latter used in the light bluish gray upper portion. This color dates from a recent recoating of the metal designed to retard oxidization. It is difficult to observe the entire tower from any single vantage point. The lower part can best be seen from inside the courtyard. The plaza around the Municipal Services Building to the north is a good spot from which to examine the upper portions. The tower is divided into eight tiers, each of which is set off by strong horizontal features. The first three tiers rise to the roof level and must be viewed from inside the courtyard.

The first tier has a semicylindrical three-story bay on the south side and buttresses to the east and west. The rounded south side has a single window at the second-story level, five windows at the third, and a row of roundels at the fourth just below its cornice. The side buttresses are pierced by a single window. The second tier has slightly battered walls on three sides, and each

has two windows. The third tier is the beginning of the tower proper, as its north side emerges above the roof. Three sides are pieced by a segmentally arched opening that is divided by a transom and two stone piers. The surface of the upper part of this tier turns to smooth ashlar, which continues upward for the balance of the stone part of the tower.

The fourth tier (view from the outside to the north and with glasses) is the largest. Its major decorative feature is a large, arched opening that has the appearance of that portion of a central pavilion typically seen above a building entrance. At its base is a balustrade balcony serviced by three arched openings. Above is a single arched opening with two square columns supporting a three-part transom. The tier is topped by an entablature with a modified Doric frieze of triglyph, guttae, and metope.

The fifth and last stone tier again has the appearance of the upper portion of a lavish pavilion. The outermost part is framed by double columns, which support an elaborate entablature with a garland-decorated frieze. Behind are two short Corinthian columns on piers that support an arch with a deep intrados. A window fills the archway. In the spandrels of the arch are cherubic figures acting out themes of the natural world: water, air, fire, and earth. The water panels are to the south, where the left cherub pours liquid from an urn, while the other holds a triton and stands over a dolphin. The earth panels are to the west, where one cherub stands on a turtle and the other is accompanied by a snake and garlands. The air panels, on the north, have birds flying above the figures. The fire panels, on the east, show a blaze on the left and a cherub holding a lightning bolt on the right.

The sixth tier begins the metal section of the tower. The twenty-six-foot clock faces are surrounded by double columns on either side and a segmental pediment above. The angles of this tier are curved and decorated. Above this tier, the roof begins in the form of an octagonal cap that simulates the look of louvers. There are roundels at the upper part of each section, each of which has a hood carrying a ball and finial. The crown of the tower is a round catwalk that surrounds the pedestal supporting the statue of William Penn. At the base of the remarkable thirty-seven-foot statue of Penn are four groups of twenty-four-foot figures portraying the two major groups of persons who greeted Penn when he arrived. At the northeast corner is an Indian and a dog; at the northwest, a female Indian and child; at the southwest, a Swedish male settler with a child; and at the southeast, a Swedish woman with a child and a lamb.

ICONOGRAPHIC SCULPTURE

No other county courthouse or city hall is so richly endowed with iconographic sculpture. Unfortunately, it is very poorly documented. Alexander Calder did not keep good records, and no full account was published at the time. We know that it was his intention to educate the populus, who were supposed to gaze on his works and be instructed. However, as one of his contemporaries observed, they were more likely to be mystified. The works are primarily rendered in marble, shaped by stone carvers who copied Calder's full-scale casts. Calder also designed numerous iron and bronze decorations, including the wonderful dragon fire hose spigots and the heavy, spiked barriers around the building at ground level.

There is some rationale to the organization of the works, but there are many anomalies. One reason is that only twenty human figures were orig-

inally contemplated, but this number eventually grew to ninety-four. In other words, the sculpture program evolved and expanded as the building was under construction rather than coming from a preconceived overall plan. Eventually over 250 works were executed, most of which are briefly noted below.

The iconography on the four central pavilions in part symbolizes the governmental functions served by that part of the building, and the exterior keystone over each portal sets this theme. To the north, the head of William Penn, the city founder, is on the key. The east portal is called the city entrance because it leads to the city executive offices, and the keystone here portrays Benjamin Franklin. On the south, where the courts were concentrated, Moses occupies the keystone. On the west, the prisoners' entrance, Sympathy is the keystone symbol. The Pennsylvania seal appears on the south side, where the Pennsylvania State Supreme Court is housed, and the seal of Philadelphia is on the other sides. Some of the symbolism on the building represents the "four corners of the earth" and the races of man. Many abstract ideas are also depicted, such as peace and repentance, and Calder used both traditional symbols from literature and his own imagination in designing the representational figures. The economic pursuits and professions of citizens in the then burgeoning national economy are celebrated. Of the occupations, architecture and the building trades are well represented. Because the tools of the trades have changed in the past hundred years, some of the portrayals are hard for us to read today. On the building exterior, the figures always appear in the same places on all four sides. Generally, the figures in a given place follow a designated theme for that location, but there are exceptions. Work on the iconography is a continuing enterprise; consequently, at times you will be invited to participate in the interpretive research. Perhaps some of you will find as yet unidentified meanings in Calder's symbolism.

In order to follow iconographic patterns, the central pavilions will be separated from the corner ones. As some of the central pavilion themes flow from the outside through the portals, the description will follow this same plan. Parenthetical terms represent alternative interpretations that have been suggested.

Central Pavilion North

Portal keystone:	William Penn
First-tier spandrels:	Left: Pioneer with ax advancing on the frontier, tall ship behind (Civilization)
	Right: Indian looking back at the advancing frontier, tepee behind (Barbarism)
Second-tier spandrels:	Left: Architecture, a female figure with a torch (the connection is not clear)
	Right: Poetry, a male (?) figure with books, plans, and a quill pen, with an hourglass to the right
Third tier, seated:	Left: Fame, a female figure writing, with a trumpet below, laurel wreath laid down
	Right: Victory, a warrior clad in armor, wearing laurel wreath
Dormer caryatids and telamons:	Northman and Northwoman (north)
Inside pediment:	Philadelphia coat of arms
Dormer pediment group:	Left: Europe, horse, religious figure in skullcap
	Right: Spanish Conquistadors (initial conquerors of the New World?)

Central Portal North

The interior of each portal differs and is appropriately symbolic in its structure. The north portal is the most richly ornamented, as befits the entrance of a building. The long, rectangular impost panels on either side of the entry have formalized foliage with grotesques; the same panels on the other three portals are wonderful natural scenes. In the first room, the walls are Ohio sandstone, which was intended to set off the red and blue granite pilasters and columns. The bronze capital decoration includes themes of art, science, and industry, subjects that are also carried out around the top of the room in the arch spandrels. Here, bas-reliefs depict with varying degrees of clarity Commerce (figure bearing bundles), Mechanics (square and sledge), Architecture, Poetry, Science (microscope), Music (pipes and tambourine), Medicine (caduceus), Navigation, and Botany, among others. On the end panels as you face south, the depictions are Freedom of the Ballot and Education. The balcony of the Conversation Room (see below) looks out over this formal setting.

Moving south to the room under the tower, the walls become blue-veined Pennsylvania marble. Here again, the "four corners of the earth" theme is used, this time with animals in the keystones representing Africa (tiger), Asia (elephant), Europe (bullock), and America (bear). The sandstone pilaster capitals represent the children of different races—Caucasian, Asian (then called Mongolian), Native American, and African—and the column capitals the adults of the same four races.

Note the encaustic floor tiles on this and the other portals. These were imported from Europe, primarily Germany. During the time the building was under construction, a native decorative tile industry was developing, and the wall tiles in the upper floors tend to be American, although most floor tiles have been covered by linoleum in the hallways.

Central Pavilion East

Portal keystone:	Benjamin Franklin
First-tier spandrels:	Left: Engineering, wheels, gears, and winches
	Right: Mining, man wielding a pick
Second-tier spandrels:	Left: Science, globe, books, and lamp of knowledge
	Right: Art, sculptress, with artist palettes above
Third tier, seated:	Left: Industry, male figure poring over a plan, with a sledge and basket at his feet
	Right: Peace, female with dove at her feet
Inside pediment:	Philadelphia coat of arms
Dormer caryatid and telamon:	Female and male Asians (east)
Dormer pediment group:	Asia: Elephant, Chinese coolie (left), and harem girl (right)

Central Portal East

This portal is called the mayor's entrance. The exterior and interior portal keystones portray the head of Franklin. The rectilinear impost panels on either side of the portal depict naturalistic American scenes, a swamp on one side and a forest with a beaver and owl on the other side. This is the only portal with exterior stairs, which lead to the second floor, where the executive offices are located. The stairwell has been described as florid Doric in style, rendered in granite with panels of red marble from Lake Champlain. The stair spandrel icons represent Navigation and Architecture. The male figure holds a map and compass, a fitting symbol for a port city, and the female figure holds a drawing board as she glances at this very building over her shoulder. Facing west, there are panels over the side arches, the one on the south depicting art and the one on the north, mechanics. At the ceiling level, the central arch straight ahead has a moose head with eagles on either side, and the side arches have mountain goats. The animal life of this portal all seems to be American. The depicted occupations can all be loosely associated with the building of America.

Central Pavilion South

Portal keystone:	Moses, representing Law, and the word "JUSTICE" carved above
First-tier spandrels:	Left: Law, holding a scroll and sitting on a lion
	Right: Justice, holding scales, partly missing
Third tier, seated:	Left: Majesty of the Law, a bald, bearded, robed man with scroll
	Right: Liberty, a female with a staff with top missing, head wreath
Inside pediment:	Pennsylvania coat of arms
Dormer caryatid and telamon:	Male and Female Africans (south)
Dormer pediment group:	Africa: Camel, Egyptian (left), and black African (right)

Central Portal South

This is the Law portal. Many of the major courtrooms, including that of the State Supreme Court, are located on this side of the building. The rectangular panels on either side of the portal arch repeat the nature scenes that were introduced on the east and continued on the west. After passing through the portal, one enters a large room with round, fluted pilasters above the wainscot. The capitals are decorated with putti in various stances. The ceiling is vaulted and has a window to the third-floor corridor. The keystone to the north on the interior of the portal arch is blindfolded Justice, with scales shown above; on the south side, Moses appears again on the keystone. On the lower walls are found cats and mice. Commission chairman Perkins was a cat lover, and apparently Calder catered to his interest by producing this

array of rather aggressive felines. There seems to have been no iconographic meaning here, just something to indulge the boss. Some wags have suggested that the cats are the building commissioners and the mice are the city taxpayers. There is a second vestibule prior to reaching the courtyard, with lion and tigers, seemingly a reference to southern or tropical climes. The keystones have a buffalo facing an owl, which is equipped with a book and pendulum. This is likely a reference to wisdom, law, and judgment. Between the two vestibules and off the inner passage is the entrance to the grand staircase, which only serves the floors with courtrooms. The first-floor entrance is now locked, and you must enter on the second floor.

Central Pavilion West

Portal keystone:	Sympathy
First-tier spandrel:	The spandrels have highly formal decorations, with no apparent relationship to the prisoner theme
Second-tier spandrel:	Left: Admonition, a female figure instructing a child
	Right: Repentance, the prodigal son returning
Third tier, seated:	Left: Prayer, with clasped hands
	Right: Meditation, holding a book in one hand
Inside pediment:	Philadelphia coat of arms
Dormer caryatid and telamon:	Indians, male and female (west)
Dormer pediment group:	America; Buffalo, frontiersman in fur cap (left), and odd helmeted figure (symbolism unclear) with rope (right)

Central Portal West

This is the prisoners' or police portal. The accused originally entered here in paddy wagons and passed through these portals on the way to trial. The sculptural images by Calder presumed that most would be guilty and they should reflect on their crimes and shortcomings as they faced justice. Below the portal keystone of Sympathy, the flora panels on either side of the arch portray thorny plants. The corridors are gray stone. While all the portal passages now appear rather gray and dingy, originally this was not the case, so these somber walls were in marked contrast to the color on the other three. The inner keystone is Pain, shown as a grizzled man with a chain across his forehead. Threatening carnivore animal heads bare their teeth along the walls. The caryatids at the intersection with the interior passage have not been identified. Unlike the other portals, this is a straight passage without vestibules or augmented spaces. It is probably intentionally the most spartan portal. If you follow through into the inner courtyard, as the paddy wagons originally did, you will find two bronze doors at the base of the round projections on the south side. Note the surviving Justice image on one of them. These were the prisoners' entrances, and stairs inside lead to the seventh-floor holding cells. Today there are no criminal trials in this building.

Corner Pavilions

While the identification of the iconographic material on the central pavilions often left much room for speculation, the record is even sketchier on the corner pavilions. The subject matter portrayed includes both the abstract, such as Resolution, and the concrete, particularly professions and sectors of the economy. From a viewer's standpoint these latter are some of the

more interesting to look at. The face of each side of the corner pavilion seems to embrace a loose theme that begins with the object between the children playing on the tops of the dormer pediment. The theme continues on the second tier and includes the spandrels and the side imposts. These are particularly interesting, as Calder has used a device with which objects varying from fruit to locomotives dangle from ribbons hung on pegs, all carved in marble. The entry keystones are mainly abstract symbols, while most of the second-tier keystone heads appear to be portraits of real people. Whether these figures have something to do with the theme of the rest of the second tier is not known. The identity of the caryatid and telamon figures in the dormers remains largely a mystery. The children playing on top of the pediments, who often seem to be peeking down on us, indicate that Calder had a sense of humor. Here are some clues to the themes.

Northwest Corner Pavilion, West Side

Theme: Commerce and Industry. Atop the dormer, there appear to be kegs or pier pilings. The second-tier left spandrel has a figure with waterfront and sea transport objects. The left figure has a caduceus. The imposts have a welter of objects of trade, including livestock, textiles, and fruit.

First-tier keystone: Knowledge

Northwest Corner Pavilion, North Side

Theme: Mechanics. The hutlike structure atop the dormer may be a kiln. The left spandrel figure may be handling textiles, and the right one has a machine above it. The imposts portray saddlemaking, locomotives, steamships, textiles, pots, and casks.

First-tier keystone: Liberty.

Northeast Corner Pavilion, North Side

Theme: Navigation. There is a capstan with an anchor chain at the dormer roof. The left spandrel shows ship rigging, and the right is holding a sextant. Nautical items are suspended on the imposts, including ropes, bollards, and fish in a net.

First-tier keystone: Warrior head

Northeast Corner Pavilion, East Side

Theme:
War. The roof symbol is a mortar. The spandrel figures are not obviously associated with the theme. The left one holds a wreath (Victory?), and the right one has oak leaves. However, the impost objects are all military items, including sword, gun, shield, helmet, spear, canteen, and drum.

First-tier keystone:
Unknown.

Southeast Corner Pavilion, East Side

Theme:
Arts. The roof symbol appears to be a lyre. The spandrel figures with a wreath and torch are not clearly associated with the art theme. However, the imposts have masks, palettes, ceramics, and a Classical column (architecture).

First-tier keystone:
Chief.

Southeast Corner Pavilion, South Side

Theme:
Science (Chemistry and Astronomy?). The roof symbol is a globe, which may be showing the astronomer's sky. One spandrel figure has a telescope and the other a retort. The imposts have various images that appear to be scientific measuring instruments or other laboratory paraphernalia.

First-tier keystone:
Inca woman.

Southwest Corner Pavilion, South Side

Theme:
Horticulture. The roof symbol is a plant. The imposts show varieties of flora. One source suggests that the figures in the spandrels may represent the growing seasons.

First-tier keystones:
Resolution.

Southwest Corner Pavilion, West Side

Theme:
Mining? Starting at the top between the children, there are gears, perhaps a hoist. The imposts have ropes, hooks, anvils, plaster tools, buckets, hammers, and tool chests. One of the spandrel figures has a hand on an arch, which suggests that all of the above may be associated with building construction.

First-tier keystones:
Unknown.

INTERIOR

The City Hall is very much a courthouse, as it contains many courtrooms. However, no criminal trials are held here now. Those take place in the new Criminal Justice Center, which is discussed below. As a result, this is one of the few nineteenth-century courthouses in this guide that has no closed entrances in the name of security. Consequently, the circulation system remains much as McArthur intended, and he gave the subject great attention. There are fourteen exterior doors for the public, two at each of the four corners and two from each portal except at the north. Inside, wide corridors on each floor go completely around the building, servicing offices on both the outside and courtyard side. Vertical circulation is also ample, starting with the stunning octagonal stairs at each corner that go to the sixth floor, special elaborate southern stairs that exclusively serve the two-story courtrooms, and two sets of iron stairs in the southern end that go from the second to the seventh floor. These are the public stairways, but numerous others connect multistory suites for employees. There are four banks of elevators that were original to the building. Only the southern stairs no longer function as they were designed.

The main building has seven floors, including the basement, which is aboveground with additional stories in the four central pavilions. The best way to see the interior highlights is to take the official guided tour, which starts in the Tour Office on the East Portal passage. In fact, some of the most impressive rooms can be seen only by joining the tour. These include the mayor's office, mayor's reception room, conversational hall, the astounding city council caucus room and chambers, as well as the State Supreme Court courtroom. The tour ends with a trip to the tower. The tower opportunity is also afforded to nontour persons as space permits. Free tickets are distributed at the Tour Office.

For those with the time and interest, here is a floor-by-floor tour of some of the other things to observe. The best place to start is on either the northeast or northwest corner. Here you will be at the base of one of the freestanding octagonal stairs, with their massive granite newel posts. It is freestanding in that it is unrelated to the exterior walls and their fenestration. The color of the granite differs on the north and south sides. Some of the original lamps on the newel posts survive. As you walk south along broad, granite-lined corridors, notice the thickness of the walls at the office doors. Because of the projecting central pavilions, the rooms on the outer side of the corridor are not all the same size, being deeper near the portal. Here is where the courtrooms, legislative halls, and other large public spaces are located. On the south corridor, two interior light wells bring natural light and ventilation to the additional offices and rooms on that side of the building. Originally, the boiler plants were located at the bottom of these wells.

On the second-floor corridor, windows at the east, south, and west portals allow you to examine the iconographic figures in the passageways more closely. The courtrooms begin on the second floor, and among those of architectural interest are 243 and 253, both located on the south side. Room 243 has more of the original furnishings. Note how well lighted these courtrooms are, as they are positioned between the portal and the light well. These and other older courtrooms in this building have an interesting division of space that employs two bars. The first is a paneled bar with bead and reel decoration that is actually the back of a long bench dividing the audience from the lawyers' area. A second balustraded bar separates the lawyers from the clerks and the witness. This is the way McArthur addressed the problems that plagued the courtroom at Congress Hall.

You can enter the monumental south courtroom stairs from this floor. This unique stairway serves only the courtroom floors, and its embellishments stress the significance of the functions that those mounting these steps would attend. The decorations are classically derived, particularly the moldings, such as echinus and astragal, which is in keeping with the "temple of justice" tradition in America. Ramped arches with bas-relief work in triangular panels support the stair flights. The first two panels show cherubs reading and a group playing marbles next to a high-wheeled bicycle. The stairwell keystones are supposed to represent the ages of man according to Faust, but one of the ages appears to be missing. Perhaps it was intended for the eagle keystone. Stone flora and fauna are abundant, with ferrets and owls among the former. On one of the upper landings you will find a memorial for McArthur, who died in 1890 before the building was completed. Its rendering is totally in keeping with the style of his building. This great stairway is now little used, as the general public no longer throngs to the trials here.

On the north side of the building, the magnificent Conversation Hall is usually, but not always, locked (always open to tours). This remarkable room was closed and turned into small offices for decades but was restored in 1983 (Hyman Myer, architect). At the time City Hall was constructed, Philadelphia had a bicameral city legislature (a common practice of the time), the chambers being called the Common Council and the Select Council. This room was intended for informal "conversations" between members of the two chambers, with the intention of facilitating cross-chamber communication. However, the legislative bodies elected to occupy the fourth floor instead, so it never fulfilled its purpose. Originally the room was five and a half stories high, eighty-six feet, but a structural flaw emerged, necessitating the installation of braces, which cut its height. The balcony allows you to examine the north portal. Details about this room are covered on the public tour. The city maintains an Art in City Hall program, and some of the display cases are outside the mayor's office.

The third-floor provides access to offices in the places not taken up by two-story courtrooms. On the south and west sides, you can have a final peek at the portal decor. Note the tiled interior passageways toward the south end of the east and west corridors. These give you a chance to look at the old iron stairs. Many of the tiled walls in the building have been over-painted, but not here. These are American tiles, and it interesting to see the patterns change on the upper floors, reflecting different suppliers. Most of these hall tiles are from New Jersey, the primary sources being Providential Tile Works, Trent Tile Company, and Old Bridge Tile Company.

The fourth floor again has two-story spaces. To the south are newly re-decorated courtrooms, including the Supreme Court on the outside (note the special doorknobs) and rooms 443 and 453 on the inside. The courtrooms are not quite as impressive as those on the second floor, though still attractive. On the north corridor around the council area, beyond the iron gate, there is more Art in City Hall and a chance to see what the corridor ceilings were like before they were dropped. The present city council room (room 400) was occupied by the Common Council up until 1920, when the city legislature was changed to a unicameral body. Room 402, which is now occupied by the clerk, was the former Select Council room. Its ornamentation seems out of place with its current use, as does room 496, which was originally the Joint Finance Committee room. During the bicameral period, this was the power center of city government and the room was decorated befitting its importance.

The fifth floor has tile wainscoting rather than granite. The octagonal stairs terminate on the sixth floor. Take a peek through the door of the newly renovated Law Library on the north corridor (room 600). On the south corridor, there are more interesting courtrooms (on the outside). The rooms are less showy as one moves up the building, becoming more marred by water streaks nearer to the roof. Above this, you are on your own.

OUTSIDE PLAZAS

This section covers the space outside of City Hall, including the surrounding square; Dilworth Plaza; Thomas Paine Plaza, around the Municipal Services building; and a few noteworthy items just beyond. On three sides of the City Hall are memorial sculptures that date from late nineteenth and early twentieth centuries. These are as follows:

William McKinley (1908), by Charles Albert Lopez and Isidore Konti (South Plaza). The assassination of McKinley evoked a national emotional response very similar to that for John Kennedy. As a consequence, a greater number of memorials were erected to him compared with other presidents of the time. Mexican-born Lopez won the competition, but he died before the work was completed, and it had to be finished by Konti.

John Wanamaker (1923), by John Massey Rhind (East Plaza). This statue, contributed by the Wanamaker family, is fittingly located across from his famous store. Rhind, who was Scottish, worked largely in Great Britain.

Gen. John Fulton Reynolds (1884), by John Roger (North Plaza). Reynolds, who lost his life in the Battle of Gettysburg, is depicted here leading in battle, his horse startled and frightened by the din, while the mounted general points the direction for the attack. Rogers was a renowned creator of small literary figures called Rogers Groups. They were reproduced by the thousands, being highly popular among Victorians. He was "loath to undertake a work of such magnitude" but was pressed in a "complimentary and emphatic manner" by the statue's sponsors.

Gen. George McClellan (1884), by Henry Jackson Ellicott (North Plaza). The statue was a gift of the GAR. Ellicott also did the statue of General Hancock in Washington.

Matthias William Baldwin (1905), by Henry Adams (North Plaza). Baldwin was the famous founder of the locomotive works that bore his name and supplied employment for many Philadelphians over many years. The monument, which was financed by the company, originally stood at Broad Street and Spring Garden Street before being moved here in 1921.

John Christian Bullitt (1907), by John J. Boyle (North Plaza).

Dilworth Plaza, to the west, is actually an enlargement of the original Penn Square. It was added to compensate for the loss of open space resulting from the construction of the Municipal Service Building on a previously empty square to the north. Dilworth Plaza was designed by Vincent G. Kling and Partners of Philadelphia and was completed in 1978. Philadelphia has an ordinance that requires 1 percent of the cost of buildings in the downtown to be devoted to the arts. The results of this ordinance are apparent all around City Hall. The sculpture to the north end of the sunken level of Dilworth Plaza is called *Phoenix Rising*, a rendering by local artist Emlen Etting in aluminum with a baked-enamel coating. To the west across the street from the plaza are three sculptures by prominent artists. Claes Oldenberg's *Clothespin* can hardly be missed. Robert Engman's looping *Triune* is on a traffic island to the left. A half block down Market Street on the left side you will find *Milord La Chamasse,* by Jean Dubuffet, tucked into a small building set back.

Across the street to the north, on the Thomas Paine Plaza, where the Municipal Service Building (1964, Vincent Kling, architect) is located, sculptures include *Government of the People,* by Jacques Lipchitz, which former mayor Frank Rizzo said looked like a plasterer dropping his load, and a bigger-than-life statue of Rizzo himself (Zenos Foudabis, sculptor). Scattered throughout the plaza are large game-board models, collectively called *Your Move,* by three California sculptors, Daniel J. Mantinez, Renee Petropoulos, and Roger F. White. At the edge of the plaza on Broad Street is *Benjamin Franklin, Craftsman,* portraying him printing, by Joseon Brown. To the west of the Thomas Paine Plaza is John F. Kennedy Plaza, designed by Vincent Kling in 1967. Here is located the Robert Indiana *LOVE* sculpture, the Samuels Fountain (after its benefactor), and the 1960 round glass visitors center (Harbeson, Hough, Livingston, and Larsen, architects). The last city office building in this direction is fronted by a rotating whimsical statue called *Philadelphia Firsts,* by George Greenamyer (1999).

The old City Hall annex, to the northeast of the building, has been converted to a Marriott Courtyard Hotel, but note its public building origins in the lobby and arcade on the north side. Across from the arcade is a modern courthouse that is worthy of attention. The Criminal Justice Center (Vitteta Associates, architects) is a building that is likely to retain lasting interest to visitors. It is in the Postmodern style and features many Classical motifs, such as columns. It is a well-secured building and adheres to the modern courthouse principle of keeping the public, prisoners, and court personnel separated. It's a handsome building and is decorated throughout. A brochure describing them is sometimes available at the information desk. The following is an abbreviated account. Phil Simkin's *Philadra Books of Just Hours,* at the southwest entrance, shows a whimsical scene of law books and legal images, including a bronze lectern designed after the crack in the Liberty Bell. The front stained-glass window is a complex, even mystical design called *Five Orders,* by John Biers, symbolizing rational orders of man and the universe: classical, legal, natural, justice, and artistic. The main lobby floor is strewn with 450 bronze symbols of justice from many cultures and tree parts suggested by the street names in the area (Michele Oka Doner, *Lexicon: Justice*). Pass through security, and there is a huge mural depicting the city from the vantage point of the Schuylkill River as it winds its way through the city (Douglas Cooper, artist). Decorative wall tiles by Neferiti are on the first- and second-floor walls, and Ming Fay's identical aluminum sculptures entitled *Spiral Ear* are over the escalators leading to the mezzanine. From the fourth to the eleventh floor, the halls are lined with stone benches featuring *Word Landscapes,* by Nancy Dwyer. On the seventh, ninth, and eleventh floors, the public areas overlooking the atria south of the elevator hall have terrazzo floor works by Cynthia Carlson based on historic map views of the city. On the thirteenth floor, secure the guard's permission to see the Erik Furubotn wall sculptures *Quadra* and *Triad* and two paper works at the ends of the corridors by Neferiti.

Finally there is the Eagle. In the old John Wanamaker store, now Lord and Taylor's, just across the street to the southeast from City Hall, is a bronze statue of an eagle by August Gaul (1904). It has been the traditional meeting place throughout the decades for Philadelphians. The bird was made for the St. Louis Exposition of 1904 by a German using a process in which each of the five thousand feathers were separately cast and then assembled by hand, a task that took five months. It was purchased by Wanamaker at the end of the fair.

Congress Hall, at Sixth Street and Chestnut Street, was originally built as the Philadelphia County Courthouse. At the time of its construction in 1789, there were Pennsylvanians who had an eye toward using the building to lure the new U.S. government to Philadelphia, some hoping the city would become the nation's permanent capital. There were skeptics who thought that the swampy land along the Potomac was not viable as a capital site. The Federal (or Georgian) style building may have been built a little grander for just this purpose. The ploy initially succeeded, and in 1793, the building was hastily enlarged to accommodate the House of Representatives, which had grown in numbers after the 1790 census. Of course, the nation's capital did move to the Potomac in less than a decade, and the state had a vacant building, which after a few years was sold to Philadelphia for $70,000 to again become the county courthouse (1800–90).

This is the only genuinely Federal style courthouse that survives in the state. Its front facade is virtually unchanged since its first inception. It is a two-and-a-half-story brick building with marble trim, five bays across the front. The first-floor windows have round tops, and the entrance is within an arch with a fan light above the door. The tower is similar to that of Independence Hall and the old City Hall. The 1793 enlargement (twenty-seven feet, seven inches) was to the rear and recreated the octagonal projection that was on the original structure.

The building is now part of Independence Park and is administered by the Park Service. It is open daily. After Philadelphia moved its offices to City Hall, the historic importance of the building prompted both preservation and reconstruction efforts. It was here that Washington was inaugurated for his second term and later gave his final speech to Congress (not the Farewell Address). Adams was inaugurated in this building, and it was the place where many significant decisions were made by the new nation. Because the early national events were deemed the most significant associations with the building, the next move was to rip out the vestiges of county occupancy and restore the look of the 1790s. However, let us look at the building as a county courthouse.

Most of what you see on the first floor, including the balcony, was removed by the county when it resumed use of the building. The room was bisected by a hallway that ran from east to west, and a west-side exterior doorway was cut through about where the speaker chair now stands. This created two courtrooms. We do not know how they were configured in terms of the location of the bench. There were no auxiliary facilities on this floor until a small judges' "retiring room" was added on the rear (since removed). In 1867, an adjacent building was constructed to add more courtrooms, but it was demolished after the move to City Hall. Until that time, these two courtrooms served all of Philadelphia. This gives you some idea of the enormous expansion of space constructed by the Perkins-McArthur team.

The double-front stairs existed in the original building. The lofty ceiling of the first-floor room made this a long climb to the second story, where the row offices and a small courtroom were located until 1793. These uses may have justified the high-volume double stairs, but they also may have been constructed in anticipation of housing the U.S. Senate. The height of these stairs may have been one factor leading later architects to place courtrooms on the second floor. But this building also supplied a second reason for doing this. The original 1789 downstairs county courtroom space was interrupted by four pillars that supported the partitioned second floor. In the 1793 enlargement, an effort was made to create an unimpeded space for the House of Representatives. Two pillars were removed and replaced by a trussing arrangement. It failed, and the Senate chamber began to sag into the room below. Bearing interior walls that divide offices on the first floor make it easier to support the monumental space on the second floor.

PIKE
County Seat: Milford

The county is named for Zebulon Pike, the explorer and soldier for whom Pikes Peak is named, who died in battle at Toronto a year before this county was formed. Milford was the creation in 1793 of John Biddis, who named the town after a place in England. Biddis was one of the original judges under Pennsylvania's first constitution, and in the course of his duties, he acquired land here, which he donated for the seat when Wayne County was formed. Milford was sporadically the seat of Wayne over the next decade or so, but the issue was not really settled until Pike County was split off from Wayne in 1814. The town was laid out on the Philadelphia plan, including the reservation of squares designated for public purposes. As the town did not grow enough to fill out the plan, there are few reminders of its origin except several Philadelphia street names, including Broad and High (the original Philadelphia Market Street name), and the public spaces, which now accommodate county buildings and the small parks, one of which (across from the courthouse) contains a monument to Biddis.

There are actually several courthouses along the west side of Broad to the north of the main intersection. The old stone one, now a jail, dates from 1815 and shows off the stone mason's skills using local materials. The red brick 1873 structure (George Barton, architect) with the tower has been sup-

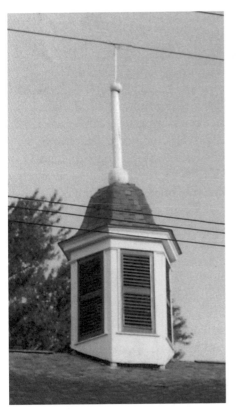

plemented by a modern 1985 administration building (L. Robert Kimball, architect). Finally, there is a 1995 addition. Our principal interest is with the Victorian courthouse, a rectangular structure that is eight bays by six bays. In addition to the tower, its principle exterior features are a mansard roof pierced by a Palladian window, a rather unusual combination, and a bracketed cornice. The wooden roof crests have long since disappeared, but a picture just inside the front door shows how they once looked. Inside, the principle matter of interest is the second-floor courtroom, which retains original elements, primarily the area beyond the rail. A recent renovation had to conform to the requirements of the federal disabilities act, and so the banked audience area, a common feature of courthouses of this era, was replaced. The tin ceilings throughout the courthouse are modern copies of what was probably the second interior redecoration.

It is for good reason that nineteenth-century courthouses had bell towers. The 1815 Pike County courthouse (the stone building occupied by the sheriff) was built without one, and the sheriff climbed to the roof and blew blasts on a large horn to assemble court officials. That proved unsatisfactory, and the horn was replaced by a huge iron triangle, a second unsuccessful experiment. The county commissioners finally had to accept the more expensive solution, a bell. When the 1873 courthouse was built, the bell was moved to it.

Note the prominent inn across from the courthouse, named for Tom Quick, an Indian fighter who claimed he had killed ninety-nine Indians (men, women, and children) during his lifetime and begged on his deathbed to have one more produced so he could make it an even hundred. After the Walking Purchase, this part of the state witnessed great fighting between whites and Indians, and Quick's father was killed in his presence by an Indian. His one-man, stealthy genocide campaign has produced numerous accounts of the killings, most of which strain credulity. There is also a local memorial to him.

POTTER
County Seat: Coudersport

This county, created in 1804, was supposed to have been named Sinnemahoning, but a state senator from nearby Centre County saw an opportunity to memorialize one of his own and amended the bill to recognize Irish-born Revolutionary War major general James Potter. The county seat is named for Amsterdam banker Jean Samuel Couderc, whose organization represented French investors in the Ceres Land Company, the original landowner of most of this county.

The courthouse occupies a full square and is an antebellum one, judging by its windows, but from the cornice up, it changes to a later style. The core of the building comes from a simple, 1835 gable-roofed structure built by a local contractor. No architect was associated with its design, and it had no Classical portico, as was the style of the time. It had a low, sloping wooden-shingled roof, which proved to be inadequate for winters in this snowy area. Snow piled on the roof, and its many leaks spoiled the interior and rotted the load-bearing pine cross beams. In 1888, the commissioners hired Homer Hall to remedy the problem. He recom-

mended a steeply pitched slate roof, which would be more durable and would withstand the rigors of the cold and snow. The interior, courtroom, roof, gable ends (dated on the front), and tower are all Hall's work. It is now a two-and-a-half-story brick (painted) building, five bays wide and six deep. The rectangular windows date from the 1835 structure. The newer Hall top includes the side gables, cornice bracketing on both the side and front gables, and triple arched windows that have peaked voussoirs. Hall probably added the quoins, as they are part of the Italianate package. Hall's tower rests on a truncated pyramid that supports a square tier with triple arched louvers on each side and a prominent cornice, heavily bracketed. Above this

is a square clock-face tier, which also has a cornice with bracketing. The four-sided convex cap has small dormers and supports a platform previously the abode of Lady Justice. (When last visited, the statue was out for restoration and destined for a lobby resting place out of the weather. When she is back, there should be information about her construction and provenance.) In the 1930s, the WPA dug a basement to increase the amount of office space.

The wainscoting that is found throughout the interior was sawed from the hand-hewn oak joists and sills salvaged at the time of the 1888 renovation. Unlike the rotted pine ones, they were solid, so they were put to good use. The oak wood, which is over 160 years old, has been recently refinished and looks in fine shape.

The first floor has a center hall, and the office openings, hardware, and transoms appear to date from 1888. Most of the office furniture is modern, except for a fine old counter in the prothonotary's office. The channel in the stairwell at one time contained the clock weights. The courtroom is still in its 1888 place and remains much intact except for an office that was unfortunately rudely carved out of its left side. Note the multiwood benches, also recently refinished.

The shaded courthouse yard has several memorials, including one for Zeisberger (plaque) and one for the Civil War veterans. The base of the latter was erected in 1876, but it looked unfinished to some. Money was raised to buy a statue of a soldier, which seems to stand rather precariously on its adopted base. The post office has a modest plaster WPA relief by Ernest Lohrmann, entitled *Lumbering in Potter County, 1815–1920*. The county historical society museum is next to the courthouse.

SCHUYLKILL
County Seat: Pottsville

Schuylkill (skoo' kl), established in 1811, is one of the few counties in America with a Dutch name, after the river that flows through it. The translation is "hidden river," and the explanation for the name varies; some say the Dutch missed the mouth on first passing, and others that they could not locate the source. Two dominant associations with the county are anthracite coal and John O'Hara. In his *Appointment in Samarra*, O'Hara states, "Anyone in Gibbsville [Pottsville] who had any important money made it in coal, anthracite." John Potts laid out the town in 1816.

Pottsville, the county seat since 1847, lies in a valley where the business district occupies one of the few relatively level spaces and the residential areas march up steep hills, a characteristic of eastern coal region towns in general. There were few mines immediately around Pottsville, but as O'Hara points out, that is where those who profited from coal lived, and thus a saunter through the old residential streets (particularly Mahantongo) is a treat.

The courthouse is removed a short distance from the downtown, but you should have no trouble finding its square tower looming over the center from its higher perch on Laurel Street. It is basically a Romanesque Re-

vival (1892) structure, but with Eclectic tendencies, designed by M. E. Beebe, whose earlier buildings of a different style are in Cambria, Huntington, and Warren Counties. This one is built of yellow Ohio (Cleveland) sandstone, five stories high (including basement), with a southern facade that is divided into five vertical sections. There is a prominent central pavilion that is brought forward in two steps, two identical outer sections also brought forward, and two intervening sections that recede. The middle and outer sections all have large arches on the first story. The arches on the outer sections enclose multiple-paned windows, and the central one also embraces a basement-level front entrance. The outer arches rest on small, short pilasters with carved capitals, and the central arch has a carved course at its springline. There are arcades of three to four windows on each section, but at differing levels. Most of the windows are replacements, but the old stained-glass arched portions have been retained. Turrets occur on six angles, beginning at the second story, while the forward part of the central sections has pairs of pilasters at the second and third story. The central section has a pair of porthole windows on the fourth story, and there is an arched dormer over the intermediate recessed sections. Horizontal lines include a water table and belt courses separating the upper floors. The decorative elements in white from the cornice upward are plastic replacements of the original metal, a fact made more apparent if you examine them with a glass. It all works well from a distance, but it is a bit disappointing on close examination. While this is a Romanesque building, it retains the mansard roof, seemingly a fixture of Beebe's buildings.

The tower rises out of the larger center mansard. Its first principle tier has triple rectangular windows on each side, piers with shell caps at the corners, a denticulated cornice, and a swag-decorated panel above. The clock-face tier has an applied balustrade at its base and pilasters on either side. The roof is pyramidal. While Beebe had trouble with towers on some of his buildings (see Cambria and Huntington Counties), evidently he learned from experience, as this one has endured. The east end of the building has essentially the same grammar as the front, but with rearranged elements, and the north side is the same as the south, except for the lower central section. There are two additions to the west: a 1931 administration building annex (Eric Fisher Wood, architect) and a modern addition that comes down to street level.

The interior has been substantially altered, but there are still things worth seeing. After entering through security, find your way to the original front entrance. Here you will see the red oak wainscoting topped by rosette molding, which once decorated much of the building. At the east end of the first floor, there are surviving original decorative iron stairs that take you to courtroom

1. The original decor features a massive Classical portico behind the judge's bench, wooden rosettes over doors and around a clock, a skylight, wainscoting, stenciling, and a mural across the front. During recent renovations, a similar courtroom was eliminated, but some of its decorative elements were salvaged. Its skylight and a portion of an old bench is in the commissioners room, and a large rosette is in courtroom 7. Just inside the north (closed) entrance, there is a tunnelike old stairwell with its original paneling on one side. It leads to the law library's skylit, marble-floored foyer. The law library, which can also be reached by elevator, is a step back in history. Courtroom 5, in the 1931 annex, features materials in vogue of

that time, such as travertine walls and aluminum detailing, including the rail.

In the 1989 renovations, a number of old paintings were found in the attic and restored. They include ones of early courthouses, now on view in the halls, and a great primitive of the county almshouse that hangs in the commissioner's room (often closed to the public). The painter allegedly was

Schuylkill County jail.

a local alcoholic who was occasionally institutionalized. He did several versions of this scene, and they are much sought after when they come on the market.

The medieval-looking jail with the tower and forbidding crenellated battlements was the design of choice in Pennsylvania during this period. Its door seems to state that it will secure forever those who must pass through its portals. It was designed by LeBrun and built in 1851 along the lines of the Philadelphia Eastern Penitentiary. Some Molly Maguires were jailed here and hung in the 1870s. The "troubles" had continued for over a decade, and the accused were convicted of murder on testimony of a Pinkerton detective who had penetrated the ranks of this "secret" society. Today, beyond the preserved facade is actually a very modern prison facility.

The most interesting political monument in Pottsville is outside the area normally covered in this guide, but it fits the political art theme so well that it is included. In a hillside park at the other end of the business district, away from the courthouse, is an iron statue of Henry Clay of Kentucky, now painted a ghostly white. When Clay died in 1851, local citizens immediately started raising funds for this memorial and had laid the cornerstone within a month. The statue, mounted on a massive iron column, was erected within a few years. Why this local interest in a politician from Kentucky? He had successfully championed the cause of a steep protective tariff on imported iron and coal.

SNYDER
County Seat: Middleburg

Simon Snyder served three three-year terms as governor (1808–17). He was from this area and was the first governor of German descent. Snyder rose from the ranks of the working class and in politics identified with the struggles of the small farmers and artisans. He was in the political faction opposite that of McKean (see McKean County), losing to him in one gubernatorial race prior to his first success in 1808. In 1855, the new county was to be named after the buffalo, but as so often happened, a name switch took place in committee. Middleburg is named for the Dutch city, the place of origin for a number of the settlers who came here.

Middleburg is a very modest-sized county seat with a modest courthouse. Arguably, it is the original courthouse, but nothing original shows. The core of the present building dates from 1855, but it was enlarged in the front by twelve feet and in the rear by twenty-seven feet in 1867. The commissioners personally supervised this expansion, letting contracts to the various artisans, such as masons and carpenters. It was essentially rebuilt in 1915, at which time the main building received its present look (J. F. Stetler, architect). Prior

to Stetler's changes, the front steps led to the second floor and directly to the courtroom. Stetler removed these steps and added the present front section to the building, which places the front entrance on the first floor through the double arches. He added internal stairs to the new rebuilt second-story courtroom. The result is that the courthouse gained this rather awkward, high-pocketed look with the Ionic columns beginning at the second floor above the flat, rusticated front of the first floor. All three versions of the courthouse have had a bell tower with the same bell (524 pounds, manufactured in Troy, New York). The present tower is a rather straightforward one. The square belfry tier has an arched louver opening and two pairs of plain,

Snyder County jail.

square pilasters on each side; the clock-face tier repeats the same styling, but with a bracketed cornice; and the roof cap is topped by a finial and weather-vane. Alfred Shrock, a local businessman and former representative, presented the 1915 rebuilt courthouse with the clock. In 1977, when the latest addition was built (L. Robert Kimball and Associates, architects), the old building interior was modernized, including the courtroom. Exterior details were added to make the addition blend with the Stetler building.

The old stone jail is around the corner. The brick building directly across the street was once the Central Hotel. The Civil War monument is on the next block, and the county historical society and museum occupies the old Lutheran church across from it.

SOMERSET
County Seat: Somerset

Somerset County (after the English county) was created in 1795 in what is historically coal country, and coal helped build a sumptuous courthouse (still heated by coal) in this small county seat. Somerset has the highest elevation of all the county seats in the state.

The courthouse, the county's third on this site, can be clearly seen on a hilltop high above the clutter around the turnpike entrance below. It is instructive to know that this gem was built despite significant opposition at the time. No less than five thousand citizens signed a petition opposing its construction, yet the county commissioners persevered, and Somerset today benefits from their persistence.

Constructed in 1905, this Beaux-Arts building (J. C. Fuller of nearby Uniontown, architect) is a fine example of this highly decorative style. It was inspired in part by St. Paul's Cathedral in London. The exterior is of Indiana limestone resting on a foundation of local sandstone, with terra-cotta adornments and crowned with a copper dome. There are nine bays across the south front, with the central five bays extended forward and the three central bays fronted by a circular Corinthian portico with a balustrade above. On the second floor are fifteen rectangular and two garland-surrounded circular windows. The rhythm of the first-floor window styles differs from bay to bay. The outer pair of bays have simple lintels with consoles; the next pair have segmental arches supported by consoles; the next have pediments; and the central bay's window has an ornamented broken segmental arch. The building's west side has similar overall treatment but with a rectangular instead of circular portico. The decorative dome rests on a round base with four pedimented pavilions. The weathervane was purchased with contributions made by sidewalk superintendents who watched the building go up. Note that the clock is really not part of the architectural design and is an

add-on. It chimes with the bells transferred from its predecessor 1854 structure. There has been a maintenance problem with the roof, resulting from people shooting the roosting pigeons with rifles.

Inside, the rotunda features a massive marble staircase with bronze-plated iron balustrades. The walls have marble wainscoting (first floor Italian, second Georgian), and the hall ceiling features decorative coffering and consoles. The basic design of the rotunda consists of columns supporting four main arches, with three decorative arches within each. The skylight has imbricated leaded glass in its central portion. In 1962, a misguided state inspector claimed the staircase failed to meet the fire code, and the county commissioners were dutifully going to tear it out until a citizen took them to court. The local fire chief testified that a fire could not be started on those stairs with "a blowtorch and a barrel of gasoline!" The judge ordered the stairs to stay.

The two original courtrooms are decorated in a style consistent with the rest of the building. The windows incorporate attractive designs in yellow glass, a color that transmits light well. The north courtroom has five large, rectangular windows and a skylight. The south courtroom has the two circular windows so prominently featured on the exterior. The north courtroom has an elaborate pediment supported by pairs of slender columns behind the bench, while the south one is a little less imposing. Both have coffered ceilings (somewhat altered) and massive rails with tablelike tops, one oak, the other walnut. When I first visited this building, a custodian proudly proclaimed that the building was "superior to the Maine capitol."

Next door is the 1856 sheriff's residence, backed by an 1890 jail, which proudly featured a double, built-in trapdoor hanging arrangement enabling two persons to be hanged simultaneously. The double device was used twice, and on both occasions convicted brothers were executed. Single executions took place three times. The buildings are now used for offices, and if the building's staff is not too busy, they will show you around. The post office across the street has a WPA mural by Alexander J. Kostellow, portraying a county farm scene. It shows a very fecund farm family, and all the gender roles are properly portrayed to fit the WPA mural policy of never ruffling any local feathers. While the artist had some difficulty with his human figures, he did capture the rolling hills of Somerset County.

SULLIVAN
County Seat: Laporte

Gen. John Sullivan, for whom this county is named, is one of the more controversial Revolutionary War heroes. He led the Big March, which avenged the Wyoming massacre. The expedition was a wartime response to public opinion, as its military merits were questionable. Sullivan demanded more troops than Washington thought necessary (Washington was right) and made a big thing of the expedition. In the critical Battle of Newtown (near Elmira, New York), Sullivan's command greatly outnumbered the Tories and Indians, who fled after about a half hour of artillery bombardment. After that victory, Sullivan failed to carry out Washington's orders to capture Niagara, but instead destroyed the numerous fields of Indian foodstuffs, a vengeful sentence of starvation for the Indian in retaliation for their massacre and torture of Wyoming Valley residents. Sullivan was also criticized for making prisoners of the peaceful Mohawks, who

were neutrals, thus stimulating another round of Indian vengeance raids on the frontier. However, his was a popular action at the time. One result of the expedition was probably to advertise the fertility of the land in western New York and stimulate postwar migration to that area.

Sullivan County, set up in 1847, is primarily a recreational area today, indeed, as it has nearly always been. Perhaps that is why Laporte is the smallest county seat in the state and is a town without the usual commercial strip. The town was laid out with an ambitious plan that has not been realized and now has an open, incomplete appearance. The red brick Romanesque courthouse was built in 1894 (Wagner and Reitmeyer of Williamsport, architects). It is a seemingly simple structure, but closer observation has its rewards. Its asymmetry reflects the fact that it originally incorporated the sheriff's house and jail (usually built separately by this date). The sheriff's section was in the hexagonal left side. On the left, the building has a residential appearance. The jail portion to the rear has been removed and partly replaced by a small, architecturally discordant addition, which contains holding cells. The courthouse roof is a very complex surface, being basically a hip roof with many projecting dormers and gables, one of the later over the front entrance. The window designs are key elements in the decorative style, being arched with brick voussoirs and stone accents set at the spring line. There is a round transom over the front door and another large, multipaned window above. Here, the stone accent is at the keystone point. The front gable is flanked by turrets, with stone corbeling. The front facade design is repeated, slightly scaled down on the west side and originally also on the north, where the modern addition is now attached. The lower part of the corner square tower has the same window treatment as the main building. Above, there are louvered openings, a double cornice, and four turrets at the corners of the roof, which is topped by a nonrepresentational weathervane. The black stripes are painted copper. Copper should not be painted, so these lines are not part of any intentional design. The new addition (Crabtree, Rohrbaugh and Associates, architects) is a sensitive effort to blend in with the older structure.

Most of the interior was modernized when the addition was added. However, the second-floor courtroom still occupies its original space and retains the simple wood wainscot, which was once used extensively throughout the building. The plain bench, rail, doors, jury box, and audience seating are all original, as are, probably, the iron theater seats. Downstairs, there are two large taxidermy displays of local fauna.

The 1884 building to the rear was constructed as a temporary courthouse for use while the present one was being built. The fact that this small building met all the county office needs for nearly a decade may have contributed to a public concern that the 1894 building was too ambitious. The "temporary" courthouse was subsequently occupied by a bank, then law offices, before being taken over by the historical society in 1960. It has since been enlarged. The park across from the courthouse was donated for public use at the time Laporte became the county seat. It has no name.

SUSQUEHANNA
County Seat: Montrose

The Susquehanna River enters the state in this county, and the county, created in 1810, is named for it.

The Greek Revival brick courthouse (1854) in Montrose is one of the few surviving Pennsylvania antebellum "temples of justice." A number of local names are associated with its design and construction, William H. Boyd and Avery Frink being the most prominent. It is picturesquely sited at the end of the short main street (Public Street). The facade is five bays wide, the outer ones having blind windows. Prominent across the front are six Ionic columns and a pediment over a first-story arcade. Square pilasters, slightly corbeled, divide the bays on both front and sides. The tower, which is a nineteenth-century replica of the original one destroyed by fire, has a square base, with the main tier asymmetrically octagonal. There are louvered openings below the clock faces and stylized acanthus decorations above them. The roof

cap has a finial. There are ten bays on the sides; the rear three (with pediment) are part of a well-matched 1883 addition. This seamlessness may be explained by the fact that some of the original contractors, including Boyd, built the addition. The long foundation stones are locally quarried, as are the windowsills and lintels. The surviving chimney tops are corbeled. There have been several small twentieth-century additions to the rear and a 1950–54 set of additions to the north. The original 1867 stone jail to the rear (built by Avery Frink) has now been connected to the courthouse by a modern glass corridor. A former school built in 1925, which now houses county offices, has also been attached to the rear. The courthouse was painted white throughout much of this century and was cleaned to the brick in 1993.

The major interest inside is the fine old courtroom, which is reached by going up one of the 1937 replacement stairs in the front of the building. It is a lofty twenty-four-foot-high room with ornamental beams across the ceiling. White Ionic columns supporting an entablature rise behind the judge's bench. There is a carved oak rail, painted church benches for the audience, and a balcony. Novel features of the balcony are the two five-foot-wide extensions reaching to the front of the room, bisecting the side windows. Additional seating capacity was obviously an issue in the nineteenth century. The portrait behind the bench is of Galusha A. Grow (see below), and the two murals were painted by the Andrews Company in 1920, when they were hired to redecorate the building. They depict the first courthouse and a train crossing the Erie Railroad Starucca Viaduct, located in the county. The room is marred by an office that has been built into the courtroom space. There is a glass case of courthouse and jail memorabilia in the downstairs hallway.

The New England origins of the town are indicated by the presence of an open green beside the courthouse, although the green is not surrounded by the major community buildings, particularly churches, as would have been the case in New England. The only other public buildings on the green are a modern post office and a 1907 library (with Palladian window), which houses the county historical society library and museum. The green is called Monument Park, for obvious reasons. The largest monument is an 1887 Civil War edifice built of native stone. It is unclear why this was deemed insufficient, but a second smaller one was erected in 1936. The more interesting memorial is for Galusha Grow, a congressman from the area who was the author of the Homestead Act of 1862. The plaque is largely self-explanatory, but it does not explain how Grow achieved this accomplishment. Grow, at the age of thirty-seven, suddenly became speaker of the U.S. House of Representatives when the Southerners walked out at the beginning of the Civil War. He seized the opportunity to push through the Homestead Act, carrying out his wish for "free land for free men." Grow was a rough-and-ready, truly indigenous, independent-minded product of the land who did not harness well in the highly organized Republican party. As a result, the party quickly ended his congressional career. Late in life, he did slip back into Congress because Boss Quay was away on an extended tarpon-fishing trip, and he served briefly, a rustic throwback among the industrial deal makers of the nineties. An elm tree was brought from one of the first homesteads in Beatrice, Nebraska, and planted to shade the memorial. It finally succumbed to Dutch elm disease and was replaced in 1973 by a green ash taken from the Nebraska National Homestead Monument.

The 1867 jail and sheriff's house, built of the familiar native stone by Avery Frink, is beyond the park, across Prospect Street. It has a massive,

Susquehanna County jail.

twenty-foot, circular wall, which encloses the jail yard, a former site of county hanginigs. While the building was under construction, the jail was enlarged, resulting in the brick section with its interesting and varied fenestration. Above is a metal-clad tower with a crenellated wood cornice.

TIOGA

County Seat: Wellsboro

The county name is after the Tioga River and is of Indian origin. Tioga county was created in 1804. The seat, which was laid out in 1806, was named for William Hill Wells, U.S. senator from 1799 to 1814.

Like many other of the northern Pennsylvania seats that show New England influence, Wellsboro has a green. The sandstone courthouse is at Main Street and Century Street, and following New England custom, it faces the Green and is not on it. While it is an early building (1835), it was not built in the Greek Revival style, as it appears today. The 1835 part is the central seven-bay portion without the portico, but including the bell tower. The gable end treatment reflects the original Federal-style appearance. Note the three handsome elliptical windows that are at attic level be-

tween the chimneys. The tower sits on a square base and is an open octagon with round columns at the corners. A delicate cornice follows the octagonal shape, and the roof is topped by a weathervane of coach and horses running from a cracking whip (binoculars needed). In 1931 (note cornerstone), there was a substantial reworking of the building (Lester, Merrit and Davis, architects), including many interior changes and the addition of the portico, as well as a rear expansion. The new portico has four fluted columns with stylized acanthus leaf capitals and four square pilasters. The county name is on the frieze, and the pediment contains a tympanum clock surrounded by garlands. The entry door, with its sidelights and semielliptical fanlight, is apparently from 1931, as early pictures show a different entrance. A wing was added in 1974–75. The attached modern yellow sandstone courthouse was built in 1974 (L. Robert Kimball, architect).

Inside the front door, there is a travertine vestibule and then a second-door window arrangement similar to the exterior one. Beyond this door, there is a small asymmetrical octagonal foyer with two clamshell niches for classical urns. The hallways have a severe contemporary look. A courtroom runs across the front of the building on the second floor. It would appear that the 1931 renovation sought to present an 1835 appearance in both the foyer and the courtroom. No documentation was found on the work done in the early 1930s.

The Green is an attractive park, with various monuments and plaques. Perhaps the most interesting item is the Wynken, Blynken, and Nod statue-fountain at the center. It is a memorial for Elizabeth Cameron Bailey. She and her husband were natives of Wellsboro but spent their adult life in Colorado, where Mr. Bailey had a highly successful career in politics and business. The sculptress of the piece, Mabel Landrum Torrey, who was born in a sod house on the Colorado plains, eventually studied at the Chicago Art Institute. A copy of this statue was rendered in marble for a Denver park, where it may have been seen by Mr. Bailey. Following his wife's death, he commissioned this bronze one for the Green, where it was dedicated in 1938. Various Wellsboro groups have attended to the preservation of the sculpture and fountain, and it is in excellent shape. Other plaques recognize Tioga countians who went on to wider fame, including George Washington Sears, John Magee, and William Stone. Stone probably practiced in this courthouse before he moved to Pittsburgh, from where he eventually was elected governor, with the backing of Boss Quay. He showed his gratitude for this support by appointing Quay, who was under indictment for misappropriation of state funds, to the U.S. Senate. Needless to say, this caused a bit of a public stir. Magee developed major coalfields in the county. Sculptor Samuel Conkey of New York designed the memorial, which depicts two scenes featuring Magee enterprises.

UNION
County Seat: Lewisburg

The name memorializes the enthusiasm for the new Union at the time of the county's creation in 1813. Lewisburg, on the banks of the West Branch, is home of Bucknell College. The combination of a county seat and a thriving college often makes for an attractive town, and Lewis is an example. Both these institutions help sustain the traditional central business district. The first county seat was New Berlin, but Lewisburg gained the honor with a little help from the political Cameron family. The town is named after Ludwig (Lewis) Doerr, an early landowner. Evidently, the practice of non-English immigrants adopting an alternative English given name began very early.

The courthouse is located a block off the main street (Market) at the end of the commercial strip and is surrounded by attractive residences (a historic residential walking tour guide is available in the courthouse). Built on the highest point in town, it is a red brick, Greek Revival (Ionic) style with four massive columns across the front. It dates from 1855 and was designed by local architect Lewis Palmer. Courthouses of this period were

usually either Italianate or late Classical style, with the order shifting from the gable end to impressive porticos over the entrance. This Union County courthouse is a good example. The facade and bell tower make an attractive sight. The bell in the tower was another Simon Cameron gift (see Northumberland and Cameron Counties). The building was enlarged and modernized in 1973 with little sensitivity to historic preservation, except for the main courtroom. It retains its Classical look, albeit somewhat altered and compromised. It is lighted by twelve six-over-six windows. The painted pine seating, judge's bench, and rails have natural finished trim, which gives the room its attractive, traditional ambience. There is a modern Justice bas-relief behind the bench.

In the halls, there is a collection of dolls in early national dress and changing displays provided by the historical society. Except for a few old portraits, most of the sterile white walls are forbiddingly bare. The floral-ringed keystone stone monument at the southeast corner was built for the veterans of the Spanish-American War, somewhat of an anomaly among courthouse war memorials.

VENANGO
County Seat: Franklin

The county name is of Indian origin, but no Seneca Indian would ever recognize that fact from the way it is pronounced, something that can be said for virtually every Indian-derived place name in use today. Along with Crawford County, Venango County, created in 1800, is oil country. The first commercial well (Colonel Drake's) was in production in 1859. It was a resource in need of a use, which was not long in coming. (The Indians used it medicinally.) One looks in vain in a city like Franklin today for signs of the boisterous oil boom and steamboat days. About the only remnants are interesting nineteenth-century houses, clear indications of past wealth (walking tour guides are available).

The courthouse (1868), with its twin towers, is similar to the one Samuel Sloan designed in Lock Haven, Clinton County. Addison Hutton, who was in partnership with Sloan at this time, was called in by the county commissioners to advise them on fireproofing their existing courthouse. He advised that it would cost no more to build a new one. At this time, the firm of Sloan and Hutton was breaking up, and Sloan may not have really participated in designing this building, but it follows ideas and plans that he had worked out previously and were available on the shelf.

The courthouse is located at a bend in the main road, at Liberty Street and South Park, where the courthouse square adjoins a well-planted park. It is a brick and sandstone (both painted) structure, five bays wide, with the central three bays within a pavilion. The first floor of the pavilion has rusticated stone surrounding the single entrance (note head of Franklin above) and two windows. These windows were originally doors, similar to the front of the Clinton County courthouse, but they were altered along with installation of the present replacement door in 1917. A decorative spindle balustrade sepa-

rates the first and second floors. All the windows in the building have arched tops, and the upper-story windows, which are the same all around the building, including on the pavilion, are very tall and narrow. Square Doric pilasters separate the bays on the pavilion, which has a pediment at the roofline. The boxed cornice features modillions and dentils. The two towers are nearly the same at the top and base, but the taller, right-hand one has an inserted middle section. The base tier on each tower has a balustrade, double recessed windows with slight segmented arch tops, and blind bays on either side. This tier has a broken cornice, which is filled with a pediment. The taller tower has an octagonal clock-face tier with a balustrade around the base and double rectangular louvers below the four clock faces. There are blind arched windows on the alternate sides, and on this tier the break in the cornice is filled with a segmental arch pediment. The metal octagonal roof caps on both towers have round dormers and are topped by the unusual finial. The bell was manufactured in Pittsburgh by a Mr. Fulton and weighs 2,362 pounds. There are seven bays on the side, and a belt course separates the floors. The building is mostly two and a half stories, except in the part occupied by the courtroom. A compatible, transverse gabled addition to the rear was built in 1932.

The interior features the traditional central hall, which serves the row offices and contains a prehistory display case at the rear. (Franklin is on the site of an old Indian town.) Both of the front sets of stairs survive (most nineteenth-century courthouses have torn out one staircase to build an elevator or add offices). They are painted in the old grained fashion. A foyer runs across

the entire front of the second floor in front of the old courtroom, which is illuminated by four tall windows with pediments on each side of the room. Other decorative features include a coffered ceiling, faux marble pilasters, and lincrusta wainscot. The bar area has some old furnishings, including a substantial rail. The bench is framed by a wooden Classical Corinthian order with entablature. The front wall features two paintings of Allegheny River scenes.

The attractive grounds are well planted, including a cherry tree allée planted by the Girl Scouts. Note the elaborate Egbert Fountain in the park and the Borland Memorial birdbath on the opposite side. A. G. Egbert (d. 1896) was a devoted promoter of the park, and the fountain was built as a memorial to his service. Egbert's former residence is next to the county historical society on South Park, facing the park area. Behind the courthouse are a Richardsonian jail and a Postmodern-style courthouse annex, which fortunately was not attached to the Sloan building.

WARREN
County Seat: Warren

Joseph Warren was a Revolutionary War hero, who fell at the Battle of Bunker Hill. Warren, established in 1800, was another of the western Pennsylvania counties that was created prior to its being populated, and a government was not really organized until 1819, when the town of Warren became the seat.

The courthouse (1877) is a Second Empire–Italian Renaissance Eclectic design by M. E. Beebe, who had a penchant for tall clock towers. The ones in Cambria and Huntington Counties were removed because of structural concerns shortly after their completion, but this earlier building and

his later one at Pottsville have with-
stood the test of time. All of Beebe's
courthouses also display a combination of the two decorative styles. The
Warren County building is located at
204 Fourth Street, in a residential
area on an ample, shaded corner lot
surrounded by a period iron fence.
The location was supposed to have
been in the business district, but town
development followed a different
logic, hence the atypical location is
accidental, not planned. This building was copied by Elk County for its
courthouse at Ridgway.

The building is red brick with
stone accents. It has six bays across the
front, with the central two bays projecting forward and rising to a pediment with a roundel at the roofline.
The angles have quoins, which are beveled on the first story below a molded
belt course and become rusticated square pilasters above. The first story is rusticated around the two arched entrances, with round pilasters on either side.
These are scarred by black strike marks from the days when smokers carried
large wood friction matches. Note the fine original doors. The window treatment is in the Tuscan Villa style. The first-story windows have segmental arch
head moldings with keystones, and the tall upper windows are round arched
with moldings. The windows have stone stringcourses at the spring line. The
cornice has heavy bracketing of two sizes. Above the roofline, the Second Empire style prevails on the corner pavilions and tower base. The mansard roofs
retain their original Vermont slate shingles and dormers featuring consoles
and pediments. The tower base has triple windows in the front. Above the
base, there is a square clock-face tier, which has a balustrade at the bottom
and a prominent bracketed cornice above. At the very top is a platform for
the Justice statue, which has been removed. Most all of the tower above the
base is metal, which is standard for the time. The massive rear chimney is still
there but is missing the large spark shield shown in old pictures. The building is ten bays deep, with alternate pairs of bays brought forward. The match-
ing rear addition was built in 1921 (Edward Phillips, architect).

The front entrance has two pairs of swinging, walnut double doors with
arched transoms and handsome original brass push plates. The push plates

were stolen in 1975 and found in a woods by a hunter. Inside is a round radiator with a marble top, marble tile floors, and broad, naturally finished walnut baseboards. Iron staircases with walnut rails rise from the foyer on either side, leading to the courtroom above; elegant bronze lamps once sat on the newel posts in place of the present plain knobs. The courtroom is lighted on either side by the tall arched windows with interior walnut shutters. There is a high walnut wainscot with a guilloche strapwork trim. The rounded corners add an unusual touch. Each door has a high arching blind wood transom containing a large rosette and console keystone. The plainness of the large arched panel behind the bench adds to its effectiveness. The rail is carved with finial knobs at the gate. Some of the furniture beyond the rail is original, including the massive judge's bench. The ceiling is not original; the room once had a massive chandelier instead of indirect lighting. Interestingly, the nearby McKean County courthouse has a similar ceiling, and it was constructed in 1940. Perhaps this one was the model. Moving back to the first floor, the hall has no wainscot, only the prominent baseboard, and the office openings are tall and narrow with high transoms. Some original hardware survives, but not the office furniture.

The 1870 Thomas Struthers House next door on Fourth Street houses the county historical society and museum.

An event that took place in this courthouse had a profound effect on most of the other courthouses. In 1954, Judge Allison D. Wade was shot and killed while presiding on the bench. In a nonsupport case, the defendant, Norman Moon, began firing at the judge, spraying bullets around the courtroom. The judge ducked behind the bench, but Moon walked around it and killed him. Moon escaped from the building, but he was soon captured. Keeping weapons out of courthouses has become a major industry. Lamentably, the security measures often disfigure nineteenth-century buildings, which were designed to be freely accessible to the public through multiple exterior doors.

WASHINGTON
County Seat: Washington

This was the second of the thirty-one counties in the United States to be named for George Washington. (Maryland recognized him first in 1776.) It is most appropriate that this particular county was named for him in 1781. Prior to the war, this area was claimed by both Pennsylvania and Virginia, and George received his early military experience here, defending Virginia Territory from the French and Indians. His observations led him to invest in land here after the war. This is the only county that the Radicals created during their turbulent stay in control of Pennsylvania government. Later, they may have had second thoughts about naming the county for Washington, because they were the ones active in the Whiskey Rebellion, which then President Washington put down with military force. The town of Washington was on the Cumberland Road by 1811, so a lot of people who developed the Midwest traveled through here in its early days.

The two sets of institutional buildings that dominate the hilly townscape of the county seat are those of Washington and Jefferson College (the first one west of the Allegheny Mountains) and the county government. The courthouse is a large 1900 Beaux-Arts (F. J. Osterling, architect, see Luzerne County) structure made of Columbia sandstone and South Car-

olina granite. It is crowned by an imposing terra-cotta dome, with George looking out from its top, 150 feet above the ground. The building shows the influence of the Chicago World's Fair of 1893, which brought ornate classicism to public architecture. Washington was a county endowed by many natural resources (oil, gas, coal, stone, and glass sand), and some of the wealth from them explains the construction of this fine courthouse. It features a massive, semicircular Ionic portico with a balustrade, which shelters a bank of three oak double entrance doors set in arched openings. These have highly decorated archivolts and blind roundels. The first and second stories are deeply rusticated, as are two substantial pillars at the street. The protruding end bays on the front are flanked by attached columns *in antis,* capped by a pediment, and have first-story windows with elaborate broken pediments. There are three acroteria on each of the front and side gable ends. The side gables are actually part of a transverse section of the building on either side of the central rotunda and contain the principal courtrooms. Their windows cannot be seen from the ground. There is a large, round central bay on the rear, which mirrors the front rotunda, but here it is as high as the building. The large dome rests on a square platform, which has small subsidiary domes at the corners, a device the architect also employed at Wilkes-Barre. An octagonal tier pierced with windows supports the terra-cotta portion of the dome proper. The terra dome has a band of round windows at its base, and the ribbed sections have eight rectilinear and round windows. There is a balustraded platform at the top, above which is a lantern with open arches. All this supports the statue of Washington. The original terra-cotta statue had lightning problems, and the present bronze one dates from 1923.

The interior is equally impressive, with its strong use of Italian marble, bronze, and brass, featuring Roman arches and massive pilasters. The central space has a grand stairway and is topped by a skylight, something that always adds an air of importance and significance. While there are many courtrooms, the ones to see are all on the second floor. Courtroom 1 has a thirty-foot coffered ceiling with skylight, red marble wainscot, oak woodwork, and generally fine appointments that pick up themes from other parts of the building. Note the unusual seating benches for the audience and the high side windows, which cannot be seen from the ground. Courtroom 2 is very similar but differs in the color of the marble, type of wood, and other appointments. The small, circular bay on the rear of the courthouse contains a courtroom on each floor, but only the second floor merits a look.

The maintenance of historic buildings is confounded not only by parsimony, but also by ignorance. Over the years, this courthouse developed leaks in the dome. The maintenance department assumed that the point of

Old Washington County jail.

failure was the terra-cotta system on the dome. The terra-cotta was variously painted, tarred, and covered with a "cementacious material," but to no avail. Finally, in 1979, the county hired a professional firm to address the problem. It found that the cement shell inside the terra cotta was perfectly sound and showed no leaks. The cause of the problems was faulty window muntins. Those were repaired, as was the interior water damage, but the various coatings were impossible to remove from the terra-cotta tiles without destroying their glaze, thus rendering them porous. The only solution was to give them yet another coat simulating the original glazing, which never needed all those coatings in the first place.

The old jail was designed by Osterling and built at the same time as the courthouse. It is no longer a jail and is looking for a new use. The old jail has a four-story central rotunda, which was designed to stage hangings. A special platform allowed the convicted to enter from the second floor. The tower had a lower shelf for the physician, who could pronounce the accused dead before the rope was cut and the awaiting coffin filled. There was a double hanging on one occasion, and those sentenced were dressed in black suits with white roses pinned to their lapels. Beyond are two large, modern structures: a 1980 office building (J. James Frillingham, architect) and a 1995 jail (Apostalou Associates, architect). The jail has reverse-mirror front doors, which add a spooky note.

WAYNE

County Seat: Honesdale

Wayne County was created in 1798 just two years after the tragic death of Gen. Anthony Wayne. Though he is more associated with the western counties in the state, it is not surprising that Pennsylvanians would be quick to name a county for him soon after his death. He was a resident and was highly renowned. The county seat, oddly, is named after a mayor of New York City, Philip Hone. As mayor of New York, Hone was interested in getting Pennsylvania anthracite coal to the city at an economical price. One problem was transportation costs. The coal started on its journey on primitive wagons and even sleighs in winter. Hone was the president of the company that built the Delaware and Hudson Canal, which developed a much cheaper water transport system to connect the coal fields with the city. Honesdale was the terminus of the canal, and it grew with the new commerce and became the county seat in 1841.

The courthouse, located one block off Main Street, is an 1880 (J. A. Wood, architect) structure with its back to the waterway that made the town. It faces a full square park, but unlike some of the other northern-tier seats, the plan was not brought by New Englanders. This town came too late for that. The setting is wonderful, as a hill rises behind the courthouse,

making a most attractive background, particularly during the fall foliage display. It is an Eclectic structure, built of stone and red brick, showing Italianate and some Second Empire features. To obtain the stone, a special railroad was built to a nearby quarry across the Lackawaxen Creek. It is an exuberantly ornamented building, with much of the embellishments rendered in metal or wood. The stone foundation is unusually decorative. The facade has a central pavilion of three double bays, with three single bays on either side of it. The entrance porch is supported by six banded columns linked by narrow arches at the outer corners. There are segmental arches over the three sides of the porch and a very prominent broken pediment at the roofline. The pairs of windows on the pavilion have segmental arch tops and are recessed below wider segmental arches in the brick. The outer sections of the building have entryways (now closed) with double doors with arched panels and overhead wood canopies. Note the faint writing on the left door transom, which indicates its original use. The windows of these three outer bays have segmental arch tops, and the narrow blind arch theme in the brickwork recurs in three differing patterns. A very low mansard roof forms the base for the tower and is repeated on the lower part of the tower. The cornice pattern makes a strong decorative statement on both the tower and the main building. It includes decorative panels on a frieze, brackets, shaped modillions, and dentils. On the tower, these elements are also used on semicircular sections punctuated by a porthole. Two later small wings were attached at the rear of the building, and a modern annex links the courthouse to the old jail.

The interior has been partly modernized, but there are remnants of the original, including some marble fireplaces, iron stairs, and hallway decor. However, the main thing to see in the interior is the upstairs courtroom. Though somewhat modified, it still has its original ample space and is lighted by large windows from both sides. The bar and bench are original. Note that the rails are accented by no less than twenty corner posts with large balls, all kept well polished. The large judge's bench has a single wide board for a top. The ramped auditorium was a convention in this part of Pennsylvania in the late nineteenth century, although some have fallen victim to the Disabilities Act requirements.

It is remarkable that this courthouse was built at all, let alone well built, considering the controversy that surrounded its construction. The 1880s were at the peak of party competition throughout the United States, and while ideology was the underpinning, the material rewards of office were often the grist. In Wayne County, the new courthouse became a party issue, and the dispute was exploited by the local press. The prior courthouse was located in what is now the front lawn of the present courthouse.

Even after construction began on the present building in 1876, there were continual legal challenges both over whether the new building was properly authorized and over the legality of the bonds that financed it. There was even an attempt to move the courthouse to another town. However, the procourthouse party won both in the courts and at the polls. The bonds were kept within legal limits, in part by postponing the construction of the tower. When it came time to add it, the cost controversy raged again, which may explain why it is so modest. Compare it to the exuberant one constructed a few years earlier in neighboring Wyoming County (Tunkhannock) on a similar building. To illustrate the petty depths of the bickering, there was a bitter attack on the commissioners for the stone plaque that is now just inside the entrance. It was called a tombstone for perpetuating the names of the sitting commissioners at the taxpayers' expense. The issue of the $35 stone plaque played for several weeks in the paper. It is difficult to have a true perspective on these controversies from our vantage point. Despite the opposition, the commissioners pursued the construction without wavering, and the newspaper accounts of opposition may have been media hype of the day.

The soldiers monument across the street in the park is one of the earliest Civil War monuments. Interestingly, the idea was started by local women who created a Ladies Monument Association in 1865. They undertook the arduous task of raising the money and employed such diverse means as fairs, sales of needlework, souvenirs, and refreshments, plays, tableaux, and benefit suppers. During the four-year effort, the local newspaper sniped at the idea (because it was a women's idea?). The city government did not seem enthusiastic either, as it set very specific limits on the amount of space that could be used in the Central Park and demanded it be fenced. The iron fence, which is still there, required a separate fund drive after the statue was in place. The statue shows a soldier, smaller than life-size, at parade rest. The ladies tastefully rejected the first suggested motif, marble cannons and cannonballs surmounted by an eagle. While the state governor (Geary) gave the oration at the dedication, it seems, judging from the tone of current accounts, that the ladies of Wayne County were ahead of their time and certainly ahead of the men (see Erie County). The pervasive Civil War monument movement happened a little later, when glorifying the war became good politics throughout the triumphant North.

WESTMORELAND
County Seat: Greensburg

Westmoreland, created in 1773, was named for the English county. In the Revolutionary War, many men from this area served under Nathaniel Greene, and the county seat was renamed for him (misspelled) on his death in 1786.

The present and fourth courthouse is an imposing Beaux-Arts structure (1906, William Kaufman, architect) on a crowded site along the busy main street. It is topped by a massive yellow decorated dome and cannot be mistaken. The exterior walls are gray granite and copiously decorated with the ornamental patterns learned at the École des Beaux Arts. It is nine bays across the front, counting each rounded section as a bay. The first story is rusticated, and the rest is smooth ashlar. The central three bays come forward over a recessed porch containing the original entrance. The porch is entered

through three arches, which have applied foliage sculpture and cartouches in the spandrels. The single building entrance is under an elliptical archway with decorated archivolt and returns. The porch has a coffered ceiling, garland and rosette adornments, and four windows, two set at angles. There are massive bronze lamps on either side of the steps. The three central bays are framed by modified Corinthian pilasters at the second and third stories, with a balustrade at the base. The second-story windows have alternate styled pediments, the third-story windows are rectangular, and the fourth's are roundels in wreaths. The pediment has statues representing Art and Industry in the tympanum and three female figures high on the roofline representing Justice (with 1993 replacement scales), Guardian of the Law (with sword), and Keeper of the Law (books). Flanking the central section of the building are round bays that lead upward to the subsidiary white domes with shell-decorated roundels. The outer three bays feature windows with pediments and keystones on the second story, two-story pilasters, and rectangular windows rather than roundels at the fourth story. There are belt courses above the first and third stories and an elaborate cornice of dentils, modillions, and two rows of beadwork. The outer angles of the building have decorations at the third and fourth stories. There is a parapet at the roofline with urns on corner pedestals. The seven bay ends are modified replications of the facade, except for a blind fourth story and a roof pavilion.

The dome rests on a square base, with the subsidiary white domes inset at the corners. At its base is a colonnade containing windows that light the inside rotunda. After several highly ornamental bands, there is a yellow-ribbed dome, which supports an open colonnade, a small plain ribbed dome, and a flagpole. Originally the dome was covered with terracotta shingles. They were replaced by new ones in 1978 at great expense, but the fabrication was faulty, and the tiles soon began to disintegrate and fall off. The present material is aluminum, which appears to be more durable but does not have the radiant color of the terra cotta.

The present building entrance is to the rear, past the Alcoa-donated sculpture by James C. Myford, at the juncture of the 1979 Courthouse Square building (Roach, Walfish, Lettrich, architects). Find your way to the 1906 courthouse and note the elaborate marble mosaics and gilded plasterwork on the first floor. The great marble stairs, with heavy bronze railings, take you to a four-story rotunda, lighted by four imbricated lunette windows high overhead and covered by the highly decorated dome. The circular mezzanines have round marble balustrades. There are two original courtrooms on the second floor. These feature gilded Ionic pilasters, ceilings with paintings by Maurice Ingres set in elaborate recessed frames, and garland-surrounded portraits of

famous local judges high along the walls (paintings restored in 1982). The furnishings are mahogany (from Saint Jago and San Domingo). The audience benches, which are also found in the halls throughout the building, are particularly impressive because of their massiveness. The balusters of the bar rail feature acanthus leaf carvings. Courtrooms 7 and 9, on the fourth floor, feature oak paneling, elaborate foliage carvings on the doors, and murals on the balcony walls.

During the 1982 renovation work, a scrap of paper was found in the walls left by two stonecarvers who had been brought from Italy to install the Italian marble. It read, in Italian, "Here we worked, two unhappy Italians for the making rich of the American capitalists," signed Stefano Martinelli and Petro Chienego.

The 1906 dedication program included a series of photographs detailing the building's features. One showed the jury dormitory, which was a barrackslike room with rows of beds and a lavatory at one end for housing the all-male jury for longer trials. Jury dormitories in courthouses were not unusual in late-nineteenth- and early-twentieth-century courthouses.

WYOMING
County Seat: Tunkhannock

Wyoming County is part of the territory that was fought over in the Pennamite War between settlers from Pennsylvania and Connecticut. While the land claims were settled soon after independence, bitter memories lingered. When Wyoming County was formed in 1842, the locals of New England descent wanted to name the county after Israel Putnam, Connecticut hero of the Revolutionary War. The legislature did not go along. The memory of Putnam was further expunged when the county village, which had born his name, was changed to the present Indian name of Tunkhannock. An Indian term may have been chosen for its political neutrality.

The courthouse in this small seat fronts on Warren Street between Washington Street and Marion Street and is about a block up the hill from the commercial center. While a portion of the 1844 two-story courthouse is embedded in this structure, what you see is the Italianate enlargement designed by D. R. Nott in 1870. At this time, it was increased to three stories and received a tower, a new facade, and an extension to the rear. The building material is brick covered with plaster. Certainly, the tower is its

most arresting feature, but the elaborate brackets around the roofline and the prominent quoins are also noteworthy. The recent paint palette has accentuated the quoins. The facade of the building has a central pavilion and three bays of windows on either side. The doorway is in an arched entrance with an ornate iron hood molding above. Above the entrance are two tall, narrow modified Norman windows with hood molding, again likely iron. The side bays have segmental arch windows on the first two stories and full arches on the third, all with hood moldings. A belt course separates the first two stories. The octagonal tower has a two-step base, with panels on the lower por-

tion and inverted consoles decorating the upper. The clock faces are on alternate sides, and the bracketed cornice has a slight arc above the faces. The belfry tier has arched louvers on each side and Corinthian engaged columns at the angles. The tower is topped by a shingled cap, finial, and arrow weathervane. The form of the building is very similar to the one at Honesdale (Wayne County) in that it is T-shaped with a highly ornamented wide facade and a more simplified narrow section behind. The purpose of the narrow rear is to provide a place for the courtroom to be lighted and ventilated from both sides. Here, as in Honesdale, there have been additions beyond the rear building. Note that the WPA-financed 1938 portion is nearly devoid of all ornamentation and has shallow eaves. The more recent 1992 (Crabtree, Rohrbaugh and Associates, architects) addition has restored some of Nott's ornamentations, which are rendered in plastic rather than metal.

Much of the interior is modernized, but original stairs lead to the second-floor courtroom with features of interest including a wooden ceiling, ramped auditorium, balcony, railings around the bar, and judge's bench. The wooden courtroom ceiling is a distinctly northern Pennsylvania feature. The rail design features an unusual fluted octagonal section that matches those on the stairs. Brief, often cryptic comments were made in the local paper about many facets of the construction. The rails and banisters were made by B. D. Jacques of Lemon (a few miles north of the borough), and

his work was complimented. It is not known whether he personally made the spindles, but he certainly assembled them and did the handrail.

There is a very tall Civil War monument and a bandstand to the rear on the courthouse square. The post office has a recently restored WPA mural by Ethel V. Ashton, entitled *Defenders of Wyoming Country in 1778*. This is not the Pennamite War, but the British-Indian action that led to the Sullivan expedition (see Sullivan County).

YORK
County Seat: York

York County was split off from Lancaster in 1748, and somewhere along the way, the two county seats became identified with the War of the Roses and adopted red and white roses as city symbols.

York ranks along with Lancaster as one of Pennsylvania's historic county seats because of its role in the Revolutionary War. The first court-house served as the national capital during a fateful period when the British occupied Philadelphia. Here, safely beyond the wide Susquehanna, the Continental Congress drafted the Articles of Confederation, welcomed Von Steuben and Lafayette, and issued the first national Thanksgiving proclamation. The historic courthouse was located in the center of the central square, Lancaster style. A replica of that building is located west of the downtown on Market Street. York claims a signer of the Declaration of Independence, James Smith, who is buried at First Presbyterian Church at Market Street and Queen Street.

The present courthouse is a 1900 enlargement of an 1837–40 "temple of justice," which has in turn been enlarged. The first enlargement is a euphemism, because the structure designed by J. A. Dempwolf, a local architect, retained only some foundations and reused the six Ionic columns from the previous building. Dempwolf's building was greatly enlarged in 1959 (Clarence L. Forrer, architect), with additions on both sides. Viewed from the front, what you see is Dempwolf's Beaux-Arts central portion refaced in red brick and pinched by the outer sections designed by Forrer. Dempwolf's central section has five square granite piers on the ground-floor level. Above are the two-story columns from the older building, which are elevated by piers. The portico has a banister at the base and pediment above, with a clock on its tympanum. Dempwolf's rather simple decorative cross pattern on the banister and towers was picked up by Forrer for his windows and balconies. The three distinctive towers, with their tile and terra-cotta adornments, are Dempwolf's. They can best be viewed (with binoculars) from the church side porch around the corner on South George Street.

While the towers are similar, the larger central one has several added elements. Its main tier is octagonal, with a pedimented window on each face separated by a pair of pilasters. There are clock faces over alternate windows, but none of the clock mechanisms seem to work. The tile roof has a window area toward the top. The bell from the previous courthouse is housed in that small central tower cupola. It appears diminutive and out of place atop this much larger building. The building was granite and buff brick originally, but the front brick has been replaced with red to match the additions. The buff brick can still be seen on the rear. I can find no account about the decision to reuse the columns. They seem too small for the

building and had to be propped up by the granite piers to make them fit the facade. One suspects that Dempwolf was told to use them.

The Forrer enlargement played havoc with the Dempwolf interior, but there are still some things to see inside. The original central corridor with its marble wainscot still runs the two hundred feet to Court Alley, but the offices that it serves are now windowless, and there are dull walls where decorative windows once illuminated the inner space. Midpoint, there is a well under the center dome, with marble beams to the north and south and plaster beams with consoles to the east and west. The Italian marble staircase has a massive newel post, but now its first flight leads to a blank wall rather than a window at the landing. Courtroom 1 is truly depressing. Dempwolf's pilasters and mosaic floor remain, but the room is now blind (lighted by hanging fluorescent fixtures). Acoustic tiles cover the original coffered ceiling as well as the walls, metal movable chairs serve the jurors, and an incongruously designed modern scale of Justice looms behind the judge. The monogrammed doorknobs remain. The second large courtroom on this floor is a little better; at least it has windows.

In a contemporary description of the 1900 building, it was explained that the toilet was located on the third floor, not for reasons of sanitation, but "to escape the vandalism of the rabble who could find access to it from the street were it located with more easy reach of the highways." Some problems never change.

Dempwolf had a brother, Reinhardt, who was associated with the firm and is credited locally with having been the artistic talent. They designed many buildings of all kinds around York. Two noteworthy nearby examples on West Philadelphia Street are the Central Market (open three days a week) and the Lighthouse Boys Club building across from it. They are both rendered in Romanesque style. One might surmise that the style of the courthouse was dictated by the leftover columns and that the three free-spirited towers come closer to the mode of expression that the brothers would have preferred.

York has a rich supply of historical street markers, reducing the need for further text in this guide for the environs of the courthouse.

TIMELINE OF EXTANT
PENNSYLVANIA COURTHOUSES
BY STYLE

This table arrays extant Pennsylvania courthouses according to the year in which the present principal appearance was constructed. Secondary styles are given after the slash for hybrid examples. A date in the second column indicates when an existing building was substantially modified in appearance.

BEFORE 1800
Chester [Chester] 1724   Vernacular
Philadelphia [Philadelphia] 1789   Federal/Georgian. Congress Hall.
1820–29
Bedford [Bedford] 1828   Classical (Doric, *in antis*)/Federal
1830–1839
Centre [Bellefonte] 1835   Classical (Ionic)
Potter [Coudersport] 1835   Vernacular/Italianate (1888)
Tioga [Wellsboro] 1835   Federal elements/Classical portico (1931)
1840–49
Mifflin [Lewistown] 1843   Classical portico (Ionic)
Chester [West Chester] 1846   Classical (Corinthian)
Cumberland [Carlisle] 1846   Classical (Modified Corinthian)/Georgian
1850–59
Lancaster [Lancaster] 1850   Classical (Corinthian)
Fulton [McConnellsburg] 1851   Classical (Doric)
Lawrence [New Castle] 1852   Classical (Ionic)
Greene [Waynesburg] 1852   Classical (Corinthian)
Susquehanna [Montrose] 1854   Classical (Ionic)
Erie [Erie] 1855   Classical (Corinthian)
Union [Lewisburg] 1855   Classical Portico (Ionic)
Armstrong [Kittanning] 1858   Classical Portico (Corinthian)
Adams [Gettysburg] 1859   Italianate/Federal

1860–69

Clearfield [Clearfield] 1860	Vernacular
Northampton [Easton] 1860	Classical (Corinthian)
Franklin [Chambersburg] 1864	Classical (Ionic)
Lehigh [Easton] 1864	Italianate/Federal (1814)
Northumberland [Sunbury] 1865	Italianate
Snyder [Middleburg] 1867	Classical Revival (Ionic)
Perry [New Bloomfield] 1868	Classical Revival (Corinthian)
Venango [Franklin] 1868	Italianate
Clinton [Lock Haven] 1869	Italianate
Jefferson [Brookville] 1869	Italianate
Wyoming [Tunkhannock] 1869	Italianate

1870–79

Forest [Tionesta] 1870	Classical Revival
Montour [Danville] 1871	Italianate
Philadelphia [Philadelphia] 1872	Second Empire
Elk [Ridgway] 1872	Second Empire/Italianate
Pike [Milford] 1873	Second Empire
Juniata [Mifflintown] 1873	Eclectic Classical Revival
Warren [Warren] 1877	Second Empire/Italianate
Blair [Hollidaysburg] 1877	Gothic/Eclectic

1880–89

Wayne [Honesdale] 1880	Italianate/Second Empire
Cambria [Ebensburg] 1880	Second Empire
Lackawanna [Scranton] 1881	Romanesque
Clarion [Clarion] 1882	Eclectic/Queen Ann
Huntington [Huntington] 1883	Second Empire/Italianate
Allegheny [Pittsburgh] 1883	Romanesque
Butler [Butler] 1885	Gothic/Romanesque

1890–99

Cameron [Emporium] 1890	Romanesque
Monroe [Stroudsburg] 1890	Romanesque
Columbia [Bloomsburg] 1890	Romanesque
Fayette [Uniontown] 1890	Romanesque
Schuylkill [Pottsville] 1892	Romanesque
Carbon [Jim Thorpe] 1893	Romanesque
Sullivan [Laporte] 1894	Romanesque
Bradford [Towanda] 1897	Renaissance Revival

1900–9

York [York] 1900	Beaux-Arts/Eclectic
Washington [Washington] 1900	Beaux-Arts
Luzerne [Wilkes-Barre] 1902	Beaux-Arts
Montgomery [Norristown] 1903	Beaux-Arts
Somerset [Somerset] 1905	Beaux-Arts
Westmoreland [Greensberg] 1906	Beaux-Arts
Mercer [Mercer] 1909	Classical Revival/Eclectic

1910–19

Delaware [Media] 1913	Beaux-Arts

1920–29

1930–39

Berks [Reading] 1930	Art Deco
Beaver [Beaver] 1933	Art Moderne

1940–49

Dauphin [Harrisburg] 1940	Art Moderne
McKean [Smethport] 1941	Classical Revival

1950–51

Crawford [Meadville] 1954	Classical Revival

1960–69

Lebanon [Lebanon] 1960	Modern
Bucks [Doylestown] 1960	Modern
Indiana [Indiana] 1968	Classical Revival

1970–79

Lycoming [Williamsport] 1970	Modern
Mifflin [Lewistown] 1978	Classical Revival

GLOSSARY

The following definitions give the usages employed in this book.
See references in brackets for illustrations.

Acroterion. A pedestal and the ornament upon it that are at the peak or corner of a roof. Often associated with the roof over a pediment and usually found on more elaborate Classical Revival buildings. [Luzerne, Westmoreland]

Angle. Corner, point of intersection of two architectural planes; often used as an adjective, as in angle bead, angle column.

Antae, *in antis*. A pier that protrudes forward, usually in pairs on the sides of a facade and forming part of the portico. The distyle *in antis* type of portico has two columns standing between the antae and together with them support a pediment. [Bedford]

Arcade. A line of attached arches. Window arcades are a common feature of the Romanesque style.

Arch. A curved structure that spans an opening. The curve can be of many differing shapes, among which are the following: The *Roman arch* is a full half circle. A *segmental arch* is less than a full half circle. A *Gothic arch* comes to a point at its apex. A *lancet arch* is narrower and more pointed than the Gothic.

Archivolt. An ornamental molding that follows the curve of the arch. Not to be confused with **intrado.**

Ashlar. Squared building stone. The outward face may be smooth or rough (quarry-faced). Regular ashlar describes stones of the same height set in rows. Random ashlar describes the use of stones of differing heights and sizes.

Regular ashlar, Lackawanna County courthouse.

227

Clathri, Bradford County courthouse.

Atrium. A major central, interior multistory space over which is a skylight.

Balustrade. A railing system consisting of a handrail, the vertical supporting members, called balusters, and other accompanying structural features.

Bay. A regular repeated element defined by some structural feature. In this guide, it usually refers to vertical sets of windows. The facade or side of a building may be divided into a number of bays for the purpose of description.

Belfry. That part of a tower that houses the bell. It may be open or closed, in which case there are usually louvers to accommodate the sound.

Blind window or arch. A structurally defined element that has the appearance of a window or arch but is filled with opaque material, usually masonry. Blind arches may simply be decorative patterns in a stone or brick building wall. [Montour]

Bracket. A brace (usually decorated) projecting from a wall to support a horizontal member, such as a cornice. A prominent feature of Italianate style linking the top of building walls to the roof overhang. [Jefferson]

Clathri. A latticelike element covering an opening.

Coffer, coffering. Usually describes a ceiling pattern of regular deeply recessed and usually highly decorated sections. Often used in courtroom ceilings.

Column. A freestanding or attached vertical, usually cylindrical, structural supporting member. In Classical architecture, it consists of shaft, capital, and usually a base. The principal types were Doric, Ionic, and Corinthian.

Console. An upright curved bracket protruding from a wall that supports some horizontal member, such as a cornice or head molding.

Coping. A protective cap on the top of a wall, roof point, or other structure to prevent weather penetration.

Corbel. A masonry device in which successive rows of stone or brick project outward in a stepped fashion, moving up the wall. Often used at the base of turrets, under the cornice, or around the tops of chimneys. Corbeling is a decorative device of bricklayers. [Lackawanna]

Corinthian. The most elaborate of the three principle Classical orders (see Erie County).

Cornice. The uppermost part of an *entablature;* generally, any molding that goes around the top of a building's wall, either interior or exterior.

Crenellation. Crenels are the open spaces along the top of a battlement, and crenellation refers to the alternating indentations and upward rectangular projections around the top of a fortified area. It alternately provides protection for soldiers and openings to employ weapons. It was a favorite nineteenth-century design for the top of Pennsylvania jail walls, giving these buildings a fortified and military look. [Introduction]

Dentils. Square blocks placed in toothlike series, used as decoration along cornices in Classical Revival architecture and at times in Eclectic and Beaux-Arts styles. [Mifflin]

Doric. The plainest of the three Classical architectural orders. [Fulton]

Embrication. An overall pattern resembling fish scales.

Entablature. A feature of Classical architecture where horizontal beams bridged the columns and in turn supported the roof. Classical orders had a rigidly prescribed form and decorations. The form was usually divided into three layers, the upper being the cornice, the middle the frieze, and the lower the architrave. Great liberties were taken in Eclectic styles.

Finial. A more or less pointed ornament that is the uppermost element of many towers, spires, or interior features, such as a newel post. Usually a spike but can be fancier.

Flute, fluting. Parallel channels or grooves carved lengthwise on a column.

Fretwork. Open ornamental carving with a repeating pattern, often in bands. Many of the patterns are named, such as zigzag or guilloche. Similar to strapwork.

Gibbs surround. Originally, a door or window with triple keystones above and protruding blocks on the jambs. There are many variations, as the one illustrated.

Head molding, drip molding. The molding that runs above and partially down both sides of windows

Gibbs surround, Clinton County courthouse.

or doors. Used extensively in Italianate and many Eclectic styles. [Wyoming]

Intrado. The inside surface of the arch.

Ionic. One of the Classical orders, characterized by the spiral scroll called a volute on the capital. [Centre]

Lantern. A glazed superstructure, often one of the uppermost parts of a tower, employed to provide light to its interior. Towers with clocks or bells required access for servicing, hence the need for a natural light source prior to electrification.

Lunette. A semicircular opening, usually glazed.

Mansard roof. Named for French architect François Mansart. Originally, a roof with two slopes on all sides, the lower one being much steeper, thus akin to a gambrel roof. The lower slope may be concave, convex, straight, or S-shaped, usually pierced by dormer windows. In American usage, the lower slope is sometimes combined with a flat roof. It is the hallmark of the Second Empire style. [Philadelphia, Elk]

Modillion. A horizontal brace supporting the cornice. May be in block or scroll form, resembling a console but with a reversal of the height-width ratio. Modillions are found in series, usually evenly spaced along the cornice. [Mifflin]

Mullions. Vertical members that separate window lights. Sometimes they take the form of pilasters with capitals.

Muntins. The secondary members that separate panes of glass in windows. Normally, they are at right angles to the sash, but muntins can also be curved. [Bedford]

Norman window. A tall, narrow, round-topped window light having two similarly shaped panes. [Mifflin]

Palladian window, Pike County courthouse.

Order. In Classical architecture, a prescribed set of proportions and ornamentation for columns and the supported entablature. See Doric, Ionic, and Corinthian.

Palladian window. A three-part window, with the central sash rounded at the top and two smaller, flanking, square-topped sashes.

Pavilion. A prominent subsection of a building located at the center facade or corners. It is usually multistoried and breaks the vertical plane of the building proper, coming forward. It is a principal feature of Second Empire style but is common in others as well. [Philadelphia]

Pediment. A usually triangular gable end found in Classical architecture and its derivatives. There is usually a cornice across the bottom and often on the two raking sides as well. In derivative styles, a segmental arch may replace the raking sides. Pediments are also used as decorations over doors and windows and can take various forms, such as triangular, segmental, split, or broken.

Pilaster. A pillar attached to a wall, derived from the column form in having a capital and base. May be square or semiround, structural or purely decorative.

Portico. A covered entryway with a roof supported by columns. The line between portico and central pavilion is imprecise in architectural usage. As used here, a portico can be part of a central pavilion.

Quoin. Building corner decoration consisting of raised flat areas in a material, color, or texture contrasting with that used on the structure's exterior walls. Used in many styles.

Roundel. Round window or opening, sometimes surrounded by a decorative flourish, such as a garland. Alternately spelled rondel.

Rusticated. A masonry practice of beveling the edges of ashlar blocks so mortar joints are strongly emphasized by the play of light on the surface. The idea is to convey strength, and this technique is often used on the foundation only.

Scagliola. A type of faux stonework consisting of applied materials, such

Quoins (and brackets above), Wyoming County courthouse.

Voussoirs, Monroe County courthouse.

as stone dust or plaster, done to save money. Real stone is usually colder to the touch than scagliola.

Stringcourse. A horizontal line on a facade made by contrasting building materials or other devices, usually between stories. Also known as belt course.

Tower. Here used as a general term to include all vertical projections above the roof line, usually housing a bell, clock, observation platform, or some combination of these.

Transom. A horizontal member over a door that separates it from a window above. The window itself is often popularly called a transom, and it is frequently made movable to provide air circulation while the door is closed.

Turret. A cylindrical tower, often corbelled into the corner of a building and rising to a conical roof. [Lackawanna] Often used on courthouse towers in the Romanesque style.

Tympanum. The surface enclosed by a pediment. Classically, a place for statues, but on courthouses a place for seals [Franklin] or perhaps a clock [York].

Voussoirs. Prominent in Richardsonian Romanesque as a design feature. [Allegheny] The wedge-shaped masonry units used to make an arch. Radiating voussoirs have alternating stone units of differing lengths.

Water table. A sloped ledge at the top of a foundation, originally designed to shunt water away from the building. Can be used as a design element to provide a horizontal line or emphasize the transition from foundation to building wall.

SOURCES

Much of the material in this book has been gleaned from the files of county historical societies. Nearly every county has such a society; however, the level of staffing, extent of holdings, and organization of the files vary from county to county. Often the best source of information was the vertical file on the courthouse, which usually contained newspaper clippings, unpublished accounts, letters, dedicatory programs, and other materials. There has been no attempt to list all of these thousands of scraps of materials. The accounts are often redundant, as the information about such matters as building materials, courthouse features, and alterations are reproduced for each generation. Only on rare occasions were there contradictory accounts. Standard county histories, which are the basic resource of every county historical society holding, were unfailingly consulted, and some of these were the major source for descriptions of nineteenth-century courthouses, as they were at the time of construction. Some counties have no historical society libraries or ones devoted exclusively to genealogy. In these cases, the public libraries usually filled the void.

Files of the Pennsylvania Historical and Museum Commission, Bureau for Historic Preservation, were consulted on all buildings on the National Register. The information on the earlier filings is sometimes meager but is much better on more recent ones.

The following bibliography lists published sources that should be available to the reader.

Archambault, A. Margaretta. *A Guide Book of Art, Architecture, and Historic Interests of Pennsylvania.* Philadelphia: John C. Winston Company, 1924.

Baldwin, Leland D. *Whiskey Rebels: The Story of a Frontier Uprising.* Pittsburgh: University of Pittsburgh Press, 1939.

Ball, Jean, ed. *Historic Buildings in Warren County.* Warren, PA: Warren County Historical Society, 1971.

Butterfield, Roger. "The Cats on City Hall." *Pennsylvania Magazine of History and Biography* 77 (1953): 439.

Cooledge, Harold N. *Samuel Sloan, Architect of Philadelphia, 1814–1884.* Philadelphia: University of Pennsylvania Press, 1986.

Crozier, Alan. "Scotch-Irish Influence on American English." *American Speech* 59 (1984): 310.

Dalzell, Bonnie. "Unlocking the Secret of Conversation Hall." *Historic Preservation* 35 (1983): 30.

Fairmount Park Association. *Sculpture of a City: Philadelphia's Treasures in Bronze and Stone.* New York: Walker Publishing Co., 1974.

Fuhrman, Robert B. *Hail Temple Built to Justice: A History of Mercer County's Court Houses.* Mercer, PA: Mercer County Historical Society, 1994.

Gillette, Howard, Jr. "Philadelphia's City Hall: Monument to a New Political Machine." *Pennsylvania Magazine of History and Biography* 97 (1973): 233.

Goeldner, Paul Kenneth. *Temples of Justice: Nineteeth Century Courthouses in the Midwest and Texas.* Ph.D. dissertation, Columbia University, 1970.

Harris, Cyril M. *American Architecture: An Illustrated Encyclopedia.* New York: W. W. Norton, 1998.

———. *Historic Architecture Sourcebook.* New York: McGraw-Hill, 1977.

Kane, Joseph Nathan. *The American Counties.* Metuchen, NJ: Scarecrow Press, 1983.

Kramer, Fay Follet. "Lancaster County's Present Court House: A History of Its Construction 1852–1855." *Journal of the Lancaster County Historical Society* 71, no. 1 (1967): 1.

Loth, Calder, and Julius Trousdale Sadler, Jr. *The Only Proper Style; Gothic Architecture in America.* Boston: New York Graphic Society, 1975.

Maass, John. "Philadelphia City Hall: Monster or Masterpiece." *Journal of the American Institute of Planners* 43 (1965): 23.

McCarthy, Jack, and Barbara L. Weir. *A Brief Sketch of the 1847 Courthouse, 1892 Annex and 1893 Judge's Bench of Chester County Pennsylvania.* Pamphlet published by the Chester County Historical Society, 1987.

Melosh, Barbara. *Engendering Culture: Manhood and Womanhood in New Deal Public Art and Theatre.* Washington, DC: Smithsonian Institution, 1991.

Page, Max. "Historical Memory of the Design of Courthouses. *Pennsylvania Magazine of History and Biography* 119 (1995): 300.

Pare, Richard, ed. *Court House: A Photographic Document.* New York: Horizon Press, 1978.

Pennsylvania State Department of Commerce. *My Pennsylvania.* Commonwealth of Pennsylvania, 1946.

Pennsylvania Writers Project. *Pennsylvania: A Guide to the Keystone State.* New York: Oxford University Press, 1940.

Short, C. W., and R. Stanley-Brown. *Public Buildings: A Survey of Architecture of Projects Constructed by Federal and Other Governmental Bodies between the Years 1933 and 1939.* Washington, DC: Government Printing Office, 1939.

Slaughter, Thomas P. *The Whiskey Rebellion.* New York: Oxford University Press, 1986.

Stanislaus, Richard. "John Mitchell Monument." *Newsletter of the Pennsylvania Anthracite Heritage Museum and Iron Furnace Associates* 9, no. 5 (1992): 1.

Sword, Wiley. *President Washington's Indian War: The Struggle for the Old Northwest, 1790–1795.* Norman, OK: University of Oklahoma Press, 1974.

Tunick, Susan, and Jonathan Walters. "The Wonderful World of Terra-Cotta." *Historic Preservation* (March–April 1982): 40.

Van Rensselaer, Mariana Griswold. *Henry Hobson Richardson and His Works.* New York: Dover Publications, 1969.

Van Trump, James D. *Majesty of the Law: The Courthouses of Allegheny County.* Pittsburgh: Pittsburgh Historical and Landmark Foundation, 1988.

Vittetta. *Master Plan for the Restoration, Modernization, and Rehabilitation of the Philadelphia City Hall. Historic Structure Report. Component I.* 3 vols. 1995.

Wodehouse, Lawrence. "John McArthur, Jr. (1823–1890)." *Journal of Society of Architectural Historians* 28 (1969): 271.

INDEX